THE LOST
CHILD

THE LOST
CHILD

A Mother's Story

Julie Myerson

BLOOMSBURY

NEW YORK · BERLIN · LONDON

Published by Bloomsbury USA, New York

All papers used by Bloomsbury USA are natural, recyclable products made from wood
grown in well-managed forests. The manufacturing processes conform to the
environmental regulations of the country of origin.

LIBRARY OF CONGRESS CATALOGING-IN-PUBLICATION DATA HAS BEEN APPLIED FOR.

ISBN-10: 1-59691-700-8
ISBN-13: 978-1-59691-700-2

First published in Great Britain by Bloomsbury Publishing Plc in 2009
First U.S. edition 2009

1 3 5 7 9 10 8 6 4 2

Typeset by Hewer Text UK Ltd, Edinburgh

For him: he knows who he is and I love him.

FOREWORD

THROUGHOUT THE TIME I spent discovering Mary Yelloly and then researching and writing this book, something painful was happening at home. Our eldest child – previously bright and sweet and happy – was drifting further and further away from us. We seemed to be losing him.

Some days it was almost impossible to concentrate on looking for Mary Yelloly. Other days, when I seemed at last to be getting close to her, I found myself too distracted and distressed by what was happening with our boy to be able to write about her far too short life. However much I didn't want it to be so, loss was all around me, in all its forms. Loss of children, loss of hope, loss of life. This book was always supposed to be about Mary Yelloly and Mary alone, and at first I tried hard to keep our boy out of it. But in the end – almost paralysed by the effort of doing so – I gave in and let the two strands weave together on the page, just as they seemed to in life.

Then, months after I'd finished writing the book, I was sorting through an old box of our boy's stuff – abandoned school exercise books, paperback novels whose corners had been ripped to make spliffs – and I found a collection of twenty-one poems, *Works From a Former Life*, all of which he had written during that time. I wept as I read them.

And later, when he'd read this book and been more generous about it than I could ever have hoped, I asked if he'd let me put some of the poems in it. He hesitated, then said yes. Nine of them are included here.

J.S.M., London, 2008

1

SUFFOLK, JUNE 1838. A day so hot the air is glass. Splash of
poppies in the hedgerows. Cow parsley high as your shoulder.
Above it all, the soaring summer sky.

Looking down. A pattern of fields, dark smudge of wood-
land, the sly grey spire of a church. England spread out on a
perfect midsummer's day. Look again. A dot on the dark dirt
road, the smallest dot, wobbling along towards that church.
Go a little closer. Zoom right in. It's a carriage – primrose
yellow, streaked with dust, a family crest on the side. A shield
and helmet, curling ribbon. *Spes Mea Christus*. Christ is my
hope.

The carriage is pulled by two drenched old horses that have
seen better days, whipped by a tired fat man in a scratchy
woollen coat – a man who should not have had ale before he
set out from Ipswich – windy, sweaty, drink-stained, trying
without success to swallow his burps. The wheels squeak and
bump, slamming hard over dirt and shale. It'll be another
hundred years before this road smooths out to a hard ribbon of
grey. Now on this summer's day it's tedious, uneven, cracked
with heat, littered with stones, dried animal dung, the sparse
yellow heads of dandelions.

The road to Woodton.

The carriage curtains are drawn tight, no chink open to let sun in. Inside, a young woman sits alone in the airless dark, everything about her black except for the pale shock of her face. A lovely face, normally flushed and teasing – empty now, voided by grief. She's done all the crying she can do. Those eyes – two pinpricks on this earth's dark surface – are dry and hard.

Sarah Yelloly, thirty-one years old. And above her un-brushed, unbonneted head, strapped to the carriage roof in a rough pine coffin, there you are. Her little sister Mary, twenty-one.

On a late winter's day in February 2006, only days – or is it weeks – after we've had to lock our eldest child out of our home, I drive to a lonely Norfolk churchyard to look for your grave. The grave of a girl who died nearly two centuries ago. A girl whose short, quiet, long-ago life suddenly feels urgent to me: something I must uncover and make sense of. Why? Don't ask me why. I'm still trying to work out why.

All Saints, Woodton turns out to be hard to find – standing some way out of the village and on high, windy ground, away from the main road. *Beautifully positioned*, says a guidebook. Lonely, it seems to me. Plague, someone mutters to me later, as if that one dark syllable explains everything.

At first, driving through the eerie quiet of Bungay and reaching Woodton at four, hurrying to beat the dusk coming down all around me, I start to wish I'd come earlier. All day it's been so dark, the sky one single, crushing slab of grey. I should have come this morning. The antique shops in Bungay might have been open.

But as I reach the church, half thinking of you and half listening to the end of a programme on the radio, the clouds shift and light spills over the Norfolk countryside and everything suddenly drowns in colour. Furious greens and yellows, blinding gold. Dazzled, I pull in by the old wall and turn off the radio. No sound except for some lone bird cawing, and the dog's eager breath in the back.

I bite the woollen finger of my glove. It smells of home. My heart tightens.

I'm approaching the place where your bones must lie.

I haven't seen my eldest son in two or maybe three weeks. The fact that I don't know the exact amount of weeks makes me wake each morning with a hard tight pain in my stomach.

I don't know his address, I don't know his phone number, though that's only because we stopped his phone after the monthly bill topped £200. We had to think very hard about that one.

Last time I saw him (two or is it three weeks ago?), I bought him dinner at the Italian down the road. I had wine, he had a beer. We shared bruschetta, talked about this and that. We managed to make ourselves chat – we're both good at that.

He'd come round earlier to collect some stuff. We'd hoped to talk him reasonably into swapping his phone contract (paid for by us) for pay-as-you-go (paid for by him). But he said he had no money. That's because you spend it all on drugs, we said.

He got angry then, refusing to hand over his SIM card: Make me, then, go on, try it.

And his father – tense with fury and sadness – suddenly lunged at him. For a moment or two, they grappled on the floor. The two of them, on the floor. No one hurt, but a moment of such despair. The kind of moment you would undo if you could.

Our son's face was greenish-white as he went from our house. He still had his SIM card.

Afterwards, because there was no doubt that he had started it, that he had gone at his son with such anger, his father wept with shame. He lay on the sofa and he wept.

We've lost him, he told me. That's it. We won't see him for years now. We've lost our boy and that's how it ended. My own stupid fucking fault.

We both cried. He cried because of what he'd done and I cried because I knew why he'd done it. Because it could so easily have been me. For two years, our boy has lied to us, stolen from us, even hit us. For two years he's done everything he can to undermine and destroy our family life, not to mention his siblings' happiness and security. For two years, we've wanted this to be over, we've wanted him gone. Is there a worse thing you can feel about your child?

Our boy slammed out of the house. But he didn't go. Two hours later we found him in the churchyard next door, playing the guitar. We went out to him.

His father said: I never meant that to happen. It was completely wrong, I'm very sorry. Please forgive me.

We love you so much, I told him.

We miss you, his father said.

He just shrugged. But then his father leaned across to touch his arm and make a little joke, and our boy looked at the ground and smiled his old heartbreaking smile, the one he's had since he was two years old.

Am I forgiven? his father said.

The boy said nothing. His father said he had to go to a meeting, just for an hour or so, something he couldn't get out of.

Come on, I said, you must be starving. I'll buy you some dinner.

My boy looked at me.

Are you hungry? I said.

Yes, but I can't stay long. I have to be somewhere at ten.

I really hoped he'd eat. That was all I could think of now – feeding him. But even though he'd ordered extra goat's cheese on his pizza, he only managed half. Said his stomach had shrunk from going without food. He sipped his beer. Panic shot through my heart.

You mustn't go without food. You have to eat.

How can I eat? I have no money.

Come and eat at home. I can't bear to think of you being hungry. You'll get ill if you don't eat. You know I'll always feed you.

He swallowed a smile.

Yeah, well.

I offered him pudding, but he told me he hadn't time – he had to be somewhere else. I didn't say anything. This is what he does, always. This is how he takes back the power. I don't know where Somewhere Else is, but when I try to picture it, all I see is the corner of a dark wet street and him all alone, cupping his hand to light a roll-up, ripped jeans dragging in the gutter, lower lip jutting. My stomach falling.

I left him at the bus stop, standing there with his guitar. I touched his head. I'm pretty sure I gave him a kiss. When I glanced back, he looked like a lonely person, a stranger, shoulders hunched, collar up. It took every ounce of energy I had not to run back and beg him to come home.

You are first put into my hands on a shrill spring morning in Mayfair, in a sun-flooded room that smells of beeswax polish, dust, old paper. A book dealer has acquired this fat leather-bound album at an auction in Suffolk. An album with your name – Mary Yelloly – stamped on the front.

It's an album of detailed watercolours begun by a little girl in 1824 when she was eight years old and finished when she was twelve. It's survived intact all these years.

But who was she? (Straight away, I like the name, the red and yellow of it. The first time it pops into my email inbox, I feel my heart tighten.)

Mary Yelloly? We don't know much about her. But you ought to see the album. It's quite extraordinary.

Two days later, in a sunlit room, I'm left alone to turn the pages of the *Picture History* – a title that doesn't begin to describe what you made, what you did. Over two hundred small paintings of what appears to be a made-up family – the Grenvilles. You've written out their full names and ages, you've told us how they spent their days. Reading, doing lessons, dancing, painting, watering flowers, visiting the sick and the poor.

Scene after scene of grand country houses and smooth, dappled English landscapes. Some lonely and wild and vast, but many dotted with tiny extravagant figures: bonneted children, bouncing dogs, now and then a baby, a stiff govern-ess, a white-pinnied nurse. Bonnets and shawls, stripes and frills – kittens frolicking, dark, gleaming wood furniture, china, silver, curls and bows.

Bright sun falls into the room. I swivel my chair into the shadows so I can see your work better.

The shades are mostly subdued, muddied and mixed, but now and then a colour jumps out – a stroke so bright and zany it could have been painted yesterday. A fuchsia swag of curtain, a lurid green parasol, a gown with the waxy hue of a daffodil. Or, the bright spines of brand-new books, a purple overcast sky, the hot crimson of a potted geranium. In the distance, always, the greeny-grey Suffolk-Norfolk landscape: hills and fields and scudding clouds.

You've written some captions yourself in ink – doing them carefully in pencil first then tracing over them with your nib. A sloping and slightly wobbly hand. Dipping the pen, concentrating, tongue wet against your lip:

Sitting Room Do. Maria Louisa and Miss Stanley.
Mrs Grenville, Eleanor – as Mrs G wished to speak to Mrs Melville about a person in the neighbourhood who was ill.
Mr Weston's Mill at Burnside near Woodlands.
And Mr and Mrs Grenville being driven in a pale yellow carriage with red wheels and bearing the family crest.

These people and these places, are they real, or did you make them all up?

Sometimes you do get the proportions slightly wrong. A mammoth chest of drawers towers above a small person with spindle limbs. Kittens big as dogs. Energetic bowls of fruit that seem to crouch ready to bound off the page. But this occasional schoolroom clumsiness only draws me closer to you. You really were here, touching these pages, your frowning breath held over this album, exactly the way mine is held now.

Sometimes a figure has clearly been cut out like a paper doll and pasted in over whatever was there before. Covering up what – a mistake, perhaps? And the pictures themselves are stuck into the album at the corners and one or two are coming loose, and I can see a trace of pencil-writing on the back. I test a corner, seeing if I can prise it further, but have to stop. I know the dealer paid a five-figure sum for this album, your album.

And then, at the end, something else. A pencilled note in a different hand. It tells me that Mary Yelloly died in 1838. She was twenty-one.

My heart turns over. She died. You died.

And I flick back through. A little girl is cutting cloth. Bonneted figures carry baskets of flowers, the trees behind them nudged by wind. It's a breezy day. A pale front door beckons. You swished your paintbrush in the water, backwards and forwards. The water turns pink. Or blue. Or muddy with colour.

And you died.

Here in this century, it's almost lunchtime. All around me, in London and the world, people still alive. Outside in the street, a beep-beep-beep, as some kind of articulated lorry backs or turns.

When we look back, his father and I, when we try to think honestly about the days and weeks and months that led up to us asking our child to leave, we slow down and then, mostly, we stop. We get confused. Darkness comes down.

What was it that took us to the edge, the place no parent can ever imagine reaching? What happened to make us ask him to leave?

You look him in the eye, the baby you once held against your heart in a warm blanket, his soft hair tickling your cheek, his breath on your face. You look at the baby you loved so much it hurt, the child whose open face still makes your heart turn over and – what? – you tell him to go.

How did we ever get to this?

8

No parent asks a child to leave except as a last, terrible resort. No parent asks a child to go unless they've tried every other possible option. Tried it a hundred times and then tried it just once more – a sliver of hope in their heart. Because – because this time, after all, it's just possible –

No parent asks a child to leave without feeling that they themselves have reached rock bottom – down there, laid out, flat and dead in the darkness. No parent rejects a child in this way without feeling they've failed in the very darkest way possible.

But we reach a point where it's him or us. Him or this family. Maybe if we had just the one child, we tell each other, if we had just him, we could let this happen. Let him undo us. We could shrug it off, that kind of obliteration. If we had just one child, if he were the only one living at home, we'd surely try and stick this out, we'd tough it out?

Whatever happened. Losing ourselves. But holding on to him.

But we don't have just one, we have two others. Two children who are slipping down too. They think they're OK, but they're not. Actually, maybe they don't even think they're OK.

And each day they need us more – they're crying out for us to do something – and most days we're just not there. Because every day is given over to dealing with the wreckage. All the joy and pleasure of normal family life has been replaced with dull-eyed damage control.

So how did we get to that place? I don't know. I do know. I know but I don't want to say.

There came a point where it felt like he was pulling the whole family over the edge and I had an option: let everyone fall, or cut the rope.

And when the moment came, I was surprisingly ruthless. I knew I couldn't let myself think about it for very long. I just did it. I cut the rope.

So when do we first know something is wrong?

Is it the day he gets up late for his maths GCSE – so unlike him – and rings his father to say he hasn't got a ruler and what should he do? And doesn't seem to care that going to buy one will make him late.

What's wrong with him? his father says later, bafflement and hurt in his voice. He almost missed the exam. He wasn't even slightly prepared. All these years of working and suddenly he's happy to throw it all away?

Or is it the day we are moving house – moving to a bigger, more rambling house with a great big basement music room for him to play his songs in – and he refuses to join in the excitement? He barely manages to pack up his own room, his own things – and then there finally comes a point where there's nothing left to move from the room but his bed. With him in it.

The removal men are embarrassed.

Look, mate, we can't just tip him out.

Oh yes we can.

We tip him out. We do. We try to make light of it.

That's teenagers for you, eh? one of the men says. You should see my son. You should see his room.

I smile, but I know he's just being kind. This isn't like that. By now we aren't like other people. Our child's eyes are furious, black.

For God's sake, he growls, what's the matter with you? Can't you see I'm trying to sleep?

But, darling, we're moving house.

Does it really have to be right now, this minute?

Well yes, it does. The removal men are here and the van is packed –

That's right, just organise everything to fucking well suit yourselves!

When we tell the story later, people laugh. Typical bloody teenager, they say. Sleeping in. Not lifting a finger to help.

We try to laugh too.

Is it possible, we ask ourselves hopefully, that they're right? That he's only doing what other kids do, that we're overreacting? How we'd love that to be true. But in our hearts we know what's true. All over the city, even in our own street, other families aren't living like this.

Because there are other things. Cash going missing. Tantrums that seem to come out of nowhere and be about nothing, but which destroy everyone's mood, leaving misery in their wake.

Threats of sudden and uncharacteristic violence. The day when, for no reason I can really explain to myself, I begin hiding all the sharp kitchen knives under the old boxes in the cupboard under the stairs.

His seeming inability to stick to any plan – our child who has always been so reliable, so easy to deal with, so very considerate and sensible. Our child who would phone if he was going to be three seconds late.

Now, his complete inability (unwillingness?) to get to school on time. Followed by his inability (unwillingness) to get to school at all.

But you don't panic. You are a good parent, a happy, loving fire-fighter, ready to deal with anything. So what do you do? You cope. You cram your work into a small space so you have more time for him. You cancel social engagements.

You try to talk to him. You stay cheerful. You look for the good things. You hope this is just a terrible phase. You wait for him to turn a corner, for things to change.

But you still hide the knives. You keep your handbag with you.

A good morning is a morning when no one shouts or cries, when life plods along. And there's one memorable dark winter's morning when life suddenly feels good again, because he gets up on his own, gets dressed and comes down and eats an egg you've cooked.

Is this it? Is this the corner?

But then there's another morning when you let the same hope bloom only to have it dashed.

Can you believe it? I tell his father, he actually got up when I woke him, came down, had breakfast quite happily, then suddenly for no reason at all his mood seemed to collapse. He told me he couldn't go in for the first lesson. And he went back to bed.

Suddenly for no reason at all. It's what we say all the time these days.

So I go up there. I put on the light and sit on the edge of his mattress and I touch his curly head. I put my hand on his waist, his shoulder. He's taken off his jeans but kept on his T-shirt and jumper and pants.

What's going on? I say softly. Tell me what's the matter.

Go 'way, I'm trying to sleep.

Darling, you can't do this.

I can do what I fucking well want to do.

But – it makes no sense.

(He says nothing.)

Do you see, it makes no sense?

(Silence.)

You did the hard bit already. You got up. You had breakfast. What's stopping you going in to school?

Gotta sleep. Go 'way.

You can't be late again. Do you realise how many late days you've had in the last two weeks?

Doesn't matter. I'll go in later.

(A sigh.) You promise? Promise you'll go in?

Yeah, now go away.

I go downstairs. Try to work. At lunchtime he's still fast asleep. He doesn't go in.

His father sits in the kitchen with his head in his hands.

There's a name for this, he says, it's school refusal. They call it school refusal.

And we look at each other almost hopefully, as if the discovery of a label might shed some light.

Two days of this and then he goes in.

He goes to school but doesn't come home. At almost midnight he bangs through the door, gripping the walls to steady himself.

My God, are you OK? Are you drunk?

He blinks at me. He doesn't quite seem drunk. His face is grey.

Are you all right? Where have you been?

When he speaks, his voice is strange. He makes no sense.

Speak to me, his father says. What have you done? You've taken something. What have you taken?

He tells us to fuck off and leave him alone. We follow him up to his room. It's dark. I put on a light. His eyes look through me. A small stream of something comes out of his mouth. Not quite vomit.

Quick, says his father. A towel. He's being sick.

But it's not like sick. Green water.

13

Should we call an ambulance? We decide not. We decide to let him sleep and to check on him. At 2 a.m. I check on him and find him asleep, his cat hunched on the bed next to him. The bedclothes are wet.

Next morning he's fine. We tell him he's not to go out on school nights. Not while he's still at school.

I'll do what I see fit, he says.

We can't go on like this, his father says. I just can't do it. I can't live like this.

A friend tells me her son can't decide whether to apply to Oxbridge or have a gap year first. I find it hard to have an opinion. Another friend tells me they had a great sixth form all lined up for their daughter, but she's gone and got a scholarship to this performing arts school – she's passionate about drama. What on earth should they do? As problems go, it's not a bad one, I say, trying to sound amused, rather than uninterested.

Meanwhile at home things are unravelling both slowly and fast.

It all happened so slowly. And yet it was amazing how fast it all unravelled.

So, it's a cold and bright February morning and, though I frequently tell myself that it could have been either of us, it isn't his father, it's me. I'm the one who tells him to go. His mother. The one who carried him and loved him and felt him move and grow. The one whose skin stretched once a long time ago to make room for him. She's the one who decides it would actually be preferable to live without him.

Though people might imagine it the other way round, it isn't his father but his mother who snaps first.

This fact is still surprising to me. No, surprising isn't quite the word. It knocks me out when I think of it. It makes me want to die. It knocks me to the ground. Where did I find it in myself to tell him to go?

Maybe I find the strength because it's no longer just about him.

That morning I discover that he's been giving his thirteen-year-old brother drugs. He and his friends – selling him cannabis. Teaching him to roll a joint when he still occasionally plays with Lego and listens to story tapes at night.

I did notice my youngest's appetite and energy fluctuations and his increasingly frequent bad moods, the way he'd rush for the Weetabix as soon as he got in from school. I'd started to worry about him. Should he have a blood test? Thinking his eyes looked rather pink, I took him to the doctor. Might he have conjunctivitis?

Later our boy tells me how much they all laughed about this, he and his friends. They thought it was the biggest joke, the conjunctivitis thing. Remembering this now makes me strong.

I don't actually throw him out. This is important, because later he will say I did – he will insist this is what happened. But I don't. Instead I do the next best thing. I give him a clear ultimatum.

Behave yourself and live in this family properly and decently, or go. Get up and go to school, or go. Go to bed at night, or go. Stop causing misery and chaos everywhere in this home, or go. Stop giving your brother and sister drugs (most of all, please, whatever else you do, stop doing that), or go. Stop stealing from us and threatening us, or go.

We cannot continue to live with you if you do all of these things.

What do I imagine? That he'll turn around and agree to change, to stay in, to give up drugs, to do all of those things? I don't think so. We've spent so many months I've lost count, maybe more than a year, talking to him, coaxing him, begging him. We've drawn up contracts, offered incentives, offered help. We've cried, we've laughed, we've told him how much we love him. We've reminded him of what life used to be like before all of this.

But nothing has changed. Or at least, something has changed – the family itself has changed. It's no longer what it was – a place of safety and happiness. It's started to come undone.

Some days we blame each other and some days we blame ourselves but mostly we just sit there and feel quietly hopeless. Someone once told me that a definition of stress is responsibility without power and that's exactly what this feels like. We feel so completely responsible and we love our child so much, and yet we have no power to act. What can we do? How can we possibly act, when the only act that will mean anything, the only one that will have any effect, is to force him from our home?

His younger brother and sister seem to know this. I feel them watching us, waiting for us to take control. I cannot bear the look on their faces. No family should have to live like this.

And it's a cold February morning, the day of one of his AS mock exams which he's just tried and failed – or tried and refused – to get up for. It's a cold February morning, the air punishingly white and sharp, when I finally say it.

This is it. This is the end. I mean it. Behave or leave.

I say it and then I walk away. I go downstairs and stand for a moment in our bedroom with my heart thumping. And something, I don't know what, makes me cross over to the window and look out and there's a big old-fashioned funeral going on down in the churchyard below. Black-clothed people, black horses with great fat black plumes, the whole lot, stamping feet, their breath in clouds. And I think, What have I done? What have I just said? And then I think something else: I think, This moment will pass. Just like everything else. It will pass.

And he goes. Surprisingly easily, it turns out. That's all it takes. I can't remember the door closing or what happens next. I can't remember much at all about what I feel on that day but I know that relief is part of it. No more hiding my handbag, no more locking my study, even if I only want to make a quick cup of tea. No more taking a breath when I hear him on the stairs, wondering which member of the family I'm going to have to protect from which aspect of his behaviour next.

The world looks different. Calm, clean, shiny with possibility. Suddenly it's actually worth wiping down the kitchen counters, getting the cupboards straight, turning lights off at night. It's worth it because they'll stay that way. The way we leave it will be the way we find it. It's even worth cooking a meal, because everyone will sit down happily around the table to eat it.

It's amazing to be able to go to bed and not come down in the night to turn off lights and check the front door isn't open, or that the ring on the cooker hasn't been left on.

His brother and sister seem strangely young. They start being silly again, laughing at their father's jokes, which is something they haven't done in ages. There's a new lightness in the family. We'd all forgotten what normal daily life was like. Slowly, happily, we relax.

Our child is gone and we can all relax. A lifetime of loving him and taking care of him and now he's out there some-where on the streets and we can all relax.

The idea is terrible to me.

That first night, his cat creeps into our room and – for the first time ever – sleeps on the bed with me. His black cat – the small black kitten with a white bib that we gave him for his sixth birthday, the cat he called Kitty because, after going through a zillion other possible names, he really did think Kitty was the best one. I curl my arm around her and I sleep too, even though my heart is hollowed out, blackened and burnt.

All of this happens just a few days after his seventeenth birthday.

Things happen. Something can happen. You're just getting used to the world and then it vanishes. Or, you love a person and expect to have them close by you for ever and then they go. Your life, your child, the world. It vanishes. It falls away. And the life you thought you knew, the one you were so certain you could count on, it suddenly isn't there any more and, before you know what's happening, the level ground you were standing on, it slopes and then it tips – and then what?

I miss my boy so much.

And something about Mary Yelloly, something about you, the loss of you, has gripped me. I'm thinking about my boy almost all the time now, yet even so, I find myself so moved by you. The loss of you.

Mary.

Cool fingers touching my sleeve. Who are you? Are you there? Who were you?

I wonder what's left of you.

If someone lives on this earth for just twenty-one years – that's just four years longer than my boy – and then they go, well, what's left? What do they leave?

It's simple, my husband says, glad for once to talk of someone else's loss, another century, a calm, dry time, she left the album. The only reason you've heard of her is because of the album.

Yes, I say, but that's not what I mean.

What I mean is, what's really left? Is there any other trace or are they blown to dust? Are you blown to dust?

You die. You paint your album, and then you die. Eight years later, just as life is getting going for you, possibilities unfolding, that's it, you have to go. You have no idea you'll die. You walk through my home, room by room. You have no idea why you do it. You just do.

You're in my head and I don't know why. It seems I don't know anything any more.

I miss you so much.

I start waking at night. Sleeping easily at first, thudding down into dreamless sleep, then waking into blackness. Three o'clock, four o'clock, five.

Thoughts jump up and down in my head. My boy aged about seven, sticky-up blond hair, licking Angel Delight off a spoon. Me standing on some high-up place as a child, some small mountain or other that we'd all been forced to climb, all of us complaining through the battering rain, only to get there and understand exactly why we came, see what it was all about: the world spread out miles below. The smell of wet anorak. Wind in your ears. Fingers mauve with cold. Perfection.

And, his baby body – pale smudges of nipples, the warm fatness of his arms on my bare shoulders, the smell of his baby skin against my face. My fragile, exhausted impatience – waiting for bedtime, longing for sleep, waiting to see him feed, change, grow.

My baby, my child. Always galloping on to the next stage. Crazy. Why did I rush? I shouldn't have rushed. Thinking there would always be enough time to hold and touch him, that he would always be there.

I find a book about your family in the British Library. *A Forgotten Past.* Its author, Florence Suckling, is a descendant of yours. She married your nephew Thomas – or at least, he was the man who would have been your nephew, if you'd lived.

On a dark and rainy Thursday afternoon, fuzzy and tired but propelled by another random burst of curiosity, I order up this book – a stout brown volume, published in 1898, complete with fold-out family trees. I order it up and take another step closer to you. Scanning the index. There are several chapters on the Yellolys and Tyssens (your mother's family) in here.

Your parents are distinguished. Dr John Yelloly is a member of the Royal College of Surgeons and physician to the Duke of Gloucester. Born on 20 April 1771 in Alnwick, Northumberland. His father was a merchant but he was orphaned and brought up by an uncle, Nathaniel Davison, Egyptian Consul and also an explorer. Davison discovered a previously unknown chamber in the pyramids – it was named after him. A famous explorer. Your father would have grown up knowing that. You'll have heard the story too.

Your mother Sarah is a Tyssen – born on 6 August 1784, the daughter of Sarah Boddicott and Samuel Tyssen, formerly of Hackney, and then living at Felix Hall in Essex. A wealthy family, landowners.

But your mother's an orphan too, in her way – her own mother died when she was only six and her father, inconsolable and unable to deal with a small girl, left her in Hackney with her grandmother while he moved to Narborough Hall in Norfolk with his son, your Uncle Samuel. When he died, your mother, just like your father, was brought up at cool arm's length, by guardians.

Your parents are married on 4 August 1806 at St Sepulchre's Church, Snow Hill in London. She is twenty-two and he thirty-two. It doesn't say how they met, but it strikes me that at the very least they have their parentless childhoods in common. They quickly set about making ten children. What a consolation it must be for them, to create this bursting, joyous family.

They live first in Finsbury Square in Hackney, where most of you are born. Then they move to a place called Carrow Abbey near Norwich, before moving again a few more miles across into Suffolk, to Woodton Hall near Bungay. Sarah is the eldest, then Jane, John, Harriet, Sophy, Sam, Nick, Anna, you and Ellen. You are the ninth, saved in the nick of time from being the youngest by the birth of baby Ellen. I wonder if that pleases you.

Ten children, running around in Suffolk. But, though you all survive childhood, only three of the ten live into ripe old age. Florence Suckling tells us that the family has a foe: consumption.

It begins at Woodton. Your brother Nick goes first at twenty-two. Followed, the next year, by Jane, thirty, and you, Mary, twenty-one, on consecutive summer days. I think your parents must really hope that Sophy, who has hung on this long, might pull through but no, a year or so later, she also succumbs. She is twenty-nine. Harriet, Sam and Ellen all hang on till middle age, but the foe gets them in the end. Sarah, John and Anna live to see them all buried.

When your mother Sarah Tyssen is twenty-two — already a whole year older than you will ever live to be — she knits a small brown purse *with two gilt tassels and rings attached*. With it, a letter:

> April 30th
> My dear Sir,
> Burns' poems and a little purse are scarcely worth your acceptance, but I offer them to you as a trifling remembrance of <u>this day</u>, of which, that you may enjoy many returns in health and happiness is the most sincere wish of your affectionate friend,
> S. Tyssen

When she wrote the book about you all, Florence must have either seen or had possession of this purse, because she describes it exactly:

> The paper is worn and yellow but its neat seal of S.T. is intact. The wrapper enfolding this letter and purse was written outside in a bolder hand – 'For dear Sarah – an old relic from "Miss Tyssen" in the spring of 1806 – July 31, 1841.'
>   The carefully preserved purse and letter were given back to her thirty-five years after her marriage, when she was fifty-seven years old (just a year before her husband's death); so the little packet has a lifetime of romance between its leaves.

A lifetime of romance. An old relic. A knitted purse with two gilt tassels and rings. Paper that's worn and yellow. It's easy to imagine your mother, the young Sarah, passionate and 'sprightly' as Florence describes her, knitting the purse, wrapping it and shyly handing the package to her darling, her future husband, your future father.

22

Does she know he likes poetry? Has he even perhaps expressed a particular fondness for Burns? Is that how they get to know each other, earnestly and passionately sharing the verses that they both love? Or maybe it isn't like that at all. Maybe your father, poor man, is beginning to regret the depth of enthusiasm he originally, in that first flush, expressed, since science, not poetry, is really his thing. He's a medical man, after all. And he fears he may have overdone the poetry thing, anxious to appeal to this accomplished and creative young woman with the interesting eyes. The woman who will one day be your mother.

And what about your mother? Does she offer the gift shyly, cautiously, with the slight trepidation those words suggest? *Scarcely worth your acceptance. Trifling.* Or is that modesty all an act? Is she secretly confident that her touching, home-made gift will be very welcome since it's already quite clear that John Yelloly, the man who will one day be your father, likes or maybe even loves her? Does she hope that he will not only accept, but treasure it too? That he'll take it out again and again in private, unfolding those poems, inspecting them for clues, a shy but certain happiness fizzing in his limbs?

I made this for you because I like you. I give it to you as a way of telling you that. I like you. I love you.

But then, thirty-five years later – when your father gives it back to her, what is it then but a dry and dusty thing, a relic? Half of their children already under the earth, Dr John himself only months from his grave. A lifetime of romance. But is that really any consolation for what came next?

I have a relic, we have a relic. It's our son's Kangaroo – a soft toy given to his sister when she was a baby. A toy which (at not quite two, having no idea of why it should be hers not his) he straight away stole and slept with for the next fifteen (though he would deny it was that long) years. I keep Kangaroo on a shelf with my sweaters. His drooping, over-washed, overslept-with body can transport me straight back to warm, safe things: nights of tucking my boy up in his bed, making him safe. Nights when I knew exactly where he was. Nights when I knew where I was too.

I rescued Kangaroo. When our boy, evicted from his dis-astrous and briefly lived-in flat, absconded, leaving us to move his possessions out in a hurry, I rescued him from the chaos and filth. I remember how I stood there in the middle of a room full of rubbish – shrugged-off underpants and jeans and unopened bills, Rizla papers, sticky beer glasses rimmed with ash – and saw Kangaroo lying there, helpless, on an old stained mattress.

I snatched him up. An old friend.

If I hadn't snatched him up, that might have been the end of him. He might have ended up in a bin bag, in a dustbin, on a dump. I wouldn't have wanted that.

What happened, Mary, to your mother's little knitted purse? How long before it was finally forgotten, thrown away, or else left to disintegrate in someone's attic? Maybe it ended up in a house clearance. Maybe it was bombed in a war, destroyed in a fire.

And how long will Kangaroo last? How many times any-way can a thing be rescued before there's no one left alive to remember why it was so precious in the first place? Bones dissolve in the earth, love turns to dust, and even relics – imbued with so much love and hope and memory – lose the meaning invested in them, once the investors are gone.

The Reading Room is very quiet now. Just the muted rattle of keyboards and the breathing that goes with so much concentration. Lamps illuminating each desk, each space, each bent head. Outside it will be dark already, spitting with rain.

Feeling my mood drop, I yawn and decide I've had enough for one day.

I can't think about you any more. I can't think about anything. I give the book back in and get the 68 bus home.

Suffolk, June 1838. The road to Woodton. But who's to say it's such a perfect summer's day? Maybe it's tearing down with rain and wind – one of those grim, wintry June days we've had so many of recently, days when the whole world has a tight lid of darkness on it from dawn to dusk, frequent showers bashing the trees, melting the countryside to mud.

A hard wind blowing. And Sam's lodgings quite cold and gritty and not very comfortable at all. Sparse furnishings, sour grey air, a meagre fire in the grate. No kind doctor to certify the death and offer reassurances.

Maybe the coach has to stand for a little longer than it should at Ipswich while they load you on, and maybe the coachman gets soaked, struggling not to swear as the rain trickles down the back of his neck.

Taking you home. Would you even have had a coffin? How long to get one made? Sarah's face glimpsed through the grey sheet of the rain, raw with tears.

Mud on her boot and the hem of her skirt.

I'll do it, she says. I'll take her home.

Funny, but you won't go away.

I have this image of you, sitting on a stone wall in breezy, dappled sunshine, legs swinging, eating apples. I don't know why apples. Apples that have ripened in a hayloft somewhere. A barn full of straw and sunshine and you outside, striped skirts, a thin shawl flung around your shoulders, long fair hair falling into your eyes.

And it's a chilly day, a bright blue windy day, almost spring but not quite, the air not quite warm enough, goose-pimpling your arms. Children are shouting. Sam and John doing something with sticks. Baby Ellen crouching for a moment then plopping backwards to sit. And you pushing yourself off the wall with your hands, kicking your legs out to jump down, apple finished, pushing the core between the hard cracks of the wall, pushing your hair out of your eyes.

Pushing your hair out of your eyes.

I go back to the British Library. Stomp up to the main counter in Humanities 1 and ask if it's possible to get Florence Suckling's book about you photocopied so I can take it home.

No, they say, it isn't. I take it to a desk and carry on reading.

It's 1816. You are born. The ninth child. But your mother Sarah Yelloly – *a comely, dark-haired matron* – is busy. She runs both nursery and schoolroom herself. Writing and drawing and painting with her older children. Teaching sums, grammar, geography.

Just like me with my kids, just like so many mothers for years and years, she keeps almost every little thing you children do. Every little scrap you write or draw, every letter, every bit of needlework. She keeps it. I keep it. I have Manila boxes marked *Kids and Baby Stuff*. In them, Mother's Day cards, yellow, poster-painted daffodils made from egg boxes. Tiny notebook stories, folded and stapled. All the little love notes they ever wrote me. Puppies and kittens, kisses and stars. The polythene hospital bracelets with their surnames on them, snipped off with scissors when we brought them home.

We keep these things because we have to. Because we want to. Because it would be impossible not to. Florence Suckling knew that your mother kept these things because, in 1898

26

when she wrote her family history, she clearly had access to them. She held them in her hands.

Your mother's system of education is strict – passionately felt and well organised, but strict. Each day's work is clearly written out, every single hour timetabled and accounted for. And when she can't be there with you, notebooks are given out and your older brothers and sisters are expected to keep daily journals which are then forwarded to her. This way she keeps an eye on your progress.

Around this time, you all get sick with whooping cough and Nick and Anna also have measles. Your parents, anxious about your health, decide to move you all from London to a place called Carrow Abbey in Norwich.

Sarah is fourteen, Jane thirteen, John twelve, Harriet eleven, Sophy ten, Sam nine, Nicholas eight, Anna six, you are five, Ellen not quite born. It is your first real taste of outdoors, of fresh sharp country air. But even in the country, education continues:

Monday, Tuesday etc.
To walk for an hour and a half after breakfast, at the expiration of that time, the school bell to be rung, everyone to come in and go to lessons in the following manner:

Sarah to teach Sophy to read. In the meantime Sam to write and sum, Sophy to do the same whilst Sam reads.

During this time Harriet to teach the little ones, and Jane to do two long division sums.

After this Harriet to do her French, writing and sums and hear Sam and Sophy parsing and geography. Sarah and Jane to do exercises and translation and a French verb.

On Friday and Saturday, if Miss Davidson is here, Sarah will only hear Sam and Sophy read; and on those days, Jane will translate Prince Chesi into English and French.

If the weather is not fine, then business is to commence immediately after breakfast; and if, in an hour's time, the weather becomes fine, they may then walk for one hour, but all at the same time, and resume lessons immediately after coming in again, which they are to do upon nurse's ringing the school bell. If the weather does not permit of going out, then business is to be gone on with immediately after breakfast, and the children may run and play for an hour and a half before tea, in the dining parlour. John to be allowed one hour and a half and two hours from the time he comes in before reading begins.

Four children to breakfast, two dine in the dining parlour.

To be up and dressed at half past eight o'clock every morning, if later a black mark.

Lessons to be done in the schoolroom, except on those days that the rooms are cleaning, and on that day in the dining room.

Go to bed at nine o'clock.

No one to go up the best stairs whilst cleaning.

If the weather is not fine, business to commence immediately after breakfast. How you must wish for fine weather. How your hearts must sink if you wake up to a black sky and the steady beat of rain. And what about the best stairs? Is there a mad, naughty morning when, giggling, you tiptoe up all the same, trying not to leave a footmark on the freshly mopped wood?

Another journal, kept by your sister Sarah during one of your mother's absences in July 1821, with answers scrawled in pencil, goes like this:

'Did you order dinner before breakfast?'
   'Yes.'
   'Have you got up in proper time?'
   Sarah: 'Yes.'
   Jane: 'Yes.'
   Harriet: 'Yes.'
   'Have you walked five times round the garden before breakfast?'
   Sarah, Jane, Harriet, Sophy each signs: 'Yes.'
   'Were you ready for breakfast?'
   'Yes.'
   'At what time did you begin your French and did you do it well?'
   Sarah: 'About half past nine but I read before breakfast.'
   Jane: 'Ditto. Ditto.'
   'Have you taught Anna and Nick and Harriet their lessons?'
   'Yes.'
   'Did the little ones do good lessons?'
   'Pretty well.'
   'Have you been ready for dinner?'
   All: 'Yes.'
   'What time did you breakfast?'
   'Nine precisely.'
   'What time did you dine?'
   'Half past three.'
   'Have you been agreeable and polite to Mademoiselle and to each other?'

Sarah: 'Yes.'
Jane: 'Yes.'
John: 'Yes.'
Harriet: 'Yes.'
'Have you behaved well in every respect to nurse?'
Nicholas, Anna, Mary: 'Yes, very well, all.'

And I stop right there. Because this is you. You just moved into the frame. Here you suddenly are, five years old and standing there just behind Nick and Anna, plump hands folded behind your back, joining in: *Yes, very well, all.* It's the very first time I've heard your voice.

My boy at five years old. Five and a half. Summer mornings before school, we have a little routine. After his father has dropped the other two – the two babies – at nursery, we have half an hour in hand, so we have breakfast outside in the garden together – French breakfast! – him drinking hot chocolate and eating baguette, me drinking coffee and reading aloud a chapter of whatever novel we're in the middle of. *Five Go Off in a Caravan Together. James and the Giant Peach.*

I read and he drinks his pink-brown chocolate from a big yellow cup and watches me over the rim. Serious and intent. The sun is hot on the metal table. He has a scratch on his hand. He wears an Aertex shirt. Birds are singing and the undergrowth – neaths of the leaves are lit up, the lightest summeriest green, and bees are already crawling in and out of the roses.

It's going to be a boiling hot day.

I look at my watch.

When it's time, we go inside – the kitchen suddenly full of shadows, cool and dark – and I wipe his mouth with a flannel and we get his bag and we walk to school together, hand in hand.

He asks me questions about the world – questions he's asked before, and new ones too. I try to answer. When I don't know an answer, I tell him so and he squeezes my hand. He doesn't mind when I don't know things.

I squeeze his hand back.

And I am entirely happy. I think these days will probably go on for ever, that this is how life will be from now on, will always be. I think I will have this same experience with his brother and sister, that I will go on having it, that I have got it all to come.

But in fact that was it. I didn't do the same thing with them. And it was just that one summer when he was five. In fact, I say summer but it was probably just a few weeks of warm weather that particular term. It might not even have been weeks, it might have been days. How many days? How many days did we do this thing of French breakfast in the garden and reading aloud, and why is it so important to me, now, to know?

And then I get to it. The page I've been dreading:

The pocket almanac for 1836, January 11, has the following prophetic entry in Mrs Yelloly's hand: 'This year seems to begin cloudy and overcast. Oh! Let it by Thy pleasure to turn these shadows to our eternal benefit.'

1837 – This prayer was answered in the following year for at least one of her children, for Nicholas passed from the night of clouds and sickness of this present world into the brightness of that land which has no need of the sun.

That land which has no need of the sun. Victorian euphemism at its finest.

Time passed and the New Year of 1838 opened on the party assembled at Woodton for the Christmas season, and Mrs Yelloly's almanac opens with its accustomed prayer of thanksgiving and of hope, and with never a foreboding of the shadows of Azrael's wing which must even then have been hovering over her home, for Mary at that time must have been ill of the fell consumption which was so soon to terminate her young life.

'In the spring John came home with the germs of smallpox, and Mary, to escape infection, was hurried off to Sam's bachelor quarters at Ipswich. John had long been consumptive but the fiercer microbe of the fever prevailed over its brother phthisis and, after his recovery from the smallpox, John was a hale man to the end of his days. Less fortunate was Jane, who succumbed to the infection on 21st June, and was buried at Woodton by night.

'Anna and Harriet were both ill of the disease at the same time and, to add the culminating blow to the poor, distressed mother, Mary died of the shock of her hurried removal, at Ipswich, on the very day of Jane's death, and was brought home to Woodton by Sarah (who had nursed her) within the week, and the funeral sermon was preached for both sisters on the same day.

'At the funeral sermon at Woodton, when Jane and Mary were buried, the preacher said: "Both were young and lovely; the one asked for, and had, the blessed sacrament on her deathbed, the other was delirious, but in her wanderings all her ravings were of singing hymns and pious words."'

Which of you is it who has the sacrament, you or Jane? And which of you is delirious and raving? If Jane dies of smallpox, then is it more likely that she's the feverish one? Or does it work the other way in that, understanding she's going to die, she has time to request a blessing?

But you – you die of shock. It's not expected. Something in you just bends and snaps. One moment you're weak, you're ill, but still very much here. Next moment, you're gone. They can't think you are going to die or they would never send you off to Ipswich. Dying in Sam's bed, away from home. Breath stopped, goodbyes unsaid. Singing hymns and saying pious words – that seems unlikely. Are you delirious? Do you even know what's happening?

And what about your mother, the twenty-two-year-old who knitted the purse full of poetry and hope? How does she cope with all of this? Is that pocket almanac stuffed with prayers really any consolation? Does she honestly believe that this – the systematic and painful decimation of her cheerful and creative young family – is some all-powerful and benign God's will?

Suffolk, June 1838. The road to Woodton. Not day at all, but night – a hot, moonless, shapeless, starless June night. No shimmering hedgerows or blue skies, no poetry or hope – just a muddy old coach hurtling through the dry, dark lanes, kicking up the dust.

So dark on this earth tonight that no one's even bothered to draw the curtains. Who, after all, is going to look in and see what's there on that punched leather seat?

Two young women, one dead, one alive. The living one holding the dead one tight in her arms. The dead one's loose fair hair already wet with the living one's tears.

FLATLINE

The long-awaited relief,
after so many a laboured breath,
it's all over now. It's been
long lost amongst for ever,
replaced by the one whining sigh,
that sings farewell over the empty form
in the bed. So no one looks now,
the eyes have been closed,
the alarms have come and gone,
and the line is left to bleed out,
in the footsteps of the departed.

2

AND IT'S ON that frozen afternoon in February, only a matter of days, or is it weeks, after I tell our eldest child to go from our house, that I find myself standing in that graveyard at All Saints, Woodton, where you must lie.

You wouldn't recognise Woodton now. If you drive from Bungay to Norwich, it's just off the B1233, a road that didn't exist in your time, a sharp left-hand turn and down into a mostly modern village with one pub. I do notice a road called Suckling Close. Along it, white-faced children with rucksacks straggling home from school. A woman in a beige anorak walking a dog. Pylons stretching on and on into nowhere.

To the left of the church – which is small and solid and pretty, covered in greyish-blue shingle, just the way you probably remember it – a kind of farmyard. Low spreading cedars, frozen mud, hens, a cockerel crowing, wooden huts, a dog barking. To the right, not much. A field, a rough little track leading who knows where.

The afternoon has turned dark again as I lift the latch on the gate. The small graveyard is a mix of very old lichen-covered stones and much newer ones – black polished marble with crisp lettering, yellow flowers slumped in little perforated metal pots. In some places the grass has been roughly mown, but a mole has been at work and even the longer grass is scattered with small, frozen mounds.

The church isn't locked. I tip the metal latch and push at the heavy wooden door and feel the hush of silence suck me in. Leaving the door slightly ajar, I tiptoe in, across the dull blue carpet towards the aisle. The very first thing I see is your name carved into the smooth, bloodless stone:

Sacred to the Memory of
NICHOLAS NATHANIEL YELLOLY
the amiable and beloved son of
John Yelloly MD and Sarah his wife
who died at Woodton Hall in this parish
on the 11th day of November 1837
aged 22 years.

Near this place and in the same tomb
with those of their brother
are interred the remains of
JANE DAVISON YELLOLY
who was born on the 16th day of March 1808
and died at Woodton Hall in this parish
on the 21st day of June 1838

and of
MARY YELLOLY
who was born on the 23rd day of December 1816
and died at Ipswich
on the 22nd day of June 1838

They were the 2nd and 6th daughters of
John Yelloly and Sarah his wife and
formed a much loved portion
of a numerous and united family

The church is silent, very cold, very quiet, my breath visible
even in here. *Near this place and in the same tomb.* But where? I
go outside again to look for your grave.

Many of the older stones are unreadable and the earliest
ones that I can make out seem to be from the late nineteenth
century – certainly nothing as early as the 1830s. There are so
many stones where no trace of writing at all is left – faceless,
nameless stones, scabbed with yellow lichen and slanting,
slumping, tipping against the earth, nothing and no one to
claim them. I can't see your family's name anywhere.

The wind drops for a moment and I turn back to look at the
church, but already the light has slipped away and I'm
standing here alone and in the dark.

When my mother married my father, she was twenty-one,
too young to know what would happen, that you had to
think about these things. She tried to leave quite early on,
but didn't have the bus fare. After that, she used all her
energy – all her bright, young, optimistic energy – to make a
go of things.

For fourteen years, she was happy. They were happy. She
made sure that they were happy.

Or, maybe not exactly happy. But when I pushed my face
between the gap in the car seats – him driving on the right, her
pretty face on the left, dappled trees overhead – and said: You
love each other and you'll never divorce, will you, Mummy
and Daddy? they both laughed and said they wouldn't.

They didn't say of course they wouldn't. They just said they wouldn't.

By the time she left him, life had got so bad that I wouldn't have even thought of asking that question any more.

There was a night – a black night rolled tight, tearful and shaky – when she came up and cried and slept in my room and promised she would do something.

Don't worry. It'll be OK. I'll do something.

I could see the shape of her in the darkness. I went to sleep. I was eleven. She kept her promise. The following summer when I was twelve, she left.

My father was a funny man who smoked a lot and watched games shows on TV and was always in his workshop. But he could make jokes and he could make me laugh. When he drove us to school, I nearly wet myself sometimes with laughing.

Back at home, two wills I ordered arrive in the post.

On 24 June 1880 while visiting Sarah at Poslingford in the village of Clare in Suffolk, your sister Anna Suckling dies quite suddenly. She is sixty-five, not incredibly old, though a good age for your family, I suppose.

Her will, written in a plump, square, slightly backwards-sloping hand, has a codicil crammed with objects, jewellery and drawings. Among the pearl bracelets and silver table-spoons and albums of watercolours of Woodton, daguerreo-types and silver coffee pots, she leaves to her third son, John Lionel:

the small diamond broach [sic] diamond and pearl ring I usually wear, gold broach [sic] with green centre, shawl pin with bird and pearl drop. Plain thick gold ring which belonged to his dearest father, gold chain which is on my eye glass, pearl half hoop ring, pair of long gold earrings which belonged to my dearest sister Mary . . .

Mary. In a few words, a few seconds, the picture changes.

You're not sitting on a stone wall any more. Instead it's night and you're looking into a dark mirror, candle flame flickering, your fair hair piled on your head, which is carefully inclined, fiddling with the screw clasp on an earring.

A long gold earring.

A quick gasp of annoyance, then a little movement of your fingers, a satisfied shake of your head. And for a second or two, with that sudden flash of gold, the shy satisfaction in your eyes, I can almost see your face, reflected there in that dark, candlelit glass.

An old friend, who now lives in Manhattan, is in London for a few days and comes to spend a night with us. As we sit around the kitchen table late at night, talking and drinking, our story spills out. More, perhaps, than we'd intended to tell. The story of daily life as it is right now with our boy.

Our friend looks more and more shocked. She's known our kids almost all their lives.

I love him dearly, she says. I remember how he was the sweetest, most responsive child. But I'm afraid he's abusing you.

We both look at her.

Emotional abuse, yes, I agree, I suppose that's how it does sometimes feel.

Not sometimes, corrects his father. Always.

You can't live like this, she says. You just can't. What about the other two children? What about your work? I can't imagine how you're keeping going.

39

With great difficulty, we say, trying to smile. But for the moment we have to. What else can we do?

She thinks for a moment, cuts a sliver of cheese.

Have you considered, she says slowly, that he may have a drugs problem?

We shrug and tell her he only smokes cannabis, as far as we know. She tells us that America is much more clued up about cannabis and its long- and short-term mental-health effects than we are over here. She tells us that everything we've told her makes her think of addiction. She says she'll put us in touch with someone in Manhattan – a kind of adolescents' psychiatrist who specialises in addiction. Even if she can't help you, says our friend, she'll know the people over here who will.

We feel – how do we feel on that evening with our friend? Grateful. Doubtful. Relieved.

A week later, back in New York, she calls to say she has arranged an hour's phone consultation for us with this woman, at her expense.

She says we are to call the psychiatrist at three o'clock on Saturday.

It's an unexpectedly hot, late-spring day and I'm weeding the garden, happy out there on my hands and knees with the sun on my head. I almost don't want to come inside and start talking about drug addiction.

But at ten to three, I throw off my gloves and shoes and run barefoot into the house. And the boy's father and I sit upstairs in the study with two phones plugged in. A conference call about our child. The window is open and you can smell the blossom outside. My nails are rimmed with soil. Manhattan is a place in another world.

We tell the psychiatrist about our concerns for our boy. We describe the straightforward, bright, happy and level child he

40

used to be, and the aggressive and chaotic person he is now. We try hard to talk matter-of-factly and not emotionally. This is a clinical consultation, after all. We don't want to waste our friend's money.

The psychiatrist asks if we know exactly when our boy started smoking cannabis. We hesitate. We tell her we don't know exactly but we're pretty sure it was around the age of fourteen or fifteen.

She asks us if we understand about the difference between skunk and old-style cannabis.

We look at each other.

A bit, we say.

Well, for instance, a lot of people say: Oh skunk, that's just like the stuff we all used to smoke, only a little bit stronger, right? Wrong. This is a very different substance, genetically modified and between fifteen and thirty times stronger in the ingredient called THC that can induce psychosis. It can do untold and irreversible damage.

I take a breath.

And it used to be thought that a young person's brain matured around the age of eighteen, but these days we tend to believe it's more like twenty-one. And if a THC-rich drug like skunk is inflicted on immature frontal lobes, then a child's neural pathways can be badly distorted. And because research into the effects of this drug have only really just started, perhaps the most frightening thing of all is that no one yet knows how to treat brains that have been damaged in this way.

So – you're saying it's irreversible?

We just don't know. We literally don't know.

But, the boy's father says, neither for the first nor the last time, what can we do? Is there anything we can do?

She gives us the name and phone number of an expert in

London whom she recommends we consult – a woman who has a phenomenal track record for getting young people clean. She also tells us we must get ourselves to Families Anonymous meetings as soon as possible.

Families Anonymous?

Support for people whose families and loved ones are addicted to drugs. Please look into it right away – you'll find it on the web. For people like you, it's a lifeline.

People like us.

When we've finally thanked her and said goodbye, I look down at my dirty gardening hands and I start to cry.

The boy's father touches my head.

Hey. Come on –

His frontal lobes, I whisper.

I know, he says, I know.

When our children were all very small – our boy maybe three or four, the youngest just a baby – I decided that a mother of three should at the very least know how to do basic first aid.

So I got in touch with St John's Ambulance and discovered that, if you were willing to get a large enough group of mothers together, say five or six, you could get a first aider to come over to your home and give you a morning's tuition in the basics. I can't remember exactly what it cost, but it wasn't much. It might even have been free.

We all gathered in my sitting room with coffee and biscuits. Mums with sleepy, laughing eyes and post-baby tummies and stains down our T-shirts. And I can't remember whether we had our children with us – my dim memory says probably not. But I do remember the calm, practical efficiency of the man in his uniform. I remember his little jokes but also his overriding respectful seriousness as he took us through all the things we needed to be able to do in case of scalding, falling, drowning, shock, suffocation, or any sudden damage to life and limb.

I remember that he demonstrated the recovery position. On your side, one leg higher than the other, checking the airways, checking the tongue was free. He showed us how to resuscitate a rubber baby doll – blowing into her mouth and pressing on her chest. The doll had a name, I can't remember what it was.

And I know he also explained that, however much you fear for your child, you should try never to panic. Stay calm and always first check the accident scene for signs of anything else that could go wrong. You wouldn't believe, he said, how often people cause a second accident while rushing to deal with the first one. We all laughed.

After he'd gone we all chatted some more over another cup of coffee. And there was a definite sense of lightness – a sense of relief and even self-congratulation that we'd done something practical to keep our children safe. Certainly, we all got the point about not causing a second accident. We doubted we would ever need to panic again, whatever dangers the future produced.

Still trying to find you, intent on finding you now, I drive back to Woodton.

A freezing day in March. A light dusting of snow has fallen overnight – just enough to make the world look clean. Though it's started to thaw on the road, it's still thick and white in the hedgerows. The ground is hard, the sky an aching blue.

As I drive into the village, the bin men are there by Suckling Close, emptying the wheelie bins. I wait ages for the van with its flashing lights until the man in a woollen hat, his cheeks dark with cold, waves me on.

I pull in on the snow-frosted verge just in front of All Saints. Cold air hits my face and I can smell manure. That cockerel is crowing in the farmyard next door and every time he crows a hidden dog howls his reply. I've never yet seen a single person there. My own dog gives me a bleak look as I leave her in the car and crunch up the church path.

There are snowdrops everywhere – great drifts of them at the entrance to the churchyard, on the path in the field beyond.

This time I decide to be more methodical, looking at every single grave that I can possibly read, inspecting each in turn, all except for the very obviously shiny new ones with fresh flowers on them.

I crunch through the snow, making my way slowly backwards, away from the twenty-first and twentieth century and back, back into the dim shadows, where the early nineteenth century lies, sunken and undisturbed, under the shade of the conifers. Your century. I notice I'm holding my breath.

These stones are almost impossible to read. I can just about make out one or two names. *Leeder. Harvey. Edward* – or Edwin? Wind gusts suddenly and powdery snow falls out of the guttering of the church, hitting the ground and making me jump.

It gets harder to walk. Further back behind the church in the very oldest part of the graveyard, the ground has succumbed to a catacomb of molehills and my feet lurch and sink with every step. Each clod of earth is capped with snow, but soft underneath. Brambles and bracken. Crunch, snap, sink. The graves shift worryingly beneath my feet.

Some of the stones have crosses, others are coffin-shaped tombs of stone, low in the grass and cracked so they look as if they've been dropped from a height. When I was small, I was terrified of cracked graves. Afraid that the dead might come climbing out of them, intent on revenge. Why wouldn't they be furious that the rest of us were still alive?

I try to read names, a date here, a Christian name there, but so many are rubbed out by time and neglect. *Emily, Luke, Richard.* 1754 is the oldest grave, two years the shortest life. No sign of a Yelloly. No sign of you.

And I'm standing in the farthest, coldest corner by the old ivy-covered wall when, for no particular reason, I look up and there it is in all its enormous splendour: Woodton Hall. Your home.

My blood stops. But – not your home. Of course not your home. It's a trick. And it takes a moment or two to work out exactly what I'm seeing. Not the Hall itself, but its ghostly imprint – the space it once inhabited somehow pulled into sharp focus by the icy winter air. Its imprint. The space between the trees, the foundations. Is it because the trees are bare and the air so cold that I can see exactly where it must have been?

Then, even though my eyes are still fixed on that spot, the sensation, the skeleton of a building, slips away. Just as quickly as it came, it dissolves again and there's nothing.

Just me and some forlorn old trees and the crumbling remnant of a wall.

I go back to the road and decide to walk up the track through the field to the right of the church that must lead up to where Woodton Hall once stood. There's no sign saying *Private.* It even looks a bit like a footpath. Great drifts of snowdrops everywhere to my left and right. Tractor wheels have made deep ruts which have filled with brown puddles, each one iced over.

But, when I get close up to what must have been the old garden wall, I stop because I realise there's a proper house –

newish, or at least newly done-up – beyond and also a lawnmower of some kind propped by the wall. Someone must live here.

I stand and listen for a moment. Nothing. Complete silence. Now I'm closer I can see that someone's been rebuilding the wall. A painstaking operation. A pile of the original old orange-and-pink bricks stacked in a corner, ready to be inserted back into the old puzzle, the wall.

A noise behind me and I turn around sharply. I don't know what I'm expecting to see. A fifteen-year-old girl in a dark bonnet and paisley shawl, gathering snowdrops? But there's nothing there, no one. Just the drip of water – snow thawing in the trees. And the dog next door who's started barking again.

Even though we tell him to go, our child comes back. First he comes back using his own front-door key, the key it never crossed our mind to take from him. When we ask him to leave, he says OK, he'll go, but we can't stop him – he'll be right back whenever he wants.

That afternoon, we get a locksmith round and change the locks. New keys for everyone. I stand and watch them being cut in the smoky shop full of beat-up shoes waiting to be reheeled.

Break-in? says the man, cigarette in mouth, turning the key.

I nod and try to smile.

Too bad. Still, you want to be safe, don't you?

The second time our child comes back, he comes in a haze of pure fury, discovering the door is locked to him, threatening to destroy the whole house if we don't let him in. He wants money. He goes away but says he'll be back. It's become quite normal for him to sleep all day and stay up all night, so it's all too easy for him to drop by exactly when we're vulnerable. Middle of the night, 4 a.m., dawn. Keeping his hand pressed hard on the bell and then, when we disable it, banging on the door, kicking it, shouting threats. When this doesn't work, he takes my large pots of geraniums and hurls them, one by one, at the door.

Three pots smashed. A grey light struggling into the dawn sky. We try to talk to him through the window.

When you'll accept help with drugs, we say softly, when you'll agree to behave like a member of this family, we'll let you in. But not until then. We love you very much, we'll always love you, but we just can't help you until you let us.

He tells us we're cunts. He says as far as he's concerned we can fuck right off. Then he takes another pot in his hands.

He'll go in a minute, his father whispers, ashen-faced, give him one more minute. I'm sure he'll go. He knows this is pointless.

One more pot, I tell my boy through the letter box, and we call the police.

Smash.

His father stands there in his dressing gown and dials. I see that his hands are shaking. To have to call the police about his own son. Dismay all over his face.

They arrive impressively quickly and seem (to our surprise) completely unsurprised, as if it's entirely normal for seventeen-year-old boys to be locked out of their homes and threatening criminal damage at dawn.

We're so sorry to trouble you, we both say.

Not at all, sir, it's fine, not a problem. Hope we can help.

The police ask us what we want. Do we want to press any charges? Oh no, no, definitely not.

A warning then? Just to send him on his way?

Thanks so much, we say, a warning would be great. We're so sorry about all this.

It is about 7 a.m. All this time, I've been very calm. I haven't cried at all up to now. So it's funny that it's actually this moment – the very moment when the friendly and sensitive neighbourhood police are talking firmly to our boy, the moment when, standing there on the pavement next to our house, our home, his home, his shoulders crumple and he suddenly looks so very tired and starts at last to move off – when I start to weep.

Maybe it's those words. *Send him on his way.* What way? Where? Isn't his way our way? Ever since we brought him home from the hospital on that sleepy, newborn afternoon. Home. I blot my eyes with the edge of my dressing gown.

We watch through the window as the police say one more thing to our boy. He seems to listen and say something back and then he shrugs and – starts at last to walk away. My heart bursts.

The next moment unrolls fast.

Shall I run after him? I ask his father, assuming the answer will be no way, but eyeing my coat and getting ready to go all the same. I'm grabbing at kitchen roll to dry my tears, stuffing my feet into trainers.

He hesitates. Well, maybe we could give him some breakfast or something?

And that's all I need. I love him for that. For his unsteadiness, his inconsistency. For giving in.

It's good that the police van has gone by the time I pull the coat on over my pyjamas and run down the street. Looking left and right, looking for my boy. The air is freezing. He's sitting alone at the bus stop, head bent.

Oh, is all he says, when I sit down next to him.

Sweetheart –

Go away. (Bottom lip jutting.)

48

Come home and let me cook you some breakfast. Go on, darling. You look hungry. Dad and I just want to talk to you calmly.

He regards me without anger. He blinks. His pupils are tiny.

You think calling the police on your own son is a calm thing to do?

A bus shudders past.

We won't tolerate you attacking and damaging the house, I tell him, you know that.

He says nothing. I try to smile.

Look at me – I'm sitting here on the Walworth Road in my pyjamas. Come on. Come and have some breakfast. Please?

The please is a mistake. His father would tell me not to beg.

I'm tired. I've been up all night. Got to go and find somewhere to crash out, he mutters.

Where? Where will you sleep? Where are you staying?

Dunno.

Then come and have some breakfast and let's at least talk about it. You can sleep at home, I add, knowing that this too is a mistake.

I don't know if I feel like eating, he says and I feel myself relax as a crack seems to open up.

I'll make you eggs. Any sort of eggs.

He says nothing. A bus draws up and my heart contracts. But it's not his bus.

French toast?

He stands up slowly.

My bus, he says.

No it isn't –

You don't know where I'm going.

49

He turns his solemn gaze on me – I can't imagine what my face looks like – and then he gets on the bus, turning back for a quick second to say: Thanks anyway, Mum.

And then he's gone.

I make my way back down the road. Holding my coat collar closed and treading very carefully, as if the ground could explode at any moment.

His father opens the door and I feel him check my face for tears.

He wouldn't come?

I shake my head.

Hey, well done. It was worth a try.

Like two extremely old people, we climb the stairs and go back to bed.

Like I said, you are the ninth child. Ninth of ten. You aren't the baby. The baby is Ellen.

Ellen Margaret Yelloly, born four years after you, littlest sister of a *numerous and united family*, does not seem to have left any works of art behind her. Nothing of hers has been bought at auction and passed around Mayfair. But she has something you never had, something far more precious: almost twenty-two years more life.

Ellen. When you die in that room in Ipswich, Ellen is just seventeen years old, on the edge, about to tip from girl into woman. What's she like? Plump or slender? Funny or serious? Does she look up to you, or does she annoy you? Is she your confidante, or you hers? Does your death make her lonely? You die of shock. She never even gets to say goodbye to you. Does it break her heart, the way I think it would break mine?

You never see her again and, because you fall out of the

50

story at this point, you have no idea what happens next. But I know. I'll tell you what happens.

In 1845, seven years after your death, Ellen catches measles and recovers – but slowly. Then, just as she's getting better, just as she's regaining her balance in life, the family foe strikes, knocking her back down. Consumption. It strikes just as it struck you and Sophy and Nick. Consumption. How your mother must have come to loathe that word.

But in January 1850, your mother thanks God in her pocket almanac for

> raising my beloved child up from her most dangerous illness and blessing us with means to give her sea air. Oh bring me safely through all my anxieties and bless all my dear children!

My beloved child.

Her prayers are answered, partly anyway, because that same year Ellen recovers sufficiently to marry your cousin Captain John Tyssen, thirty-eight, son of your Uncle Samuel Tyssen of Narborough Hall. Your mother adores her brother Sam. That marriage must delight her.

There are other cousins too. Sophia, Charles, William, Henry, Honora and John. You must have played together. Gone on visits to Narborough Hall to see them. There's a painting of Narborough in your album, so you must have known it well.

Ellen and John are married at Cavendish in Suffolk and they have three sons, none of whom live. All die within days or weeks or a year of birth. But on 8 May 1856, she finally gives birth to a healthy daughter, Honora. Another daughter, Eleanor, follows in spring 1860.

But by then your sister is severely ill and she dies a week later. She is just forty. Your cousin Captain John is left alone to cope with two little girls. And, with Ellen's death, your mother has just lost yet another child, her baby. First Nick, then you and Jane, then Sophy and now Ellen. How does she bear it?

Dear Narborough Local History Society
I wonder if you can help me. I'm an author currently writing a book about a girl called Mary Yelloly whose uncle (Samuel Tyssen) lived at Narborough in the eighteenth century. Is there anything you can tell me about Narborough Hall beyond what's on your website? I'm hoping to visit soon – also is the Hall ever open to the public? Are you by any chance able to put me in touch with its owner? Any help you can give me would be hugely appreciated.
Very best wishes and thanks,
Julie Myerson

Dear Julie,
Just back from holiday and replying to emails. The present owners of the Hall are Robert and Joanne Sandelson. They are good friends of mine and I am sure would help. The gallery in the Hall is open on Sundays in the summer, also the grounds, and there is a fair at the end of May. I can check the dates and let you know. Last year *The Book of Narborough* was published by Halsgrove Community History series, which I edited. Information on the Tyssen family is included and I am happy for you to use any information of interest to you. I have several original letters relating to the disputes between the Tyssens and the local vicar, details of the Tyssen collection of coins and medals, and a few other bits and pieces about Samuel

Tyssen, his son (also Samuel) and Charles Tyssen. You are most welcome to visit to see if anything is of use. I have been trying to think where I have heard the name Yelloly before.

Best wishes,

David Turner, Chairman Narborough History Society

David Turner is waiting for me as he said he would be at the low wooden gate which is the entrance to the Narborough Hall estate. It's a shrill and windy late-March day – mauve sky with flashes of sun, clouds scudding. On the distant lawn, a small white dog bouncing.

I'll hop in with you, if you don't mind, he says.

I apologise to him for the smell of dog.

Oh goodness, I'm used to it.

As we crunch up the drive to the Hall, he tells me that he was born right here, in the Gatehouse. His mother and father met at the Hall in the 1920s, when his father was the gardener and his mother was in service as a maid. Every summer the Critchley-Martins, who owned the place back then, went away and the Turners would move into the Hall for the whole six weeks and look after it.

We'd have the place entirely to ourselves – we kids would spend the whole summer running wild around the house and grounds.

I look at him.

That must have been amazing.

Oh, certainly it was, it was. But my sisters were much older, you know, so it was mostly just me on my own.

I ask him if he still lives there in the Gatehouse now.

Oh no, no, I live in the new part of the village. Sadly.

★ ★ ★

We park by the side of the house. Beyond the gravel area is an enticing glimpse of a well-tended walled kitchen garden. Old walls dappled with chilly spring sun. The same crumbly orange brick I saw at Woodton. Your grandfather's house. Is this what you would have seen, hanging out of the windows as the Yelloly carriage cantered up the drive?

We walk round to the front of the house.

Ah, and there she is! says David and he points proudly to a small, dark-haired woman in a lilac fleece and wellingtons who's bent over the flowerbeds.

Joanne Sandelson pulls off one gardening glove and shakes my hand. Sun flashes across the garden and she shades her eyes with her other hand. The little white dog – who turns out to be a retriever puppy – is still jumping up and down at her feet. In front of her looms the house, elegant, ancient and enormous. Beyond, acres and acres of formal garden giving way to misty grey-green parkland, stretching away as far as I can see.

This is the most incredible place, I say, and she smiles.

It is an incredible place. Your grandfather Samuel Tyssen buys it while in the throes of grief, inconsolable after the death of your young grandmother, Sarah.

Your grandmother is an heiress who, according to Florence Suckling, comes with a *handsome dot* and she and your grand-father are married with some pomp in Hackney in 1782. There were a couple of miniature paintings which Florence must have seen. She describes your grandmother as having frank and innocent blue eyes but a slightly peevish mouth. Your grand-father's face was refined and intelligent but his eyes were merry.

The refined and intelligent man and the girl with the frank blue eyes live at Felix Hall in Essex, where they quickly have five children. But only two of them, Sarah (your mother) and

Samuel, survive. By the time the fifth baby dies, your grand-mother is very ill indeed – yes, the family foe again – and all she wants in the world is to be back home with her mother. So her husband takes her back to Hackney, where she dies and is buried with her ancestors. She is thirty-five.

And your grandfather is so heartbroken at losing his wife that he can no longer bear the sight of Felix Hall. Too many memories. Too much loss. That's when he sells it and instead buys Narborough, where he lives with his son, your Uncle Sam, while five-year-old Sarah, your mother, remains with her grandmother in Hackney.

Ten years later, your grandfather dies without making a will, and the trustees sell off all of the Narborough treasures at auction, letting out the old Hall itself. Sam is away at school and your mother finds herself under the legal care of guardians but otherwise completely alone in the world. She is fifteen.

It is your cousin Charles Tyssen – older brother of Ellen's husband Captain John – who finally inherits Narborough in 1845. He extends the existing watermill and adds a small cottage at the back, but in 1850 he sells the whole estate to a wealthy linen draper from Norwich. It is sold on to at least two more owners before it becomes the property of the Critchley-Martins, who employ the yet-to-be-born David Turner's parents.

We drink tea out of Cath Kidston cups in the homely kitchen at Narborough Hall. Cream floors and squishy sofas and, glimpsed through the back door, children's brightly coloured tricycles flung down on the patio. David tells me that, back in his childhood, this used to be the gun room.

Really? You actually remember it as the gun room? Joanne asks him and he nods vigorously.

Oh yes, yes.

It's clear, when I explain to Joanne why I'm interested in the Hall, that she doesn't know a single thing about the Tyssens. But then, I think, why would she? For her this place is about the future, not the past. She's brought her own young family here. She's not interested in making a museum. She's doing the garden. She's making a home.

On the wall are striking black-and-white photos of beautiful dark-haired children, their faces daubed with mud. They look like warriors – ferocious and androgynous, huge dark timeless eyes.

Your kids?

Joanne nods.

Those pictures were taken in the earthworks over there. You should get David to tell you about it. It must have been there in your Yelloly girl's time.

David explains that there's an old Iron Age fort just across the garden beyond the lake. About an acre wide. Trees, mud, a clearing. He played there as a child and Joanne's kids now play there too.

I expect children have played there for centuries, he says.

It's ideal, Joanne agrees. The kids love it. Perfect for creeping up on people and shooting arrows, that sort of thing.

After tea, Joanne takes me on a tour of the house and David follows. She explains that they've only been here three years and, once they'd bought the house, there really wasn't any money left over for furniture.

I mean, if you're wondering why the rooms are so bare, she laughs.

I ask her how she found the house.

Would you believe, it was just advertised in the back of a glossy magazine? We knew we couldn't afford it but we just had to see it anyway. It sounds crazy, I know. We wanted to live around here but we never set out to buy something like this. Some days I still can't quite believe we did it, that we really live here.

We cross a dim, wide stone-flagged hall, and go into a very grand drawing room, vast, high-ceilinged. Joanne tells me this was the Chinese room and that right up until the 1920s or '30s it had the most amazing mauve-and-green silk wallpaper, which was almost certainly original – dating from the first Samuel Tyssen's time, perhaps? The bay window looks straight down the drive and lawns. Joanne points out that the plaster ceiling rose is decorated with dragons. I tip my head back to look at it and, rather wonderfully, see about fifty yellow balloons also nestling up there.

My son just had a birthday party, she explains.

Must have been some party, running around this place, I say, and she laughs.

Do you have kids? she asks me.

I make a face. Horrible teenagers, I say.

Bet they're a handful, says David, and I don't answer as we walk into a room that's in darkness. Joanne goes across and flings open the shutters.

The billiard room. There used to be a conservatory joined on, built in Victorian times, but it's gone now.

And there was a little stage in here once, adds David.

I didn't know that, says Joanne, visibly surprised.

Oh yes. I don't know what it was for, but there definitely was, just here.

I look at David as he gestures with his arms. It's hard to decide who has a greater claim to this place. The new owner, whose party balloons cling to the ceiling. Or the boy, the servants' child, who spent whole summers haunting its vast spaces.

A very long corridor takes us down to the old kitchens where Joanne shows me the cold store – a room with marble surfaces, stone-flagged floor, fly screens on the window.

So useful, she says, running her finger along the marble. Things really stay cold in here.

Then she takes us through into a dining room with an enormous stone-and-marble fireplace, but no table.

We haven't really decided how to use this room, she says, but you can imagine the grand dinners they'd have had in here.

We go back into the grand dark hall and up the stairs. The broad stone staircase sweeps grandly upwards, the effect somehow enhanced by the fact that every single step has a soft toy sitting on it.

My kids! laughs Joanne.

David tells us that as a boy he used to slide down these banisters regularly with no hands.

Joanne shakes her head.

I wouldn't let my children do that.

Oh come on, goes David.

They'd crack their heads open, she says.

She's right, I say, partly because it's the truth and partly because it seems only polite to be on her side. This floor would be lethal.

We go up and David follows. At the top I glance back. It's a long way down. It must have been the biggest thrill, whizzing down with no one around to stop you, and I doubt that David was the first child to do it.

Upstairs, seemingly endless bedrooms open out on to one another – intricate panelling, tall sash windows giving breath-taking views of the distant grey lawns and trees, the acres of parkland, the fast-moving clouds.

I stand for a moment at one of these windows and am so effortlessly zoomed back to your grandfather's time that it's actually the plastic paraphernalia of a twenty-first-century female childhood – bright toothbrushes, pink-and-blond sparkly toys and the lurid splash of a duvet cover – that seem out of place.

OK, that's nearly it, Joanne says. But before we finish, I'll show you one more thing.

On the landing she opens a small wooden door, a door so low you have to bend your head to go inside, and we climb a winding wooden staircase just like in a fairy tale. Dust and cobwebs and a strangely familiar smell, neither musty nor old.

We're standing in a long, low attic – or series of attics really. Dark, tattered remnants of ancient wallpaper on some of the walls. Ceilings that slope so you can only stand up in certain places. The remains of a white candle collapsed and spattered on the floor. You down there on hands and knees, skirts grey with dust. The swing of your hair.

The oldest bit of the house, says Joanne as we all three stand looking around.

A moment of silence. I can hear the wind moaning in the eaves.

How old?

Oh, sixteenth century at least. I know it was used as a hospital in the First World War, this room up here, wasn't it, David?

He says it was. And we all gaze at the stained walls, the peeling plaster, the greyish light.

I feel myself shiver.

Did you come up here? Did you and your cousins know about this space?

Hey, come out on the roof, says Joanne – and, after crouching down through a little doorway, suddenly we're out there on a small parapet in the bright March wind. An intricately red-tiled rooftop – right on top of Narborough Hall.

You can see right over Norfolk from here, says David.

Hey, I say, holding my hair out of my eyes, it's amazing.

Isn't it? says Joanne.

And the wind lifts David's hair. David the man who was David the boy. Who says exactly what I know he'll say next.

We played up here as kids.

Did you? What an amazing place!

It was pretty good, yes.

Before I leave, David takes me for a walk around the Iron Age fort, while Joanne resumes her gardening.

We walk through the garden, across a lawn, past rows and rows of daffodils, to the lake. Passing an eccentric-looking wooden landing stage designed to look like a dragon – built in Victorian times, David says – and, skirting round the edge of the lake, we walk up into the earthworks. The mad white puppy, who has decided to join us, rushes backwards and forwards, catching the twirling leaves in her mouth.

It's a place full of gnarled trees and thick, low-lying branches. Perfect for climbing. Piles of leaves and sudden dips in the earth, an ideal place for a warrior to hide. It's easy to imagine boys and girls shouting and running here. John and Charles, Sophy, Sam, you and Ellen. Dirty nails, flying hair, stout boots coming unlaced, pinafores buttoned high up your backs.

Daffodils and narcissi bend in the wind.

So did you play here all on your own? I ask David.

He considers.

Well, sometimes I'd have friends over. There were plenty of kids in the village. But yes, I suppose I was often alone. I didn't really mind. They were good times. I lived for those summers.

Driving back to London down the A12, my mind caught somewhere between you and David and the mad white puppy and that madder attic space, I'm not even going very fast, certainly no more than 50, when it hits me. Pure panic.

My heart moves into my throat. Cheeks burning, mouth drying. Breath moving up too high in my chest. I'm suddenly aware – catastrophically aware – that there's nowhere to pull in, that I can't stop. I don't need to stop, but if I did need to, I couldn't. I could not stop.

Macy Gray is singing – loud and laid-back, unconcerned. I turn her off. Nowhere to stop. I need to stop. There are lorries in front and behind. Speed is swallowing me up. I need to stop.

At last there's a metal farm gate slightly back from the road, a dried mud area, deep with tractor-tyre marks. Just enough space to slow down and swerve in.

I do it. I indicate, pull in, swerving slightly, braking fast. The car shudders to a halt. Relief. As I turn off the engine, my limbs melt. I have no idea what has just happened.

The boy's father starts going to Families Anonymous meetings as the psychiatrist ordered. Every Wednesday, seven o'clock, for an hour.

Because we don't want to go out together and leave the children alone, we agree we should go on different days of the week, to different meetings. They take place all over London.

He comes back from his first meeting and doesn't tell me much about it except: that he cried. That most of the people there had children older than our boy. Mostly harder drugs too. That he's not sure yet how helpful it was, but he thinks he'll probably go again.

We both agree that I must find another meeting, a different venue and on a different night. I make a note in my diary to do it. And do nothing about it.

He comes back from his second meeting looking upset.

Are you sure it's helpful? I say. You don't have to go, you know. Should you do it if it makes you feel worse?

He shakes his head and something about the look in his eyes makes me feel very far away from him. He's been where I haven't been. He tells me he's sure it's the right thing.

Just listening to the other people's stories, he says. I don't know why but it helps. It's hard to explain what it's like. You really must put aside some time to find a meeting and go.

I tell him I will, and I do manage to find one up in north London but, when the evening comes around, I decide I have a headache and I mow the lawn instead.

And we take our boy back.

I still remember the length of time that he's away from us (not ever actually on the streets but sofa-surfing, sleeping on the various floors of various friends) as a long, bleak period of dark and frightening winter months. But in fact it's only a couple of weeks. All right, maybe three.

Three frightening weeks. I can't do it.

All day I pace the house, unable to concentrate. Every night I surprise myself by somehow managing to fall into sleep, his cat hunched against my legs. Every morning there are balled-up tissues all over the floor on my side of the bed.

Things keep on coming back. Things I haven't thought about in years. Pulling a vest over his fidgety blond head. A white vest with cap sleeves. How it felt to do up the poppers on his Babygro, his wriggling body warm inside, the bulk of his nappy getting in the way. Kissing his three-year-old fingers and toes till he laughed so hard he kicked me in the stomach. Staying up late to make him a *Power Rangers* cape. Letting him come into bed and watch a film with me because he couldn't sleep. Trying to explain the grown-up plot in six-year-old's language. Snuggling up, the biscuity smell of his hair. Serious, tearful conversations about God and death and bad things happening to animals.

His father and I make an effort to go on as normal, we try to work. But again and again, drifting around the house, we'll find ourselves grinding to a halt at the same time and in the exact same spot, and then that's it. The day is over. We're lost.

Long sad hours of talking about him, hours of sitting and going over and over it. What to do, what might be the best way to help him. Why we mustn't ask him back, why we must. What sort of expert help we should seek. Whether or not it's right to tell his grandparents. What exactly to say to his teachers. Which of our close friends it's acceptable to bore with this. Because we know that this is the truth – that we've turned into dull, one-track people. People who've forgotten how to have a good time. People who just aren't very good company any more.

The friend in Manhattan who paid for us to talk to the psychiatrist also sent us a box of American books about coping with cannabis addiction. Tough Love. I read them in one quick sad burst and for a few days they did seem to give me a kind of strength. The stories were so depressingly – reassuringly? – similar to ours, the symptoms so clear, the cure so clean and brutal, so obvious.

The books described a method known as *intervention*. You get a whole crowd of people, relatives or friends who really care about your child, people who have been a part of his life, to tell him he needs to go to rehab.

But it has to be a surprise. So the addict is either lured somewhere – a hotel room, somewhere he can't easily get away from – on some false pretext, only to find all these people there waiting for him. Or else maybe they burst into his bedroom, wake him up at dawn. And he – blinking and baffled by sleep, presumably? – lies there and listens while they read out letters that they've written. Passionate, upsetting letters that tell him how much they care for him but also tell him the truth: that, unless he goes to rehab, they don't know how to be a part of his life any more. Unless he goes to rehab, they don't want him around them. They won't see him any more.

If he agrees to go, then great: the car is waiting. The plane ticket. His bag is packed. It's very important he goes immediately, before he can be distracted or change his mind.

But if he refuses, then that's it. He's out and the door is closed to him. And hopefully, that soon sends him to rock bottom, which is where he has to go, that place of no hope. He has to bottom out. You have to lose your child to that terrible, no-hope place, in order to find him again. Hopefully.

That's the idea anyway and, while I was reading the books, I thought I could almost imagine finding the strength to do this.

This really could be the answer! I said, turning, elated, to his father, and I explained what this thing called intervention was, and we discussed which friends and members of the family we might be able to line up: his grandmothers and his grandpa, his uncle and aunt, his lovely old primary-school teacher?

He'd just tell them all to fuck off, his father pointed out.

No, that's the point. He wouldn't be allowed to. It would just be too powerful – seeing them all there.

His father looked at me, unconvinced, but I think I really did believe this for a moment. But then, as soon as I closed the book, all conviction and energy seemed to drop away and all I could think of were the poppers on his Babygro, the way he'd shriek when I kissed his tummy, the tender way he used to talk to his cat.

I told his father he should read the books anyway, just in case. And he said he would, he promised he would, even though we both knew he wouldn't. And how could I blame him? I'd said I'd go to Families Anonymous and I hadn't. The broken-hearted can't make themselves do anything.

And then one day we can't do it any longer. We can't be without him. So we do exactly what we said we wouldn't do, what the experts categorically say you should not do. We take him back without negotiation, without having secured any promises about behaviour. We take him back unconditionally. We tell him we love him. We just take him back.

All right, for a quick few moments, we do pretend to weigh up the pros and cons: What exactly are we doing? Is this really right? We have two other children to protect, remember.

But then again, they miss him. We know they do. It's just not natural to live without your brother. It's too unnerving, surely, to know that he's out there somewhere, adrift and alone, moving from sofa to sofa?

And although it's true that we all felt relief when he went, it's been too long now, too painful. It feels right to try and put the family back together. This is what we tell ourselves.

If we can just draw up a set of conditions, his father says brightly, already excited at the prospect of living with his boy again, if we could just manage to negotiate something that he could try and adhere to –

I tell him I agree, that would be good. But in fact I'm barely listening. It's too late, I'm gone, I want my boy. Love shoots through my veins. I want the mummy-fix of seeing him fast asleep, safe and warm in his own bed.

When he comes home, we do at least try to talk to him about the possibility that he needs help.

Help with what?

Your addiction to cannabis. We know an awful lot more about it than we did a few months ago. There are people you can talk to – people we can take you to see.

As usual he laughs loudly.

You guys. I can't believe it. You're just cracked.

OK, maybe addiction's too strong a word. But we think you're smoking far too much.

What's too much?

I take a breath.

We think you're smoking pretty much all the time.

He rolls his eyes but he does not look at me.

Fuck's sake, Mum, I'm smoking when I want to smoke. Now and then I do a bit more than I want to, yes, sure, who doesn't?

But then I pull back.

So when did you last smoke a joint?

None of your fucking business!

Have you smoked one today?

I told you, it's none of your business. But I don't have one every day. Last week, for instance, I didn't smoke for three days.

Three days? I say, looking at his pale, pale face. You think that's a long time?

He shrugs.

It means I can stop whenever I want to.

But darling, three days is nothing. You need to try and stop for three weeks at least – three months maybe. Three days proves nothing. In fact, to be honest, it just makes me feel even more certain that you're addicted.

Now he looks at me with real anger.

I'm not sure I can live here with you guys if you keep on treating me like some fucking junkie. It's quite insulting, you know.

I'm sorry, I say, but I'm not always going to be able to say what you want to hear.

It would be nice if you could learn to mind your own fucking business.

I give him a long look.

Well, let's just see how it goes, shall we? I say.

When we take him back, we do it because we hope that, with love and patience and understanding, we can get through this.

You'll get him back, well-meaning friends have told us again and again, you'll see. It'll be all right in the end. We're not just saying it. We know it will.

But it's not true. They are – just saying that. They don't know. No one knows.

He returns sometime in March, sometime after my visit to Narborough Hall.

Soon, he is keeping everyone awake by coming home at 2 a.m., making cheese on toast, watching *South Park* DVDs, playing the guitar till four or five in the morning. Sometimes, coming home late, high and wired, he fries eggs and leaves the gas ring on. Or else wakes his brother up for a chat.

Please, darling, I beg you not to wake your brother up on a school night!

What the fuck're you on about? What's it to you? I swear he doesn't mind.

He tells you he doesn't mind. But look at him, he's shattered.

But I needed someone to talk to. Seriously, what else was I supposed to do?

His brother and sister stagger around, tired and bad-tempered. Both go off to school looking like they've been punched in the eyes.

Meanwhile he sleeps in. Despite being woken by me and offered breakfast each morning, he hardly ever gets to school on time and sometimes doesn't make it in at all. He skips school and sleeps in, his cat hunched on his shoulder, a satisfied, protective look on her face.

He starts almost every day with a roll-up, smoked in the garden with his coffee.

What is it he's smoking, his father asks me as he glances out of the kitchen window. Is it just tobacco?

I think so, I say. I smelt it just now. It's not cannabis.

And a part of me thinks how it's quite funny really – his father and I have never smoked cigarettes in our lives, and I never dreamt the day would come when we'd both be openly, innocently relieved that our baby was inhaling tobacco smoke.

He sits outside in the sun and smokes and writes poetry in a red leather-bound journal.

Where did you get that book? I ask him, because it looks expensive and we know he has no money.

He smiles. His eyes are as frank and blue as when he was five years old. He hesitates a moment.

I helped myself to it, didn't I? he says.

You mean you stole it?

He shrugs. Call it that if you like.

That's the only thing I can possibly call it.

He shrugs, carries on writing.

Do you mind? he says. You're disturbing me. I really need to get on with my work.

Sometimes we try to talk to him.

We can't live like this, we tell him.

What do you mean? Like what?

You're disrupting family life. Making life impossible for all of us.

Oh yeah? So what're you gonna do? Kick me out again?

You know that's the very last thing we want to do, we tell him.

He says he wants money. He needs money. He says that if he just had some money, everything would be all right. He'd feel more relaxed and he'd be able to behave. So we try to draw up a contract.

We'll give you a generous allowance (so you don't have to steal) and total freedom at weekends to do what you want, stay out all night if you like. In return, you stay at home in the week, eat supper with the family, do some studying, don't wake your brother and sister, get to bed on time.

He tells us these conditions are cracked, warped, insane. He calls us cunts. He says our standards are ludicrous, restrictive, monomaniacal, middle-aged and middle class.

We plead guilty to the last bit.

All we want, we tell him, is for you to be able to fulfil your potential.

He laughs. He says it's up to us. If we don't give him money, he'll take it anyway. He'll help himself. And by the way, it's no good our putting locks on our study doors. Because he'll just kick them down anyway. A few cheap little locks aren't going to stop him.

Please don't make threats like that, his father says.

But a few days later he does exactly that. Takes a running leap with his foot up the way he's seen them do in the movies. Our nice Victorian bedroom door is broken, a jagged fist of splinters sticking right out. I pull the lock out of the wood and lay it carefully on the windowsill. Then I go on making the bed.

Everyone in the house is exhausted now. Everyone is having trouble getting up in the morning.

We ask for a meeting with his teachers. He hardly ever gets to school on time now and – unsurprisingly – we keep on getting phone calls, warning notes.

We sit in a little room in the art block, sunshine pouring in.

Please, we tell his warm, open-faced young tutor, be as tough with him as you like. We'll support you all the way. He needs to know that the rules still apply, that he isn't special, that he can't get away with this kind of behaviour.

She and her colleague hesitate, glance at each other. They speak very carefully, clearly anxious to handle this matter as sensitively and appropriately as possible. They say they do know there have been some problems at home of late. They know, for instance, that he was out of the house for a while. That must have been very traumatic for him. They hear what we are saying, but at the same time they know we'll understand that they want to be as supportive as they possibly can.

I tell them that we do understand this. And I mean it. I think how glad I am, really, that our boy has these sympathetic, nurturing people behind him.

But, the boy's father tells them, his voice cracking slightly, that's all very well, I do understand where you're coming from. But the trouble is we're pretty sure he has a drugs problem.

He shoplifts, I tell them then – because a part of me wants so badly to shock them, to make them see how dramatic and sad all this has become. He just can't stop smoking cannabis and he's reached a point where he'll do anything to enable himself. And we just don't think him getting away with coming to school so late is helping.

He needs clear boundaries, adds his father. I'm not saying we're managing all that well to set them at home. But it would help so much if school could be firm with him.

His teachers regard us with real concern. We can see they are trying so hard to keep an open mind and it's hard to blame them. They are exactly where we were a year or so ago. While they know what cannabis is, I'm not sure they know about skunk.

His father tells them some facts. The strength of it. The mental health implications. The fact that we only know all of this because we've been forced to educate ourselves so fast. I glance at his face – taut, sad, a touch too passionate – and hope they won't think he's lecturing them.

If they do, they don't show it. They regard us both with real sympathy. I feel tears springing to my eyes but I swallow them back. And his tutor explains – carefully, diplomatically – that our boy is incredibly bright, really seriously intelligent, and they've known other boys like him go through similar phases and come out the other end. She really does want to reassure us. She and his other teachers fully understand that his behaviour at the moment can be, well, challenging. But if we don't mind her saying so, she's known a lot of seventeen-year-old boys.

And I've spoken to him, she says. We've had two long chats. He's been very receptive.

Receptive, I think. Of course. His biggest skill.

Please don't believe everything he tells you, I say and my heart sinks as I realise how cold, how destructively unmaternal and unsupportive I must sound. He's so plausible. Everyone wants to believe him. Everyone does believe him. The denial, the self-delusion. It's his biggest problem, in a way. I mean I love him so much, I add, but I just think it's time someone saw through him.

The look of careful kindness she gives me makes tears of frustration spring to my eyes.

His life could be so great, I tell her. He has so much life ahead of him.

I know that, she says.

OK, says the boy's father a touch harshly, so, cutting to the chase, how're we going to get him to come to school?

Calmly, the tutor shows him a piece of paper. Squares and boxes. A series of targets. He has to report in each day to various different teachers. They will all have to sign a sheet of paper. He will be encouraged very strongly by her to meet these targets.

I gaze at the boxes and squares.

Very strongly?

We'll be monitoring him very closely.

And if he doesn't meet the targets?

She blinks.

Let's just give him a chance first, shall we?

As we walk back to the car, I tell the boy's father off. How on earth can we hope to get the teachers on our side if he loses his temper and shouts like that?

I didn't shout, he says, jutting out his bottom lip. And anyway you cried.

72

I didn't cry. I nearly cried but I stopped myself.

I saw tears in your eyes.

OK, but I didn't let them come right out.

You nearly did.

I nearly did. OK, great, thanks, punish me for that.

We drive home in depressed silence. We know our son well enough to know that a set of targets will make no difference whatsoever to his attitude to school. But we also know the school well enough by now to understand that his teachers are doing all they can – doing everything they can to support this bright, likeable, plausible boy who has experienced a traumatic time at home. Because no one can say that being thrown out of your home isn't traumatic. I think of how that fact must shock them.

I understand why they want to give him a chance, I tell his father. I just wish I still felt optimistic enough to want to give him one.

His father says nothing. I see tears standing in his eyes.

What none of us know at this point is that by April he will be stealing from us again and we'll have to put locks back on our doors. By early May he will have punched his father, who was, yet again, trying to stop him kicking one of these locked doors open. And by late May he will have hit me so hard on the side of my head that I'll find myself in A & E with a perforated eardrum.

CYCLONE

I'm a cyclone,
making trouble wherever I go.

I'm a cyclone,
I end up hurting whoever I know.

Just scratching at
the essence of life,
to see what lies beneath,
but all I find
is grey tarmac streets
that never end.

Under my feet, a trail
of destruction follows me.

Smashed feelings,
splintered fragments,
of other people's lies.
Why won't you please leave me behind?

I'm a cyclone,
problem child wherever I roam.
I'm a cyclone,
the only thing I'll ever know.

Regret is slow
in coming,
but it knows the truth
from lies,
same way I always did,
when I looked in your eyes.

I'm a cyclone,
I know it now and I've known it before.

I'm a cyclone.

3

ONE NIGHT ON the Internet, hopping between drug-information websites and Yelloly-related searches, I find something interesting. A page from the *East Cambridgeshire News* dated December 2003, with the headline *Cromwell Returns After Three Hundred Years But Keeps His Silence on Mystery Message:*

A unique oak carving of Oliver Cromwell said to have been sculpted from life has been donated to the Cromwell House Museum in Ely and will be put on public display for the first time next year. The ancient statue, carved at least three hundred years ago, is reputed to possess a centuries-old unsolved secret involving a mysterious silent message meant to be sent to Cromwell's generals. The distinctive two-third life-size statue, the only one of its kind known to exist, was presented to the museum on Friday by Tony and Bryony Yelloly from Warwickshire, who said that the carved figure of the man who signed the death warrant of Charles I and became the Lord High Protector of the Commonwealth after a bloody five-year Civil War had been passed down through his family over five generations, although the carving was much older even than that . . . Mr Yelloly said the statue is known to have been a treasured family possession at the time his ancestors lived at Cavendish Hall in Suffolk . . .

Yelloly. Cavendish Hall. Your parents later moved to Cavendish and your sister Ellen was married there. Definitely the right Yelloly, then.

I call Directory Enquiries and give the name, the initial (A for Anthony?) and the area and am immediately given a telephone number. Before I can lose my nerve, I dial it and when I get a man's voice on the answerphone I leave a quick, apologetic message.

He calls back the very next day.

Tony Yelloly here.

His voice is warm, friendly, he sounds about fifty.

This is all very exciting, he says.

I try to explain, better than I did on the answerphone, my interest in his family.

Well, he says, I can tell you right away that John Yelloly came from Alnwick in Northumberland and there are certainly plaques in the church there put up by his family. And he was a surgeon and I know that he had all his children immunised against smallpox, which was a very new thing to do in those days.

He did?

Yes. Dr Jenner. He was famous for developing the vaccine. I think he was a friend of the family or something.

That's strange, I say and I tell him how I read in Florence's book that smallpox was brought into the house and that Jane died of it. He agrees that doesn't quite make sense. But then maybe the childhood vaccination only protected a person for so long? He says I should talk to his daughter Julia.

We're in our seventies, Bryony and me, but Julia knows an awful lot about the family history. She's definitely the one to talk to. Oh and by the way, I have a couple of oil portraits – one of Dr Yelloly and another of his daughter Sarah.

Oh, I say, I'd really love to see them.

Well, you can, you can. I think I also have some pictures by Sophy Mary Yelloly.

Mary's sister?

That's right or – I'm getting confused here – they could be by Mary herself. Anyway I know for a fact that some years ago my daughter swapped some old surgical instruments that belonged to Dr Yelloly for a book of pictures, a sort of album, it was.

You mean there's another book of pictures? By Mary?

Oh dear, I don't know who it's by. I'm afraid you'd have to ask Julia.

And do you know who has them now, the surgical instruments?

I've no idea. Again, Julia might know. They weren't very interesting. Just some old bits and pieces, you know. The pictures are much nicer.

I ask him what they're like.

Watercolours of Woodton, I think. But I'm really not sure which family member it was who did them. Mary was the youngest, you say?

The second youngest.

Oh well, you'll have to ask Julia.

I tell him that any paintings done by the Yellolys are probably quite valuable now.

Valuable? Oh I doubt it. Of limited interest, I imagine.

I can't resist telling him, then, how much Mary's book went for at auction. I hear him take a breath.

That's very interesting, he says and then, after a little beat: You're not serious?

He tells me that his grandfather was born at and lived at Cavendish Hall and the place definitely still exists.

A nice lady lived there, an American, I think, called Mrs Matthews or something beginning with M. And I dropped by one day a long time ago and she very kindly let me look around. She was very cordial and she said we must have a party in 2002 as the Hall was built in 1702! But I never did hear back from her. I expect she must have died.

He asks if I've been to Woodton. I say I have, a couple of times. But I don't know exactly where Woodton Hall was in relation to the church. Is it all gone now?

Well, Woodton Hall was just behind the church. Pulled down eventually, yes. But there's the remnant of the garden wall still there. It's perfectly visible if you know what you're looking for.

I tell him I never noticed it.

Oh well, you have to know what you're looking for, you see.

For a moment I remember the suggestion I sensed – the immensity of the Hall's great bulk – on that icy day.

I tell him I've been trying hard to find the graves. That I've looked everywhere. Does he have any idea where they are?

Oh, he says, the graves are there. I can't remember exactly where. I know they take some finding but they're definitely there.

I ask him then if he knows of Florence Suckling's book, the one I've been reading in the British Library.

He laughs.

Oh yes, we have a copy of that. A very treasured volume, but you'd be most welcome to borrow it. I think Julia's got it.

He tells me he's amazed I'm so interested in all of this.

Well, it's pretty amazing, I tell him, to be talking to a real live Yelloly.

He chuckles.

Well, we'll have to meet. I haven't got much but I'm more than happy to show you what I've got.

He invites me to lunch in three weeks' time. He says he'll pick me up at the station. I tell him that's really kind but there's no need to do that. I'll get a taxi.

Oh no, but I insist.

Only a day later, a casual late-night Google on the Internet throws up something else. A page from Yale University:

Yale Center for British Art, 2003 Acquisitions: three sketchbooks by Miss J. Yelloly, with drawings of London tradesmen and nearly eighty watercolours of Norfolk (1831–40) Paul Mellon Fund.

Is it really possible? Can there be Yelloly paintings over there as well? I send off an email and get an almost instant reply:

Dear Ms Myerson,

Amy McDonald has passed on your inquiry to me. I realize the press release you saw online is not quite accurate; the three sketchbooks are not all by Miss J. Yelloly and I apologize for any confusion. We do have three albums by members of the Yelloly family, dating from 1827–45, and only one is by Jane. We have the following in our collections (these are the labels for a display we just did of our Recent Gifts and Acquisitions):

Three albums by members of the Yelloly family of Norfolk, 1827–45. Paul Mellon Fund
1. Sarah Tyssen Yelloly, 1785–1854. Sketchbook, 1827.
2. Jane Davison Yelloly, 1808–1838. Sketchbook, 1831–38.
3. Sophy Mary Yelloly, 1811–1840. Sketchbook depicting local tradesmen and villagers of Norfolk, 1839.

I saw the Grenville album last year at a bookseller's shop in London but it was too expensive for us. Do you know where it has ended up? In any case, you are welcome to come and consult these works. We have only begun doing the research on them and anything you can tell us would be marvellous. I think there was another sketchbook that appeared on the market some years ago but I don't have access to my notes on that as I'm working at home today (24 inches of snow is blocking my door!). I can pursue that if you'd like and let you know.
Best wishes,
Elizabeth

On a bright, warm, early-summer evening, we drive to see the addiction counsellor that the Manhattan psychiatrist originally recommended. She lives some way out of London, in the country. Because of work, we end up having to go at rush hour and we drive for ages, getting lost in the country lanes.

For a while – me reading the map and getting it wrong, him pulling in so he can have a look, me complaining that he never trusts me to navigate him anywhere, him saying: Yes, and I wonder why not – it almost feels like fun. Long-ago carefree holiday afternoons when getting lost didn't matter. When we had no one else to look after and weren't due anywhere and could make life up as we went along.

The air outside London is fresh and golden, cows lowing in the distance. A smell of manure as we get out of the car. And the counsellor doesn't look at all how I imagined her. Homely, kind-faced, but reassuringly authoritative, she reminds me of my old piano teacher.

She makes us tea. There are biscuits. And we sit on comfy sofas in her large, pale-carpeted sitting room and, taking it in turns, try to tell her our story. A slightly enlarged and more detailed version of the story we told the psychiatrist.

We tell it haltingly, struggling to get the timelines right, struggling to be absolutely fair to our boy, handing the narrative back and forth between us when it gets too tough. Once or twice I have to bite my lip. But, although there is a big white box of tissues on the low coffee table, I don't cry.

When we've finished, she looks at us both. Asks us a few things about our boy. Does he do this? Is he like this?

Yes, we say, Oh yes – slightly amazed as she somehow guesses accurately about so many specific aspects of his behaviour over the past year.

What you're describing, says his father with an exhausted face, well, I couldn't have said it better myself. That's exactly what he's like.

She looks at us carefully.

Then, just like the psychiatrist, she asks if we know the difference between cannabis and skunk.

Now we're quick to tell her we do. The frontal lobes. The potentially irreversible damage. We tell her we worry for our youngest child too, who was given the drug by his brother when he was only just thirteen.

The look on her face makes me feel momentarily sick.

Certainly all the evidence says the younger they start the more likely the damage is to be irreversible, she says gently. But there is hope. First, your youngest may well never develop a problem with the drug. Not everyone who tries the drug gets addicted, remember. And even addicts can get clean and lead normal happy lives again.

That's what we want, I tell her quickly.

It's a tough one, she says, because so few people understand the true nature and seriousness of cannabis addiction. There's an awful lot of denial out there. And ignorance. Skunk's been around less than ten years. Back when cannabis was reclassified from B to C, there was no such thing as skunk – not that anyone had heard of, anyway.

She tells us that she is currently working with many families whose children are either in denial, like our son, or in and out of rehab. She tells us that addiction often runs in families. She's working with several families where two or more siblings are affected in exactly the same way.

More than one child? I whisper, thinking of our youngest.

She reaches to pour more tea.

The children who're experimenting with it now are guinea pigs, in every sense. For instance, I'm treating some people at the moment, a lovely couple, you couldn't ask for better parents, both of whose teenage sons are out there on the streets right now, trying to prove they're not addicted.

And they are? Addicted, I mean?

She looks at me.

Of course they are. And as soon as they realise that, we can help them. Meanwhile, though, their parents, these poor people, are going through hell.

People think cannabis is a soft drug, she says. And in some ways the old-style cannabis was. But it's actually harder to deal with than almost any other drug, because the addiction is far more mental than physical. And of course social attitudes don't help. In my opinion, she says, skunk is more dangerous than heroin.

We both stare at her.

Unlike heroin, it's being used regularly by children. And unlike heroin, it's much less likely you can make a full recovery.

Because of the damage to the brain?

I'm afraid so, yes.

Silence as we take this in. I can't look at the boy's father's face. I know he is feeling what I am feeling: pure despair.

Outside the evening sun slides over the warm green slope of the garden. I have a brief sense of freedom – of floating out of my body and up, up into that bright evening sky. At last I think of the question I want to ask her.

So, if this happens to your child, to someone you love so very deeply and feel so responsible for, then what do you do? How do you go about getting them clean?

She takes a breath and looks at me kindly, hands me a box of tissues.

There's a photo of our boy, not an especially good one, just a snap really, which sits on a chest of drawers at Granny's in a little silver frame. I know this photo so well. It's been there on that polished chest of drawers for years.

In it, he's about nine or ten years old, dressed in cricket whites, leaning rather self-consciously in the hall doorway at our old house, hand on hip, one leg crossed over the other. He's beaming – one of those smiles that use up his whole face. And it's Sunday and I've probably just picked him up from cricket practice and am asking him to lay the table for lunch. And this is something he will do cheerfully, with good humour and without complaint.

I know that, in the kitchen, his father will be baking fish and roasting vegetables, Van Morrison or Springsteen playing or else some political discussion programme turned up loud on the radio. And the boy and I will be having the same old tired debate about whether or not he should change out of his whites before lunch.

He'll insist that he doesn't need to, that the trousers are already all grass-stained and dirty, so why does it matter? And in the end I'll probably give in and let him change afterwards. He's so good-natured when he argues, so reasonable most of the rest of the time. What's the harm in letting him get away with this?

And it's a sunny day and outside in the garden the dog's probably barking a little bit too much and his brother and sister are shouting and laughing and our boy is about to lay the table, and yes, he will wash his hands, but first he pauses for one quick moment in that doorway so that someone – is it Granny who has come to lunch? – can take the snap.

Our boy after cricket practice on a Sunday.

The other day when we were round there for some reason or other and, for a moment or two, no one else was in the room, I found myself reaching out for this photo, picking it up and staring and staring at it, my face close to the glass, greedy for whatever it could give me. A clue? A jolt of pain? A taste of what we'd lost?

★　　★　　★

You don't know this, but your eldest sister Sarah, the one who brings you back home to Woodton from Ipswich after you die, has a late marriage. She is fifty-seven when, in 1864, she marries a widower called Samuel Severne and goes to live with him at Poslingford House near Clare, not far from Cavendish, in Suffolk.

It's a summer wedding and Sarah and her new husband give a generous supper for all the villagers in celebration of their marriage. It's even reported in the *Bury & Norwich Post*:

On Tuesday night the populace of Poslingford were regaled by Mr and Mrs Severne to a most plentiful supper, all labourers' wives and children above the age of 12 years assembled in the most capacious barn which was decorated with flowers and evergreens. Hot joints of beef and mutton-plum pudding and vegetables were liberally supplied to the company by the many helpers of young people from farming families. A band from Clare added to the cheerfulness and the evening passed pleasantly and the large assemble of near 200 separated in good order.

Their happiness is short-lived, though. What Sarah and her new husband don't know, as they celebrate their union in that capacious barn with the villagers, is that he has only seven months left to live. He dies the following spring and your sister lives out her remaining thirty-two years as a widow.

On Friday, 24 October 1896, in her ninetieth year, Sarah dies in her chair. In her *Last Will & Testament*, written in an elegant, sloping hand, she asks to be buried

in a coffin similar to those which my brothers and sisters had and not in a leaden one, and I direct my executors to erect a neat tablet in Woodton Church (the last resting place of many of my dear family) to my memory and that of my late brother Samuel and my late sister Ellen Tyssen, the expense of the tablet and the erection thereof not to exceed the sum of Twenty pounds (exclusive of a proper fee which I wish to be paid to the Rector of Woodton on the occasion).

Just like her sister Anna, Sarah leaves a huge quantity of possessions and ornaments, but unlike Anna she seems to have a much longer list of friends and relatives to leave them to. She makes careful provision for her servants too – making sure they have money to buy mourning clothes as well as something to spend on themselves.

Even the lad who works in the garden is told he may help himself to *any loose numbers of British Workmen, Animal World and The Vet.*

We had our babies too fast, too easily. I didn't think it at the time but it's what I think now. I think we were having much too good a time of it, taking for granted how easy it all was, jumping in there without much thought or fear.

We were so young. We thought we were perfect. We didn't know that bad things could happen. As soon as we tried for a baby, a baby came, just like that, boy, girl, boy. And we were so absolutely caught up in the rhythm of it – the nappies, the night-time feeds, the exhaustion and exhilaration of holding one new person after another in our arms – that we just kept on going. We didn't look down.

But I'm looking down now – from the dark, churning centre of my middle-aged anxiety – and certain moments make my heart stop. The time I let an inexperienced friend hold our baby girl on his knee over our stone-flagged kitchen floor and when, as he took one hand off her to reach in his pocket for something, I saw her wobble for a quick second, some kind of crazed politeness stopped me diving forwards and snatching her away. The time I raced back from work in my lunch hour to check on our nine-month-old, our boy, who was being looked after by a temp from an agency. And found her smoking and chatting on the phone while he lay in his cot crying so furiously his face had turned a whole new colour I'd never seen before.

Not only that, but he had on two woollen cardigans buttoned up to the chin and, when I touched him, felt like he was running a fever. And what did I do? I unbuttoned and soothed him, asked her steadily and politely if she could take him out in his pram, before heading straight back to work, anxious not to be missed. Why? Was I completely insane? Why didn't I just stop right there, fire the nanny, and lose my job if necessary? What job is more important than the welfare of your child?

In the bleak middle of the night, I punish myself with these questions. In the bleak middle of the night, I remember that, when our boy was about thirteen, his father and I went through a difficult patch. And I think now that I was very much to blame for the atmosphere that this generated. Temporary, but potent, and all my fault.

And even though I thought – we thought – that we were still being genuinely good parents, loving and caring for our children, I think for a while we were very centred on ourselves. It took us a year or so to sort out our problems. A year of self-centredness. And because we managed it, because we came through, I automatically assumed the family would be OK too. But is that when he started smoking?

There was the day we were looking for something in his room and we stumbled on a DVD case labelled *Hands Off*. Straight away we opened it and found a little bag of weed. Not that worrying, really, not that surprising. We'd always known our kids would come across drugs, would probably try cannabis, maybe Ecstasy, hopefully nothing much else. And we prided ourselves on not being so naive as to think these substances any more dangerous than alcohol, for instance. We really hoped they would never take up smoking tobacco, but a little bit of cannabis? Where was the harm in that?

So on that day, after a quick discussion – and faint guilt that we'd invaded his privacy in the first place – we put it back exactly where it was and agreed to say nothing. Our boy was bright, happy, energetic, easy-going. He was working very hard at school. So what if he occasionally smoked with his friends? Was it even any of our business?

We go over that scene again and again. So many times we replay it, question our actions. And again and again, we do the same thing. We put the cannabis back, close the case, leave the room, say nothing. I can see us doing it right now. Closing the case, leaving the room. Leaving his things as they were, walking out quite carefully, with respect for his privacy, pulling the door behind us. Closing the door, smiling and shaking our heads – leaving our child to his fate.

The moment haunts me. How did we miss the signs? And would it really have made any difference if we hadn't?

An old schoolfriend who lives in Canada emailed me recently to say that her youngest child – her late baby, her joy, the apple of her eye, the one who'd never caused them any problems – had developed eating and self-harming issues. We certainly didn't see that one coming, she wrote.

I hadn't seen her for years and could only really remember this child as a baby – dark-eyed and plump-cheeked. And that sentence – so lightly written, without anger or self-pity, yet somehow loaded with parental responsibility and remorse – made me want to weep.

The boy's father sometimes says that a bomb went off in our family. That it went off without any warning and left destruction in its wake. And there was nothing we could possibly do except sort through the wreckage, salvage what we could. That's how he looks at it.

But I don't really see it like that. For me it's not a bomb, but a tidal wave. There we all are, a little family group standing on a beach with our backs to the sea. Holding hands. Happy. Stupidly happy, because just behind us – towering and terrifying – the wave is approaching. A vast dark curve of water just waiting to knock us off our feet.

I come home one night after doing a late-night TV programme to find our boy sitting alone at the kitchen table, head in hands, face raw with tears. Arranged in front of him, eight or nine pieces of sodden and scrunched-up kitchen paper. And three kitchen knives.

Hey. I touch his shoulder with my hand. What's going on here?

He says nothing.

I get a glass of water and sit down at the table next to him, kick off my shoes.

What are these doing here?

He picks one up, gently rests the tip on the pine table, lets it drop. He looks at me with pinprick eyes.

Dad threw them there.

Why?

He says nothing.

I stand up again, my bare feet sticking to the kitchen floor.

Why would he do that? I say.

No reply.

I gather up the knives – which have only recently been allowed back into the drawer from their hiding place in the cupboard under the stairs – and carry them back over to the drawer where I lay them carefully, blades pointing down. I make a mental note that they might have to go back into hiding tomorrow. These kinds of precautionary measures have now become a normal part of our daily lives and no longer strike me as strange or tragic, the way they did at the start.

I sit down again. I'm starving. I pick up a banana, start to peel it.

Did you have a fight? I say.

Believe what you want, he says. I don't care.

Did you have a fight? I say again, my mouth full of banana.

Why don't you go and ask him? He's the one being a fucking insane idiot.

We sit together for a few more moments. He doesn't say anything else. He doesn't need to. I know how the evening will have gone. He will have threatened and his father will have stayed calm. Then he will have threatened again, he will have done one more destructive and outlandish thing – maybe looked around for money, maybe tried to kick a door down – and his father will have cracked. Or maybe he won't have done anything else. Maybe he didn't have to. Maybe his father will have cracked anyway. Sometimes the threats are enough: one moment you're trying to be a calm and loving parent. The next, you're shouting, screaming, weeping.

Recently, we've returned to the old, depressing dialogue. We can't live like this. We really do mean it this time – behave or go.

If we don't do as he wants, if we don't give him the things he wants, he punishes us. He plays guitar, turning the amp up so loud the house shakes. He shouts and he throws things. He broke my vintage phone – a present bought on eBay by his father – by slamming it against the wall because he couldn't get through to someone. If I refuse to give him money, he sits on my study floor, his whole body blocking the door, his eyes on my face, smiling because he knows I won't be able to write a word.

This last kind of menace – not violent exactly, but making full and calculated use of his physical bulk – is the worst. At times like these I'm shocked to find myself feeling little love for him. It's all been squashed out of me, squeezed out through the smallest hole. Is this what abuse is? Is this a definition?

One time, when he's followed me all around the house for an hour demanding cash, I lock my study and, grabbing the car keys before he can stop me, rush out to the car and drive away. Just around the corner, I pull in and sit in a side road, shaking and crying, till I think he'll have given up and it's safe to come home.

Another time, I walk right out of the house without a coat or bag and have to stand in Superdrug, pretending to look at the nail polishes, swallowing tears of loneliness and frustration. The security guard eyes me. He knows something's up, he just doesn't know what. I'm tempted to beg him to come home with me.

And then another time – the time he picks up a little set of espresso cups that he and his sister jointly gave me for

Christmas, and walks outside and proceeds to drop them, one by one, on the pavement.

I remind him that I actually gave him the money to buy me that Christmas present as he'd spent all of his. He grins. I then plead with him not to do this terrible and destructive thing, because didn't his sister pay for half the set with her own money?

He looks at me.

You're right, he says. I didn't think of that. And he smashes exactly half of the cups, leaving the rest on the kitchen counter.

You shouldn't have watched him do it, his father tells me later. He was only able to do it because you gave him the satisfaction of watching.

And I know he's right. Of course he's right. But the instinct to beg him to stop, the instinct to prevent damage if you can, is strong. Still, I think I'm tougher now. Replay that situation today and just watch me walk away.

He's almost eighteen, people remind us, he's almost a man.

What they mean – and they mean it kindly – is don't feel responsible. Let him go if you have to. And intellectually I know this, of course I do, but it's not what I feel. What I feel is a great big burning grief. And deep, deep responsibility. And shame, that I no longer know how to comfort him.

And now, tonight, at 1.30 a.m., this. Knives and tears.

His cat jumps on the table and pushes herself on to his lap. I see that he's crying. He doesn't often cry these days, except just occasionally in rage. He doesn't cry, even though he's made all of us cry, often. A small cold part of me decides that maybe this is a good sign. At least he's feeling something.

Tell me what you're thinking, I say gently.

He says nothing. His cat pushes her head into his hand, purring.

He makes a noise, sucking in tears.

If I have to go from here, he says, then what the fuck am I going to do with Kitty?

Much later, when he's in bed and so am I, it's that small practical question that reduces me to tears as well. If I have to go from here. Again. If I have to go again. If I have to go from here, from my home – then what provision do I make for my cat, this cat I've had all my life since I was six years old?

When he was about seven and Kitty about a year old, I went into his room to find him lying on the bed, sobbing. Really sobbing, wet and hard and loud. I asked him what was the matter and, when he wouldn't tell me, I sat on the bed and pulled him on to my knee. Kissed his warm, honey-smelling hair.

In the end he told me that he'd been cutting something out of his *Beano* with scissors and he'd suddenly got the idea of trimming Kitty's fur. Just a little bit. A little haircut. But he'd done the little bit, and then a little bit more until suddenly he saw that he'd gone too far and now there were great chunks of her fur all over the floor and she had a bald patch. He showed me, sobbing harder.

I'm so worried I've hurt her.

Kitty was fine and I showed him that she was. I told him the fur would soon grow back.

But you frightened yourself, didn't you? I told him. And that's a good thing really, because cats don't need their fur trimmed and you might have hurt Kitty and you don't want to hurt her, do you?

He looked at me and shook his head, still sobbing silently, a thin line of snot hanging down.

And I kissed him and he kissed his cat, who pushed her face into his hands, as trusting as ever.

94

You're good with animals, I told him. You're a good owner and a kind person. And you learnt something today and you won't forget it. You won't cut her hair again, will you?

He said he wouldn't and he never did.

He never did, but a whole six months or so after that night of the knives and the kitchen towel, a whole six months later when he's long gone from our home and just been evicted from that flat after neighbours have complained to the police about noise and fighting; a whole six months later when he's briefly had Kitty living there with him, but has finally absconded and left town; a whole six months later, when we go to that place one sticky summer's night to see if she's all right, I find her huddled alone on the bare floor, facing the wall, no food or water. Hunched and resigned, a prisoner doing time.

I lift her gently and she doesn't make a sound. I lift her and her black legs with the little white socks hang heavily. I put her in the cat basket and drive her back home. There, after a drink of water and some gentle stroking, I persuade her out into the garden. She wobbles down the back steps like a drunk.

When my mother told my father she wanted to leave him, he said she couldn't take anything with her except one suitcase because this was how she'd come to him. And she couldn't take us, her daughters.

She left him at 4 a.m. on a balmy August night with a removal van, while he was away on holiday with us. She took exactly half the furniture and all the pets – dog, duck, budgie and hamster – to a secret address, a house in the red-light district of town which she'd bought and done up on the quiet.

95

Then she came and collected us. It was easy to do this because it was her turn to be on holiday with us. That was how they did holidays by then – taking it in turns. So he said goodbye and drove home, unsuspecting, to find half of everything gone. He was furious.

Meanwhile she took us to the secret address. We cried all the way. Actually my middle sister and I cried. My littlest sister cheered up once we stopped for fish and chips.

It was the summer holidays and our mother said she just wanted to spend a few weeks with us without our father knowing where we were. A few weeks of calm. After that, the courts would sort everything out and it would be fine, we could visit him.

It was fun in the new house, even though we didn't have a TV. We went for walks and bike rides, played charades, stayed on a caravan site with a swimming pool. It was a great relief not to live with two people who were always crying and fighting.

But I thought about my father in that half-empty house and wondered what he was doing. Drinking? Smoking? Watching TV?

I didn't miss him but I worried about him.

Tony Yelloly stands waiting for me at Banbury Station on a raw and windy spring day. He's a rosy, round-faced, incredibly genial-looking man, intent, alert, generous. He holds out his hand, smiling.

I can't believe I'm actually finally shaking the hand of a real live Yelloly, I tell him and he laughs and leads me to the car, which is even more of a mess than our own – dog hair, leaves, dried mud.

As we drive to Dog Lane (*Dog Lane, ha!*) he tells me all about their dog Fred, a rescue greyhound who was discovered in a miserable state, completely emaciated, abandoned and cowering in someone's greenhouse.

Anyway it was our forty-ninth wedding anniversary and we saw this sign in a shop window saying he needed a home. And so we said: well, all right, if you haven't found a home for him by Monday, we'll take him. And of course, we phoned on the Monday and . . .

Outside their cottage, primroses and snowdrops stand up stiffly in the cold. The air is blue and clean, hardly a cloud.

Here you are, here you are, he laughs as we stand shyly for a moment in the hall and his wife Bryony emerges from the kitchen, wiping her hands on a tea towel. More shaking of hands. For a second or two we all just stand there.

Now – goodness, sorry! – would you like to use the cloakroom?

I say I would. I go in and shut the door. It's an old-fashioned bathroom – reminds me of the wonky 1960s bathrooms of my childhood. I play for time. Flush the loo. Take a breath. I turn on the cold tap and the handle falls off. I put it back on carefully, wipe my hands. I go back in the kitchen to find Bryony struggling to open the apple juice.

Can I do that?

Oh would you? Thanks, it's very stiff.

Fred the greyhound sticks his silky snout in my hand.

What a lovely dog, I say as he gazes at me. Hello, boy – oh, isn't he nice! What an amazing coat.

Bryony looks pleased.

Well, we do actually wonder if he's part Saluki.

As I put down my bag and sip my apple juice, Tony takes me straight into the dark hall – coats and photographs of daughters – and points out a large oil painting high above the front door. We both tilt our heads back.

There he is. Dr Yelloly!

Wow.

He's handsome, definitely, but fatter-faced than I'd imagined. Stouter, better fed? This is the man who was given the purse and poems. Dark, clever eyes. The lover, the doctor, the dad.

He vaccinated them, you know, Tony reminds me. He introduced vaccinations. Very ahead of his time, he was.

He takes me upstairs then, to the top landing. Fred follows, his long, loping heaviness making the stairs creak. Right at the end of the landing, we stop and look at a small oil painting. I peer at a woman's lit-up face.

Sarah Boddicott Yelloly, Tony says, gently triumphant.

Mary's sister?

The same.

I go in closer. She's really lovely, your sister, dark, wispy-curly hair, the same strikingly round and rosy face as Tony, in fact. Thin arched brows and delicate features. A real, timeless sparkle in her eyes. Even by modern standards she'd be pretty.

It's not the original, Tony says. It's actually a photograph. My cousin Margaret has the original. And look what she's wearing, though. Could those possibly be the earrings?

I'd told him on the phone about your earrings, the long gold ones mentioned in Anna's will.

I peer at them. They're certainly long and gold.

But then it was your Mary who had them, not Sarah, wasn't it? Tony says.

I look into Sarah's smiling eyes. She's not telling.

Maybe they each had a pair, I say.

Downstairs Bryony is serving lunch out of the Aga. Salmon and mashed potato and lentils and peas. Fred, whose bed is right in front of the Aga, is quietly getting in the way, but no one seems to expect him to move.

Now don't worry, says Tony, we've remembered you don't eat meat –

Oh I really hope you didn't go to too much trouble, I say, even though it's obvious that they did.

Not at all, not at all. It's not every day we have someone here who's interested in Yelloly history!

Tell her the story about Mary dying, Bryony says, moving the apple juice out of the way to put the peas down, the awful story –

Oh, but that's not her. That's Mary Webster, Tony says.

Mary who? I scuffle in my bag for a pen.

Mary Webster – she married John Samuel de Beauvoir Yelloly, my grandfather, who was the son of Samuel Tyssen and his second wife.

You mean the Samuel Tyssen who was Mary Yelloly's brother? There are so many Samuel Tyssens –

That's right. Well, Mary was the mother of Claude and Sam – Claude was my father. And she was diabetic, you see. And anyway, she was lying there dying of puerperal fever after giving birth, poor woman, and it was a snowy day and the boys were making such a noise outside her window that they were told to play more quietly, but they didn't and then she died. Poor boys, can you imagine that?

At the other end of the table where we're eating lunch is a large wooden box covered in faded tattered paper, enticingly old. Also, a big pile of papers. Tony is sifting through these papers now with great enthusiasm. Unable to bear the sight of his elbows swishing up and down, I move both his and my glasses of apple juice out of the way. Fred, quickly seeing my hands are occupied, takes the opportunity to sidle straight in close to my plate.

I'd watch your salmon, if I were you, Julie. That dog is a thief, I told you. Get down, Fred!

I stroke Fred's silky head.

Good boy, I say.

Now you're encouraging him!

Sorry.

Of course my main claim to fame, Tony continues, giving up on the papers for the moment, is that I once had tea with Beatrix Potter.

You didn't!

He grins.

Oh yes, yes, I did. I was all of eight years old and we were up near Alnwick in Northumberland, you know, which was where the Yellolys came from, and I was taken to see her by some member of the family or other. And she arrived riding side-saddle, I remember, and really did manage to dismount very gracefully, given that she must have been quite an old lady by then.

I gaze at him, my pen in the air. Even though this has nothing to do with you, still I can't resist the picture. The stout, elderly Beatrix Potter looking down at a small male Yelloly.

And what was she like? I ask him. I mean was she friendly? Was she nice? Did she even like children?

Children? says Tony. Oh no, I shouldn't think so, not very much, not at all really. She certainly didn't want to have to hear us make a noise or anything like that. Children weren't really interesting to anyone in those days. But I still do remember one amazing thing – that in her cottage there was Tom Kitten's fireplace!

Bryony is smiling. She tells me she saw the film with Renée Zellweger, and I'm about to ask her if it was as bad as it sounded, but manage to stop myself just in time.

I really enjoyed it, she says.

Now this. Tony hands me a tiny ancient book. You use it for writing blank verse in Latin, I think. And look inside, look who it belonged to.

I open the flyleaf. John Yelloly, 16 August 1826. I feel its impossibly small weight in my hands. This book would have been in your house. Your father's book.

Dr Yelloly, I say.

Exactly. And do you know how I got it? A friend at school found it in a second-hand bookshop, would you believe, and fleeced me for it. Really fleeced me. Seriously! I dread now to think how much I paid but I had to have it. I just had to. It's one of my most treasured possessions, you can imagine.

I can see why you had to have it, I tell him and he smiles.

But, I say, reading the name inside again, I still don't understand – what do you mean your friend found it? I mean how come he had it in the first place? You mean by accident?

Tony nods.

Complete coincidence. Can you believe it? He just came across it and bought it. Funny, isn't it? Incredible really. Just one of those strange things that happen. I mean it's no use to anyone really, he says happily. Unless of course you have a sudden desire to write blank verse in Latin, that is!

We eat our lunch. Fred comes and plants his nose on the table. Tony chuckles.

Look at that dog. He's a thief, a total thief. He can't help it, poor boy, can't even disguise it – look at him.

He shakes his head.

Bryony offers me more potato.

I don't think he'll ever stop thieving, she says. I suppose when you've had to scavenge the way he did –

Just to stay alive, poor chap, Tony agrees. And he pours more juice, and I look at the dog, who sighs a sigh of pleasure, relieved to be understood.

As we finish our salmon and the plates are pushed aside, I show them your death-register entry and Jane's:

Mary Yelloly, female, spinster, 21 years, died 22nd June 1838. Cause of death: consumption.

Jane Yelloly, female, single woman, 30 years, died 21st June 1838. Cause of death: [?] eterus together with affections of chest and head.

I'm not sure if it's *teterus*, or *jeterus*, I tell them. I looked up *jeterus* and it seemed to indicate a yellowing, in plants. A type of jaundice maybe?

Tony and Bryony are making startled noises. He bites his lip, emotion on his face.

They're just copies I ordered up from the Family Records Centre, I tell them gently. But Tony holds them in his hands, the entries that recorded your deaths. He holds them and looks from one to the other for a very long time.

Goodness, he says at last, this is very – I mean, it's very affecting. Very sobering indeed to see these.

He looks at me as he hands them to Bryony, who also inspects them carefully.

No doubt those children, he says steadily, they all had TB. There's no doubt about it whatsoever in my mind. They'd have caught it from the milk, from a family cow. That was how you caught it in those days, you see.

Was it? I ask him, not sure whether I already know that or not.

Well, it was certainly one of the ways.

Tony had it, Bryony says then, putting the certificates back down on the table, and I wonder for a second if I've heard her correctly.

I look at him.

You? You had TB?

He laughs.

Isn't it funny? At first the doctors couldn't figure it out. They said I had a bit of tomato skin stuck to my insides, to my gut or something. Imagine that. But it turned out that yes, it was TB.

I'm sure some families are genetically prone, Bryony says.

Really? I say. I didn't know that. Does it run in families?

Oh, certainly, absolutely. I'm sure it does.

I gaze at Tony. A descendant of yours, who once contracted the disease that killed you.

But you're better now? I ask him hopefully. I mean you got better?

He leans across the table to me.

One word, he says: penicillin. None of those poor Yellolys would have died if they'd only had access to that.

We're all silent for a moment. Bryony starts to clear the plates.

I'll do that, I begin to say. But then I worry that she might prefer to do things her own way in her own kitchen. So I just take a couple of plates through and put them by the sink and then sit down again.

Fred flops down in his bed with another huge sigh and, while Bryony sorts out the pudding, Tony tells me that his grandfather John Samuel de Beauvoir Yelloly had to sell Cavendish Hall in the end.

Such a shame. They couldn't even rent out the land. Four hundred acres of Suffolk! I was educated on the proceeds. He was colour-blind, you know, John was. He was also a bit of an inventor.

Really? What kind of an inventor?

He invented some kind of a device to coil a land-chain, something that they still use. He was quite proud of it. And then another time he developed some kind of a thing that was, I don't know, halfway between a bat and a glider. Anyway he climbed up into a tree with it and he got his wife to pile all these mattresses under the tree – seriously, I'm not joking! – and then he jumped. It didn't work, I don't think, but at least he wasn't hurt.

We eat our stewed apple with crème fraîche. Bryony offers me a shortbread biscuit and Fred immediately gets up and comes over to watch me eat it.

Look at him. He's certainly decided you're a soft touch, Tony says, shaking his head with pleasure.

Finally, as Bryony boils the kettle for coffee and we're brushing the shortbread crumbs from our laps, he reaches out and pulls the big old falling-apart box towards him.

I don't even know what's in here, he says, pulling out envelopes and papers and spreading them out here and there. I quickly wipe the table with my napkin. He holds up some faded watercolour figures with jointed legs, painted on stiff paper. These, for instance, what are they?

I look at them. I inspect the rosy faces and harlequin-patterned clothes. They look as if they could have been painted by you. And I'm about to suggest that, but Tony's already busy finding something else.

And I really have no idea what any of this is, he says as he takes out a long, slim, yellowing envelope. For instance, look at this – what on earth is this old thing?

And he pulls something out of the envelope – a folded piece of yellowed paper with a blob of bright red sealing wax on it and out slides something brown and lacy, crocheted or knitted.

Knitted. Brown and lacy, hand-worked. Little gold tassels. Suddenly I can't speak.

I put my fingers out to pick it up. And in that instant everything slows down. The spring sunshine outside, Fred's slim neck, the crème fraîche carton on the table, knives and forks and crumbs – all of it recedes. I read the yellowed envelope Tony has just handed me:

Family Romance. Purse worked by Sarah Tyssen and given to Dr Yelloly with a note in the spring of 1806. They were married August 1806 and in July 1841 the year before his death he returned it to her in the enclosed wrapper.

What is it? Bryony asks me, watching my face.

Do you know what it is? asks Tony.

Sarah's purse, I tell him and my hands are shaking. This is her purse. The one I read about. This is it. I can't believe it. This is the actual purse.

I hand it to Tony.

This is the purse that Mary Yelloly's mother knitted for John, before they were married. It's in the book – you know, Florence Suckling's book?

Tony's laughing.

I just can't believe it, I tell him. I honestly didn't think it could still exist. And here it was all along –

In our loft! says Tony, sitting back and handing the purse to Bryony, who looks at it and solemnly hands it back to me.

This is it, I'm holding it in my hands. Your mother's little purse. It's tiny, fragile, a sausage of knitted brownish-maroon cotton, very fine and delicate, gold tassels on each end and two gold bands to hold it shut and, yes, in the centre, a tiny folded piece of paper. *1806.* I read the wrapper aloud:

April 30th
My dear Sir,
Burns' poems and a little purse are scarcely worth your acceptance, but I offer them to you as a trifling remembrance of <u>this day</u>, of which, that you may enjoy many returns in health and happiness is the most sincere wish of your affectionate friend,
S. Tyssen

The outside of the piece of paper is addressed to Dr Yelloly, and there are some small tears and rusty age spots and the red sealing wax has had a stamp or ring with the initials S.T. – Sarah Tyssen – plumped into it. If you slide one of the gold bands along the purse, you can get the tiny folded piece of paper out.

I look at Tony.

Is it OK? Do you mind if I take it out?

Good heavens, of course not. Go on, go ahead!

We all watch as I unfold the shred of paper – just a little Manila strip which has been folded over about four times. I'm half expecting it to be the Burns poems, but it's far too small for that. Instead there's just one inked line. I hold it to the light and try to read. *With kind . . .* something illegible *. . . and many thanks.*

Kind regards? says Bryony.

I don't know. It could be. Or it could be *wishes*.

On the other side is written, so small it could almost be a mistake, *Dear Miss J.* or *S.* and then something else crossed out.

I fold the piece of paper back up, put it back in the purse, pull the gold band tight.

I look at Tony and feel myself breathe again.

I can't tell you how incredible this is, I tell him and he looks very pleased.

Well, there you are! he says, and straight away Fred looks up, in case he's talking about food.

Do you mean, I ask Tony, sorry but, you seriously mean you've never looked in this box?

He waves his hand.

Oh well. A bit. Not much. No, not really.

But – does Julia know about all of this? I ask, remembering that he said she was the family historian.

He smiles.

Oh, I don't think Julia would be all that interested. She's more into athletics, you know.

With the purse still on the table in front of me, I delve into the box. I can see handwritten sheaves of paper, drawings, watercolour pictures, an exercise book or two.

The thing is – I think it must all be in here, the Yelloly stuff I've read about, I tell them. I think she must have had this box.

Who?

Florence Suckling. This must be it, it must be the archive she used. The papers she referred to when she wrote her family history.

Well, it's just been sitting up there in our loft, Tony says again, still beaming. No use to anyone.

I think for a moment, suddenly embarrassed, trying to decide how exactly to frame the question. Should I ask how they feel about me coming back on another day to sit and look properly through the box? But it turns out I don't even have to ask.

And of course, Tony says without any prompting, if you want to, take it all away with you. I mean it. It's not doing anyone any good here. Please feel free.

I stare at him.

But – this is your entire family history.

He smiles and his eyes are warm.

Feel free. I mean it. I would love you to have it to look at.

I'll guard it with my life, I tell him, amazed by his generosity.

Well, as I say, I really don't know what's there, he says and he fetches a large, bright blue Tesco carrier bag, the type you buy to use again, and together we put the box in it. It won't go in the right way up, but we manage to fit it in sideways.

Will it be OK? I say.

It'll be fine, look, it's a strong bag. I just hope it's not too heavy for you to carry, that's all.

I don't tell him that if it had weighed eight tons I would have found a way of carrying it.

He drops me back at Banbury Station to catch the train to Oxford, where I tell him I'm meeting my husband. I don't say that we're also going to a Regina Spektor gig at the Town Hall, because I haven't yet worked out quite how I'm going to manage the bag and the gig. But nothing would persuade me to part with it now.

When my husband picks me up in the centre of town as we arranged and I tell him what I've got in the bag, he offers to put it straight in the boot.

No way.

He looks at me and starts to laugh.

Come on, a locked boot? It'll be quite safe.

I couldn't possibly relax with it in there.

So what're you suggesting? You're going to keep it with you all night?

I'll have to.

You're going to stand holding that great huge thing all through the gig?

This is two hundred years of Yelloly history that I've just been trusted with, I tell him. It's staying with me.

And so the box stuffed full of your family comes with me. It comes, held tight under my coat, down the windy street now spotting with rain. It comes into Café Rouge for a cup of tea. And an hour later it sits next to me in an All Bar One while I drink a warm gin and tonic. Finally it comes with me to the Town Hall, to the Spektor gig, where it accompanies me to the loo, the bar, and then sits at my feet while we stand listening to the music.

Regina Spektor has long black clothes and a crooked little smile. She sings about love and loss, pain and longing. It doesn't seem especially odd that the little purse that your mother knitted for your father in 1806 – the purse that outlived every single one of you, sole remaining witness to a lifetime of romance – is accidentally there to hear her do it.

SMASHED AND TORN

Outside, the crockery, it gleams,
green, blue and purple black,
not an inch of which
I would not take back.
I love your sighs?
But we won't compact.
Is it simply lies or fact?

Oh how we glow,
to let ourselves go
to each other,
but it's love and hate,
if not one, then the other.

If we felt the same,
right from the start,
why do you twist
and tear our love apart?

4

THE DAY MY son hits me, I'm all dressed up to go out. High heels and lipstick and perfume.

A director friend has a first night in the West End and it's a hot May evening, hot and light, and I've really been looking forward to this. We go out so rarely at the moment and I'm all ready to leave and I don't want to be late. So I'm watching the clock when I see him dragging his amp through the hall to take out on to the lawn.

Where are you going with that?

Outside. We're gonna practise, when you've gone.

Not outside, you can't.

Why not?

Come on, darling, not with an amp. It will be far too loud.

Oh for fuck's sake.

He tries to push past me, but I get there first and lock the door and put the key on the shelf.

It's not fair on other people, I tell him. That amp really is louder than you think. Practise outside without an amp by all means if you want to.

Without an amp? he almost shouts. You really don't have any fucking idea, do you?

His father comes in, car keys in hand.

What's going on?

She won't let me take the amp outside, for Christ's sake! Please tell him it's not fair on the neighbours.

It's not fair on the neighbours, says his father. End of story.

Fuck's sake!

Oh come on, you know you can't make such a noise, not at this time of night.

It's not night. It's early fucking evening.

Still too late. Look, darling, there's the church out there and then all the flats. It's just not neighbourly to inflict that on people.

But I'm not fucking inflicting –!

You are. You are if they have no choice.

I look at my watch.

Come on, I say, we've said no, and now we really have to go.

The key of the door is on the shelf where I put it. Our son walks over and grabs it.

Put that back right now, I tell him.

He holds it high above his head. He is over six foot tall.

How're you going to stop me?

I stare at him. I'm so tired of this.

You absolutely cannot practise outside tonight. We are forbidding you.

How exactly are you going to stop me, Mother dear?

Come on, darling, says his father, who is closing the door of the dishwasher so the dog can't lick the plates and putting down a fresh bowl of water for her. Give her the key. Why do you always have to be so aggressive about everything?

You call *me* aggressive?

I look at the clock. We are now cutting it fine. This isn't fair.

You're being extremely selfish, his father adds.

Give me the key! I shout and I take a quick step towards him. And I really am quite cross now. Give me back that key right now!

No.

If we don't leave right now, this second, that's it, we can't go, we're late.

Go. I'm not stopping you.

Please just give me the key!

No.

As usual he is intimidating me with his size. As usual I feel small and sad and staccato, powerless in my green satin high heels, a strand of hair sticking to my lipstick. I feel a surge of anger and I lunge at him and –

And what? What exactly is it that I do next?

In the muddled dark of my memory, it's this: I jump up and grab his sleeve with one hand, try to wrestle the keys out of his closed fist with the other. And yes, I am definitely shouting and almost certainly swearing, but do I hit him? No, I do not hit him. This is important because later he will insist that I did.

But did I hit him? Might I have hit him? Sometimes, later, late at night, months and months after this moment, I will still be wondering if I did.

If you keep on doing that, he says, I am going to have to hit you.

Keep on doing what?

His face and voice are very steady, very calm. And – why? – those words don't stop me in my tracks as maybe they should.

Don't you dare threaten your mother like that, says his father (who will reassure me later that I absolutely did not hit him).

He is standing very still now. He is still and I am the one shouting.

If you keep on doing that.

His face is pale.

I said stop it, Mum. I am going to have to hit you if you don't stop.

Outside it is hot and light. The birds are singing. Somewhere in another world, people are arriving at the theatre, queuing for the cloakroom, ordering interval drinks.

I am going to have to –

I don't remember the next moment as a single moment, more a series of neat segments. One segment is that I am definitely somehow on the floor, a crackling-fizzing sound in my ear. Another segment may be shock. Another may be pain.

No one has ever struck me before. Never in my life, I've never been struck. My bottom smacked, yes, when I was four or five, quite hard as I remember it, even once with the back of a hairbrush. But never struck, not knocked to the ground. There is even a touch of exhilaration in the newness of it.

I don't know what I say but I hear my own voice coming from somewhere inside me. Muffled. I put my finger to my ear, half expecting to see blood, but there's nothing. Just a fizzing silence. The boy's father is picking me up. I look at the clock.

Great, I say, that's it. We've missed it now.

And my legs give way again.

I sit on the orange plastic chairs in A & E, still dressed up and feeling stupid. The pain has almost gone and I'm calm. I look at my face in my compact – eyeliner all smudged, lipstick gone, cheeks drained of colour. I think I look OK.

Do you think there's a chance we could get there for the second half? I ask the boy's father.

He looks at me strangely.

No, he says.

The consultant asks what happened and, when we tell him, he says nothing, but concern flicks across his face.

OK, let's have a look, he says.

He shines his light in and tells me my eardrum is perforated.

Not both ears? I say, confused, because I seemed to feel the blow in both.

He checks.

No, the other one's fine. When you receive a trauma in one ear, you can sometimes feel it in both. There's a little blood. No treatment required, but it will take about three months to heal completely and you must get it checked. And it's absolutely vital that you don't let it get wet during that time. No swimming.

What about washing my hair? I say, more worried about that.

Put a cotton-wool plug in it – cotton wool and Vaseline – and be very careful. If you get water in it, you could get an infection and it won't heal.

We thank him.

Watching us as we get up to go, he hesitates.

You do know that this is assault? he says. You do know that? It's quite serious. You've been assaulted. Even though it was your son – what I mean is, you need to think about that.

We say something like yes, OK, we do. Something apologetic. I feel exactly as I did that early morning at home when the police came round. And we say goodbye.

It isn't until we get back out into the main waiting area, among the drunks and the people complaining and frowning and drinking water out of white plastic cups, that my whole body starts to shake.

A strange thing happens with me and the Yelloly box, your box. I can't open it.

Even though, the morning after Regina Spektor, at my desk at home in Elephant & Castle, I go to take it out of the Tesco bag. Even though I manage to lift the brown, battered, falling-apart lid and pull out the first envelope, the one containing your mother's knitted purse. Even though I do quite easily manage to put my hands in among the unknown bundles of papers underneath – noting in one tantalising glimpse a piece of greyed linen, the mysterious slant of a name with a lick of a Y written in ink, the purplish smudge that is the edge of a painting. Even though I get as far as doing all of this, something always happens. The doorbell rings. The phone goes. The dog starts. My nerve just dissolves.

In the end it's a whole eight days later, alone in Suffolk on a Saturday afternoon, that I finally put it on the clean kitchen table. There, as the day turns grey and geese honk loudly over the sea, I find whatever courage is required to touch the things that were once a part of your life.

I take out a small red leather-bound notebook with marbled end-papers and a broken, tarnished metal clasp. Untouched for many years, its dusty texture on the ends of my fingers. Many of the pages seem to have been torn out and put back in the wrong order. Some are printed: *The Churchman's Almanac for the year of our Lord 1851 – being the third after leap year*. There's an engraving of Ely Cathedral. Written at the top in pencil: *Mrs Y.'s Bible Jan 15th 1851*.

The pages underneath, again torn out and stashed together, are covered in minute, sloping pencil writing. I pick one of them up and hold it to the light of the anglepoise that I've set up on the table. On 1 January 1829:

Oh Lord God! Accept my humble thanks for Thy great goodness in having preserved to me my dearest husband and children. Forgive me all the weaknesses and misdeeds which Thou has seen in me and give me strength to perform my duty in that state of life to which Thou has been pleased to call me. Be pleased to present to me my husband, children and friends and give me those blessings which Thou seest I am able to heed, and support me under whatever trials it may be Thy will to send me. S.Y.

The little page, written on rough, cream-coloured paper, measures about 2 inches by 4 or 5. A prayer from almost two centuries ago. I look up for a second. Outside it's dusk now. The sea, the horizon has turned black. Here in my hands, I'm holding your mother's precious pocket almanac.

A raw cold day, the start of the year. A room at the end of a long corridor, the door slightly ajar. An arc of soft light. In it, a woman, your mother, her head bent over a desk. Skirts bunched in the chair. The toe of a slipper peeping from under her skirts. A strand of hair loose over her ear. The glass of the window peppered with rain.

Give me strength to perform my duty . . . support me under whatever trials.

These are her words, her prayers for you, her family, written about five years before the first of you began to die.

Then, on Sunday, 1 January 1831:

Accept oh Lord my humble thanks for all thy mercies particularly for preserving to me my dearest husband and children, though Thou has pleased to call away one of our household, yet let me acknowledge thy wonderful goodness in suffering 24 years to pass over without visiting our house with death!! Grant oh Lord that we may be improved with every visitation of affliction and be pleased to give us all the blessings of this world which may be for our good and therewith make us content and preserve us all to each other as long as it may be Thy good.

This is 1831. You're all still fine. Even Nick is still alive. So who has been *called away*? Which member of the household? Is it a servant, perhaps? The prayers go on. 1833, 1834, 1835, 1836. On a cold, bleak day at the edge of each year, she sits and writes her annual prayer. Makes her deal with God. Gives profuse thanks but also begs for continued mercy. She is in his hands, in his power. What can she do but beg that no one should die?
But then, on 21 January 1838:

Oh Lord God who hast brought me to the beginning of a new year, accept my best thanks for sparing to me my dearest husband and so many of my dear children. I grant that I may be resigned to Thy will for the one Thou hast taken, Thou only knowest what is for our real good and hast [illegible?] taken my poor child from a world of temptation and sorrow thus to Thine everlasting kingdom where he cannot again know pain. Enable me oh God to be patient, resigned and cheerful under whatever sorrow and disappointments Thou mayest see good to visit me with and grant me the grace of Thy holy spirit . . .

Sparing so many of my dear children. So many, but not all. *Taken my poor child.* So Nick has been taken. And although she doesn't know it yet, just six months later, so too will you and Jane be taken. Your mother pleads. She pleads with so much articulacy and gentleness and good grace, with so much decency and humility – but still he helps himself to two more. He helps himself to you, Mary. But your mother doesn't know that yet. This page I hold in my hands doesn't know what I know.

I look up from the yellow light of the anglepoise, seeking familiar things. The sofa with its cotton throw. The carton of V8 juice, the coffee pot by the sink. The dog asleep on her cushion, paws bundled together. The black-and-white photograph of my children taken on a long-ago summer morning before school when they were small enough just to gaze at the camera without smiling.

There is nothing for the rest of 1838, the year of your death. No note, no prayer, no entreaty. A blank.

The next page is from 1839, 13 January:

Hastings

Oh God, I thank Thee that Thou has given me this haven of rest after the waves and storms Thou has seen it necessary in Thy infinite wisdom to bring upon me and mine. Take me and my dear husband and children oh Lord under thy protection this year and for all the remainder of our lives. If Thou seest fit, oh Lord, to restore my dear invalid to health and keep her in her earthly views and if Thou seest good blessing all this family with health and prosper our endeavours, to obtain this blessing. Grant that the heavy affliction we have been called upon to suffer may lead our hearts to Thee and may we never again forget or lose sight of our entire dependence upon Thee . . . I hope through the merits of Thy blessed son that my most dearly loved children Nicholas, Jane and Mary are with Thee!

My dear invalid. That's Sophy. And I already know that, despite the continued passion of your mother's pleas, God does not see fit to restore her to health. Almost exactly a year later, on 11 January 1840, the family foe gets her too. She is twenty-nine and in love, engaged to be married to a man called Robert Groome. But that doesn't seem to cut any ice with God.

Three months after Sophy's death, on 22 April, your sister Anna marries Robert Suckling, and just three days after that, on the 25th, your father is thrown from his phaeton and suffers a head injury which causes a right-sided stroke. What a year. He recovers from this sufficiently to buy and move into Cavendish Hall, but dies there two years later in June 1842. On 20 April 1843:

Oh Lord have mercy upon us and give me the help of Thy Holy spirit to resign myself to Thy Will. This is the first year for 37 years of my life that I have entered upon without my dearest good and kind and affectionate husband – Thou knowest how great a loss it has been Thy pleasure to call upon me to submit to and may it produce such a frame of mind by Thy help.

Finally, inserted in the almanac, a flimsy sheet of paper, and written on it in brown ink something from that dark year, 1838:

Sarah Boddicott Yelloly
A last token of the affectionate remembrance of my beloved sister Jane.

It's cold, really cold. I hadn't realised how cold it was. I'm shivering and my fingers are stiff. And it's now completely dark outside. The dog heaves a sigh, paws twitching as she dreams. And as I push my chair back, ready to get up to go and draw the curtains, turn on the lamps and turn up the heating, I see what I hadn't seen before. My lap is full of human hair.

When I tell people – not many people but just a close one or two – that our son hit me, they always say the same thing: Oh, but I bet he felt so terrible afterwards?

And that's where this story gets harder to tell. Because if he did feel terrible – Oh, they say, but he must have! Come on, there's no way any boy could do that and not feel the most extraordinary remorse? – if he did feel terrible, then he did not show it. Even now. He has not showed it.

Ah yes, but even if he didn't show it, he felt it?

Well . . .

After we got back from the hospital that night, having given up on the theatre and sent an apologetic text to our friends, after we got back home and saw the tea towel which we'd briefly used to hold ice to my ear still damp and forlorn on the kitchen table, the knocked-over chair, the amp still scowling at us from the dining-room floor, we felt so sad and sorry for our fractured family. So we took all three children out for dinner down the road – the Italian again, the same cheap and cheerful family-run Italian we always go to when we need to be put back together again.

We sat at the table in the window, the one we've often sat at. Our boy had spaghetti carbonara. I probably had risotto. I don't know what the others had. We drank wine, the kids drank Coke. Someone might have had a pudding. We were careful and affectionate with each other. There was a strong, unspoken sense that we were being kind to ourselves because we'd all had a shock.

I'm not sure how I felt. Vulnerable, probably. But, in a way, also elated, euphoric even. As if some terrible thing I'd been vaguely dreading for a long time had finally happened. It was over now. It could not hurt me again.

If you don't stop, I am going to have to hit you.

We didn't talk about what had happened – odd for a family like ours who always seem to talk too much about almost everything. We just told the children that my eardrum was perforated, but they needn't worry, that it wasn't as bad as it sounded. It would mend, it would be OK. After that, we talked about other things. Talked and laughed. The boy didn't tell me he was sorry and I didn't ask him to.

At the time this felt like the exact right thing to do, the only thing. If someone you love hurts you, how can you respond except with love? Every other possibility is just too painful to contemplate.

Looking back now though, I think I felt such pity for my boy that night – so sorry for what he had done to me, for what that meant, for the way it might somehow have altered the set of his heart for ever. It wasn't all that different from the time he cut Kitty's fur when he was seven. A part of me just wanted to protect him from what he'd done. The only difference was that he'd been able to express remorse about Kitty.

And later, months or weeks later, when things had escalated to a whole new undreamt-of level of despair, his father told me he thought, with hindsight, we'd been wrong to behave so normally that night, wrong to take him out for that cheerful dinner.

I should have told him to leave the house there and then, he said, I should have acted. I feel ashamed that I didn't protect you, express my outrage. I'm a little bit ashamed. Maybe then he'd at least have understood what he'd done.

And though this wasn't quite what I felt, by then it was hard for me to argue. Because when, in the intervening months, we'd tried – so many times – to speak to our boy about that terrible evening, to elicit some sort of an apology or suggestion of remorse from him, his response had been that I had driven him to it. It was all my fault. It was no more than I deserved. And by then I think he believed it. And so, almost, did I.

Tony Yelloly tells me that the hair might belong to Charles I. He remembers – or thinks he remembers – that the family were supposed to have owned a lock of the King's hair at some point. But then again, it could all be rubbish, he could be wrong. It could have come from a locket or something that perhaps was once kept in the trunk.

It could be anybody's hair. It could be Yelloly hair. It could be your hair, Mary.

Whoever's hair it is, on that evening in Suffolk, I gather up as many of the strands as I can – they're long and thick and straight and dark – and put them in a plastic Zip 'n' Seal freezer bag, squeezing it shut carefully. Whoever it belonged to – a king or a Yelloly – it's been loose in that trunk all these years. And though the sight of those long wiry strands through the clear plastic of the bag makes me shudder a bit, still gathering them into one clean, safe place seems the only respectful thing to do.

After that, I brush down my lap and hoover the tiny hairs and flecks and crumbs left on the table, as well as the floor underneath. If the hair really did belong to Charles I, it doesn't seem quite right that it should end up in a Henry Hoover bag.

But I know I can't live a single moment longer than necessary with those sinister dark strands all over my floor.

Next morning, sun streaming in, coffee made, I decide it's time to be methodical. I open the box and take out every single object, every little picture and scrap of paper, inspecting each and every one in the order in which I find it.

A dozen little white cards, each with a delicate silhouette of a child's head on it. Sarah, Nick, Jane, Sophy, John, Anna, Sam, Harriet, you. None for Ellen – maybe she wasn't born when they were done.

I turn each card over, trying to match the faces to the names. Each of you has the same close-cropped hair curling slightly in at the neck. The little girls have on dresses with frills at the sleeves and chest. Sam and John each seem to have some kind of a ruff around the neck, but Nick – bafflingly – is dressed like the girls. On the back of his card someone has begun to write *Sophy* in pencil, then crossed it out and put *Nick* instead. I turn it over and study the face again. It looks like a girl.

At first the faces all seem to be very similar to one another. But the longer I look, the more they separate into individuals. Sarah's nose, for instance, is definitely more adult, no longer even slightly retroussé – and her lashes curl upwards prettily. I like Jane. Something about the way she holds her lips together indicates curiosity and a touch of amusement.

Harriet looks just like a younger, fatter-faced version of Sarah, the same straightish nose and thick lashes. Sophy's is a young face, small features, pretty. But Anna's nose tilts upwards and there's something more genuinely babyish about her face. Sam's lips are small, he has a slight overbite, and his nose is quite long and sharp.

And you? I hold your card in my hand for a long time. A round face, babyish like Anna's, plump-chinned, your little button of a nose tilting up at the end. I don't know what I expect it to tell me, but nothing comes. It's just the silhouette of the face of a baby who turned into a little girl who painted a book of pictures then shot through adolescence and died before she could do anything else.

In a stiff white envelope, marked *Sarah and Jane*, four letters scrawled in childish writing:

To Mrs Yelloly, Drawing Room, Second Floor, Finsbury Square

My dear dear Mama,

I hope I shall get all my lessons ready for you tomorrow that you may not have to wait as you did this morning and as you have for these last two or three mornings and I hope that I shall be able to come downstairs tomorrow evening after dinner. I hope I shall be very good whilst you are away and I hope you will hear a good account of me and of us all from Mrs Greenacre and I hope that the time you are gone there will be nothing in my book but 'good', 'good', 'good', morning and evening. I will endeavour to do as much as I can what you desired and what I think will please you for I like you to be pleased with me more than anything you can give me ever.

I am, my dear dear Mama, and I hope I always shall be,

Your affectionate and dutiful daughter,

Sarah Yelloly

It's a note that only an eldest child could write. Unquestion-ingly affectionate and dutiful, anxious to please almost to the point of pain. The eldest child's lot. I am an eldest child. So is my boy.

My dear dear Mother,
I hope I shall be good and practise my dancing and I hope I shall do it well and command my temper and not let it (naughty thing) get the better of me for I am determined I will try and master it. I hope I shall remember to teach Sophy and Sam. I hope I shall do all my lessons well and do as much as I can that you bid me. I don't know what more to say so therefore I have any [sic].
Your very dutiful daughter,
Sarah Yelloly

And then Jane joins in:

Dear Mama,
I will try to be good on my birthday and do my lessons well and I will try to please you dear Mama and I will not quarrel with my brothers and sisters at all.
I am my dearest Mama your affectionate daughter,
Jane D. Yelloly

My dear Mama,
I hope you will soon get better and be able to hear us our lessons and go out again as you used to do. And dearest Mama I will try not to make any noise while you are ill and dear Mama I will try to do all my lessons well and I hope you will be well in a few days.
I am your very affectionate and dutiful daughter,
Jane Yelloly

Underneath is a child's pencil drawing of a house with windows and doors and surrounded by a few stick trees.

Another note from a child comes folded over on a piece of yellowing paper, dated 1821. The lines have been ruled in pencil and even the letters – at least an inch high and done in thick black ink – have been traced once in pencil and then gone over:

April 20 Carrow Abey [sic] 1821
My dear Sarah,
As it is your Birthday I have sent You some Spanish Liquorice [?] & I bought from nurse on part case [?] to give you some. But I would not be like the greedy children in Fanny and Mama's book.
Your dear sister Anna has sent you this.
Anna Yelloly

20 April 1821 is your sister Sarah's fourteenth birthday. Her dear sister Anna is six. And Sarah keeps this little scrap of paper for the remaining seventy-six years of her life. Later, still intact, it resurfaces in Tony Yelloly's loft.

And now here on my kitchen table.

Running my fingers over the paper's rough surface, I can still, almost two centuries later, feel the deep grooves made by a six-year-old's pen as, frowning slightly, tongue hanging out, she presses just that little bit too hard.

There's also fabric in the trunk: a pale blue watered-silk needle case, hand-stitched, containing about six sharp needles each about 5 inches long, most of them furred with rust at the end. Each has a kind of two-pronged claw on it and the loops of thread – in scarlet, royal blue and brown – are still attached to the beginning of a piece of work.

Still attached. Two hundred years later, they're still attached, threaded, ready to be continued.

Someone starts making something, gripping the needles, a whisker of cotton pulled taut, slim hands moving briskly – then she breaks off suddenly, never finishing it. Who? Why? Who is it who begins this piece of work, gets halfway through and stops? And why is the unfinished piece then kept so carefully afterwards? Do they hope one day to take it up again, finish it? Or is there a darker explanation? Does it memorialise something – a day, a moment, a loss?

I just can't face throwing it away, that's all. Stuff it in the back of a drawer. Don't think about it.

A hot late spring and summer. May and then June. Long days spent watching by the bedside, hands kept occupied as you move in and out of fitful sleep. You open your eyes for a moment, just to check she's still there. Sarah. Eyes down, working the thread and needles, crocheting, tatting.

Sarah?

Mmm.

What is it you're making?

What's that, my love?

What is it? What's it going to be?

I don't know. I don't know what it is yet. I haven't thought.

What it is is something to do. What it is is something to carry you on through those long, dark and frightening days that end – as I know and you don't yet know – in this:

Lodgings in Ipswich. A dark and sweaty bed. The rough ride back to Woodton. The smell and taste of damp earth in the churchyard at dead of night.

Two pieces of fine cotton lawn have a dead insect folded in between them, a husk of a thorax, translucent pale-brown limbs. A nineteenth-century spider? Or a more modern stowaway from Tony Yelloly's loft?

Another scrap of fine white cotton, long and thin and sad, folded over, looks like a sleeve for a very thin arm. A child's arm, or were you all so very skinny? A frill has been carefully worked at its end. I lay it down on the table next to the needlework, my fingers getting drier with each dose of dust.

Next to it, attached to a scrap of crinkled brown paper, a series of a dozen or so small patchwork circles, tacked together – gingham and stripes and flowers. Pinned to the brown paper, a scrap of white: *Mrs Severne's work done when about 82 years of age. I gave her the pattern and she found out how to do it.*

Mrs Severne. Your sister Sarah in her brief seven-month marriage and achingly lengthy widowhood.

And then an intriguing little pencil sketch of your mother teaching you and Nick and Anna your lessons on a wintry Friday afternoon in 1823. Close-cropped hair, pinafores, hands clasped behind backs, attentive faces. And look at you, the smallest – fat, baby-faced girl, your pinafore quite swamping you, the wispy curls on the back of your neck almost kissable.

Card pictures of a bird and its cage, finely detailed in watercolour, are looped together on silk threads. *For Sarah Yelloly with her mother's affection and love, Aug 1837.* I pull gently at the threads, but nothing happens.

On a larger piece of octagonal board, a house and garden, the flowers dewy and bright. With a fine blade, someone has made tiny slits all over the surface of the picture and at the centre is a loop of brown ribbon. Very gently, I lift it, and the house becomes a three-dimensional version of itself. Underneath, painted on the card itself, two mice are busy attacking a piece of cheese:

129

This wire-fenced mansion
Mr Souri's Hall
Is now on sale
And may be viewed by all
Lift up the latch
And peep into the house
But move with caution
Lest you scare the mouse.

A letter has been written by a child on a piece of paper edged in black. The initials in relief at the top, *A.M.S.* Anna Suckling?

> My dear Uncle Sam,
> I have got the toothache and couldn't eat no dinner hardly. I am very sorry that I didn't say goodbye and I'll ask him where he was that I didn't say goodbye. Which station did you stop at and how did you find your chicken and Grandmamma's horses and how is Harris and please how is Phyllis and Vilet and I forget the others and how is Aunt Sarah's room and all her things and I'll ask him how is the pony chaise and Constance and me and Anna were going to breakfast with Grandmamma and Aunt Sarah and Aunt Harriet, are you not surprised to hear it and I hope it will be fine tomorrow and I send my love to you.

Aunt Sarah and Aunt Harriet. This is from your sister Anna's daughter, also Anna.

A fold-out painting of Temple Bar in London, done by Sarah, quite crude yet ferociously detailed. And a small sampler of the alphabet, stitched in red cotton, also signed *Sarah Yelloly 1819.*

And then something that I instantly recognise. A small white card printed with the following words:

ADMIT
Thos Howe & wife, & George & Maria
to a SUPPER on Tuesday next, July
26th, at ¼ before six o'clock.
They are to bring a Knife, Fork, Plate and Mug
with them
By order of
S.A. Severne Esq

It has to be one of the invitations to your sister Sarah's wedding supper in the *capacious* barn. *Admit Thos Howe & wife, & George & Maria* . . . Straight away I see a family, husband and wife and two children, making their breathless way towards the barn on a late-summer's afternoon, knives and forks and plates clutched in their hands. Long shadows in the hedgerows, music slipping across the fields.

How, then, did the card survive all these years? Did the Howes drop it on the ground as they went in, leaving it to be kicked around on that hay-strewn barn floor? And did your sister pick it up later and decide to pocket it as a memento, slipping it fondly between the pages of her Bible, or else lodging it among the pressed flowers and sketches in the top drawer of her writing desk?

Something else: wrapped in a piece of paper with *Sophy Yelloly* written on in pencil, is a tiny painted envelope with forget-me-nots on the front tied with a pink bow. A hand-painted view of Snowdon on the back.

Inside in tiny writing: *Robert from Sophy and Snowdon from the* [illegible]. In the little envelope are two bits of what look like very old paper, a tiny black piece and a larger transparent one. Nothing written on them. I put them back, somehow subdued by the sense that I've just intruded on something intimate and private.

Another envelope: *Harriet Yelloly Flowers from the Field of Waterloo July 23rd 1847.* Inside, some long-dead mouldering stems and petals, brown and dried out. And a piece of folded paper containing watercolour cut-outs of wigs and hats which look like they were made to fit on paper dolls.

There's an 1837 edition of the catechism and a *Table of Etiquette* showing how one should properly address the King of England as well as various peers of the realm.

A sketch of Clare Castle, Suffolk, drawn *from an old print.* And some engravings of other British landmarks – Snowdon, Conway Castle etc – pulled from a book and saved. Are these what you copied when you painted your album?

A whole bunch of little watercolour cut-out dolls and figures, some of them with cotton carefully threaded in and knotted, as if they were about to appear in a toy theatre. The best one is a jester – red hat, green waistcoat and red-striped tunic, yellow stockings with garters and inward-pointing feet in red shoes. If you jiggle the cotton his head moves.

Deeper in the trunk, there's an envelope with a coin inside: *Royal Medical Society to J. Yelloly Esq. SIG SOC REG MED CHIR LOND. Non Est Vivere Sed Valere Vita.* Also, a copy of a letter, undated, but written by your father to *The President and Members of the Court and Assistants of the Honourable Artillery Company:*

Gentlemen,
The late Act of Parliament for the defence of the kingdom afforded me as a Physician exemption from that military

service which everyone, except medical men and clergy-men, were called upon to perform. I did not however consider it right, in the present momentous crisis of affairs, to avail myself of this privilege, and therefore became a member, nearly three months ago, of the Hon Artillery Company, well assured that in this corps, my humble services would be respectably and usefully directed.

Within a short time it has been suggested to me that as my profession may even be more useful than military services . . .

A folded-over piece of brown paper has the words:

Miscellaneous manuscripts chiefly written by our dear Groome when he was a young man, for sweet Sophy my sister to whom he was engaged. She died of consumption before their marriage.
Woodton – A Satire – Oak Room, Woodton, April 27th 1837 presented by me, R.B. Groome and dedicated to the Lady Sophy by her Humble Servant The Author.

And that's almost it. Except that, at the very bottom of the box, under Robert Groome's collected poetical works, are two faint pencil sketches done by your sister Anna. Two girls.

The first has a sharp, intelligent face, slender nose, hair piled on top of her head, a couple of long ringlets hanging down. Earrings. A rope of pearls around her neck. It's captioned *My Dearest Jane* and is dated September 1838, three months after her death.

The other girl is younger, her hair loose, curls tumbling down to her shoulders. Her dress is a young person's dress – sash and bows. On the back is written: *My Beloved Sister Mary* and the same date. It's you, drawn three months after your death.

The only difference between the picture of you and the one of Jane is that, although your hair and clothes are drawn with care and in some detail, unlike Jane – for reasons unknown to anyone but Anna – you have no face.

Last of all, right at the bottom of the trunk, among the hairs and dust and a few stray pins, some slim notebooks.

Sarah's Journal of a Visit to London May 1829. And four volumes of a journal written by your brother Sam when he was living in London and in Ipswich and seeming to span the years 1835 to 1838, the year you died.

But that's not all. There are two others. One flimsy and small, dated July 1828. Another, dated 1830, fatter and bound with an emerald green silk ribbon. The handwriting is neat, but childish. The author is Mary Yelloly aged thirteen and a half. My heart speeds up. These are your journals.

My stepfather was a chartered surveyor and when I was thirteen and a half he brought me something he got free at the office. A white, ring-bound Halifax Building Society diary with pictures of Winston Churchill and Charles Dickens on the front. On 1 January 1974, I wrote: *I have decided to keep a diary. I hope it will be a comfort for me to read through it occasionally and see how lucky I am.*

Your journal for 1830 – covering just a few brief summer weeks when you were that age – is a thin brown home-made book about 8 inches by 4, a few sheaves of rough brown paper gathered together and stitched, a bit of green silk ribbon threaded through.

The lines and margins have been drawn by hand. The handwriting is faded – brown ink, twirls on some of the larger capital letters.

My own teenage diary is written mostly in Biro.

Monday, 13 May 1974:

Back to school. Went into Arboretum in art. Drew primroses. Had a lecture on Macbeth in the afternoon. Oh why am I so sad? I don't like Daddy, imagine, my own father! He is on the verge of a nervous breakdown, Mummy says he is mentally ill . . . Lily (my doll) is staring at me . . I think she knows. Now I'm crying. Oh dear.

Thursday, 13 May 1830:

From 8 to 12
Heard Ellen her music. Had breakfast. Went to Mrs Hudson wrote English Ex, practised half hour.
12 to 2
Squeezed lemons helped to divide A's margins put on [illegible].
2 to 5
Had dinner. Helped to make cake then made part of a frill practised half hour.
5 to 7
Had tea made lemon sponge had fruit turned out lemon sponge the Hudsons came.
7 to 10
Read.

Thursday, 25 July 1974:

We 3 made a beautiful cake for Mummy's birthday. Mummy came in and found Mandy and I fighting. She was so angry. I apologised and I meant it but she sent me up to my room when I told her the truth. I hate her for it.

Friday 26 July
Quite a nice day.
Saturday 27 July
I'm afraid I don't understand myself.
Sunday 28 July
An extraordinary weekend. I don't know if I enjoyed it or hated it.
Monday 29 July
Fairly ordinary day. Didn't do much. Baked a cake, finished my novel, wrote my diary. Felt a bit sick in the night.

Tuesday, 31 May 1830:

From ½ 8 to 10
Worked at chemisette, had breakfast.
10 to 2
Bound screen. Made sago. Had luncheon.
2 to 5
Read prayers, bound part of screen. Took a walk down Trowse.
5 to 11
Had dinner. Worked at chemisette. Finished chemisette. Wrote journal.
Wednesday June 1st
½ 8 to 10
Took some inks spots out of chemisette.

What I Must Achieve 1974
Write to tea company
Finish my novel
Write to Dr Barnardo's
Make some pies
Write to RSPCA about little dogs in Trinity pet shop

Books Which I Have Read 1830
Tales of the Crusades
Flirtation
Grandfather's Tales
The Country Curate
Part of Mrs Beroc's [?] Journal
Caleb Williams
Rhoda

I began writing my first real novel in the bitter winter months after our daughter was born. Our boy was just two, his little brother (though we didn't know it then) just a couple of months from being conceived.

It was pure coincidence that my father decided to kill himself the night our girl was born, but it didn't feel like it. New Year's Day 1991 was exactly when she was due (and when, in the early hours, after we had drunk a little too much champagne, she decided to come). It was also the time for suicides. As the edge of the old year tipped into the new, our daughter (6lbs 12oz, blue-eyed, pale-skinned, no hair) slipped into the world and my father – drunk on whisky and gulping exhaust fumes – slipped out.

I could hardly take it in. Cushioned by happiness and hormones, I was unable to experience the full shock of it. It really took another whole year – and the birth of another baby

(7lbs 14oz, black hair, ruddy-faced) – before it really hit. Then I made up for it. As if I'd finally grasped what had happened, I panicked.

I developed scary headaches, saw flashing lights, felt I could not breathe. My heart raced. Sometimes I felt as if someone was sitting on my chest.

I tried to focus, literally and metaphorically, on my newborn baby, but his small face was getting further and further away. Convinced I was about to die, I finally saw a neurologist, who told me I was fine and said: By the way, what a lovely baby boy. He told me all I needed was a bit of rest.

I don't know if I believed him. I wanted to believe him. I said I believed him. I didn't believe him.

As far as I can remember, I continued to care for my three small children quite normally throughout this time, but what if I didn't? I didn't think my hysteria extended to them. They were my darlings, my saviours, they were all I desired in this life. I did not believe for one moment that they could pick up on what I was feeling. But what if I was wrong? What if they did?

In photos taken at the time – one baby on my lap, one in my arms, one at my feet, I look: fine, happy and shiny and pretty. Or: thin and young and petrified. It all depends what you're looking for.

I remember then, just as now, finding fast cars a bit too much to deal with. The impulse to stop, to pull in. And I remember thinking about death quite a lot too – not especially my father's death, just death generally.

And I remember a good friend of ours coming to tea and bringing her toddler, who was the same age as our boy. And I know that we spread a rug and some toys on the lawn and all lay around laughing and talking and drinking tea in the sunshine and daisies, so it must have been a happy afternoon.

But in my memory, the proportions are all wrong and it's dark and skewed and it doesn't look like my life.

Two startling things about this time. First, that it passed. I came out of it. And second, by the end of it, about six or nine months after that third baby was born, I'd written a novel.

I don't know whether it was before or after the novel was published that my boy wrote me his first letter, but I still have it now on my wall in a little clip frame. Written on an upside-down postcard, the letters are individually drawn, like stick animals. *You wrote a good novel I love you very much Jou, Julie*

He never in his life called me Julie except on that card. And he didn't know what a novel was. Nobble, he used to call it. He was about four years old. He was delicious. I loved him so much. We loved each other.

I suppose I would like to think that little scribbled postcard might survive the next two hundred years.

We meet up with some people the addiction counsellor put us in touch with – the couple she told us about, who have two sons who are both addicted. We meet in the members' bar at the top of the Tate. Sky pouring in through glass.

They are slightly older than us – attractive, good-humoured, friendly and charismatic people. The kind of people who, in more innocent times, we'd choose to have a drink with anyway.

The mother tells us their story. It's worse than ours, if only because it involves two children and a whole lot more years. As she speaks I feel tears welling up in my eyes, but I don't know whether they're for her or for me. Certainly there's something heart-stopping about hearing a total stranger reveal themselves in such an open, undefended way. The loss of children. Not many things are worse.

We all drink coffee. And we tell them our story too. And the light spills in and downstairs people are wandering through white spaces, leaflets in hand, looking at art.

We tell them how much it means, that they're willing to talk to us about this, sharing like this.

At least you know you're not alone, says the man, who has colourful socks and, when he's not talking about his children, twinkling eyes.

Out there all over the country, plenty of families are dealing with this, says the woman, flicking a look at the London skies. Far more than anyone realises. Seriously. It's a whole new way to lose your kids.

I look closely at her face and I recognise the weight of grief behind her eyes. Her face, but also mine. *A whole new way to lose your kids.*

SOS (SAME OLD SHIT)

Welcome to the loamy darkness,
between slick bodies
and the glow of mobile phones,
a meaningless moment in which to forget,
get off with strangers, loose our heads.
In which to forget there's a world outside,
come on cheer up, we're here to socialise,
in here there ain't no serial killers,
to pick off girls of the night.
But somehow though everyone's smiling.

For me something's not quite right,
can't sleep, can't eat,
can't force myself to go along for the ride,
I suppose I have two options for how to see out tonight;
the conversation's dwindling, and so is my thrills,
I can keep popping till all I can say is pills,
bouncing off walls till the morning trills.
Or I can go home and sleep,
grab a bite to eat.

All sounds fucking boring to me.

5

THE FIRST TIME Julia Yelloly and I are due to meet we have to cancel because snow lies thick all over Suffolk and the trains aren't running.

Now, on a warmish Sunday afternoon a couple of weeks later, I'm waiting on the road outside All Saints, Woodton when a pale yellow car turns on to the road. Primrose yellow. She's already waving to me as she pulls up and parks half on, half off the grassy verge.

Your great-great-great-niece.

She's thirty-something, dark wavy hair, lively eyes. She's been in Bungay training for a triathlon and she has on blue trousers and a red fleece. No make-up. Cheeks blazing with cold. I ask her if she realises that her car's the exact same colour as the old Yelloly coach, and she laughs but I'm not sure she knows what I'm talking about.

After several weeks of emails, we're shy with each other, both talking too fast, interrupting then apologising, falling over each other's words. Together we make our way through the little wrought-iron gate, up the gravel path and into the dim silence of the church. After standing a moment to look again at your family plaques, we settle ourselves in a pew about halfway down the aisle. There's no one else here. Just us and the vaulted ceiling, stained-glass windows and *Yelloly* written over and over on these walls. Your familiar coat of arms with its frothing red plumes. *Spes Mea Christus.*

Julia pulls her bag up on her knees and shows me what she's brought. First, her copy of Florence's book, which I'm welcome to borrow. No more having to go and read it in the British Library. I tell her I'll take huge care of it.

And two smallish watercolour paintings in frames – not the original frames, she points out quickly – both clearly and recognisably Woodton Hall. There's a little bit of land in front and it looks as if the view is probably done from just here, by the church. On the back of one a typed white sticker:

> Taken from an album . . . this book was given to me by my dear amiable daughter Mary Yelloly in April 1838 and is now sent to my dear son Samuel Tyssen Yelloly in memory of her who was so deservedly and so truly beloved. 17 July 1838.

I've never taken it out of the frame, but I'm presuming that's what it says on the back of the painting, Julia says.

I look carefully at the picture. Misty grey-green Norfolk copses, brush-blobs of colour – a suggestion of brightness and wetness in the air. *Given to me . . . in April 1838 . . . who was so deservedly and truly beloved.*

Painted just weeks before your death.

It must be one of the very last things Mary painted before she died, I say.

A moment's pause as we both think about this. In the foreground of both pictures is a small male figure, red waist-coat, a dark hat and what looks like a gun.

Do you think that could be one of her brothers? Julia says. Or else maybe a servant?

Nick was already dead, I say. It could be John or Sam.

I ask where she got the pictures.

Would you believe, I was just given them, she says. It was so lucky. I was on my way to see Cavendish Hall, you know where my father's family had lived? And I stopped off at an antique shop in Long Melford to ask directions and when the man heard I was a Yelloly he said: Oh well, then you'd better have these. He just gave them to me!

I smile. She has the same bright, frank warmth as her father. I wonder if it's a Yelloly quality. Were you like this?

Well, that's it, she says. That's all I've got.

Feeling slightly awkward because it still doesn't really seem right that I should have looked at it first, I ask her if she knows about the box her father has lent me. I tell her it contains some wonderful stuff.

It's funny, she says with a little frown, I never even knew anything about it. He's never ever mentioned it to me.

I'm not sure he knew he had it, I tell her. Or at least he'd never really looked at it. Not until I came to lunch and he got it down.

It's incredible what families can sit on for hundreds of years, she says, smiling.

I tell her I still haven't managed to find your grave even though I've tried so hard, searching this whole churchyard more than once.

She thinks about this.

Well, I was pretty sure my father knew. But now I think he was perhaps referring to the other graves, you know, the ones at Stansted. That's Stansted in Suffolk, by the way, not Essex.

144

We decide to go and walk around the churchyard anyway – see if we can tell where the pictures were done from – and, as we walk out into the weak winter sun, I realise what's been bothering me about Julia's face.

That portrait on your parents' landing, the one of Mary's sister Sarah, with the long gold earrings. It's just so incredibly like you!

Really?

Seriously. The expression, the colouring, everything. I can't believe no one's ever said it before.

She laughs and shakes her head and tells me no, no one ever has, but, out here in the chilly spring light, it's true. If your sister Sarah had hennaed her hair and worn a red fleece, turquoise hood and blue combat trousers and come straight from triathlon training at Bungay, this is exactly how she would have looked.

The ground in the churchyard is hard to walk on – soggy and muddy. Fleshy turf caving in underfoot.

Because of all the snow that's melted, I expect, says Julia. A couple of weeks ago this must have been several inches deep.

And now it feels almost like spring, I say.

Blinking in the sunshine, we make our way across to where the older graves are, each of us carrying a framed picture done by you in our hands. We're facing out from the back of the church now, away from the road, looking out towards where Woodton Hall must once have stood.

Wow! Look at that! Julia shouts as something flaps away. A barn owl!

We watch as its dark shape disappears between the trees.

Definitely a barn owl, she says again. A good omen!

Really?

Of course.

Afternoon sun falls in slants over the grass. I ask her if the pinkish wall we can just glimpse through the trees was once part of the old hall.

Yeah, I think so. I'm pretty sure. My father and I had a look quite a few years ago. We just went a little way up the path.

I tell her I did exactly the same a few weeks ago.

I didn't go far, though. I wasn't sure if people lived there or not. There's a house up there that looks like it's been recently done up.

Now Julia glances at the path.

God, I'd so love to go and see where the Hall stood, she says.

I know. So would I.

She gives me a look and I begin to laugh.

Well, I don't see what's to stop us going a little bit further up the path than we've already been, she says.

The worst that can happen is we just have to apologise and leave, I agree.

She looks triumphant.

And look, we don't even need to go round, we can easily get over here.

And she hands me your picture to hold and begins to hoist herself up, easily, gracefully, over the grey stone wall, stopping only to cast a critical glance at my clothes. They're not exactly urban, but they weren't put on with wall-climbing in mind.

Will you be able to do it? she asks me.

Of course!

She slithers down on the other side and laughs. I hand her the pictures and follow her over without too much difficulty, keeping quiet as a nettle licks my shin.

Together we walk over a carpet of snowdrops towards the space once occupied by Woodton Hall.

★   ★   ★

Reaching the top of the path, we find ourselves under the spreading branches of the old cedar I found before. We stare up into it. It has to be hundreds of years old.

So why isn't it in either of Mary's paintings? I say.

Julia holds hers out at arm's length and squints.

Maybe she was standing more to the right when she painted it?

It's either off the edge of the picture, or the tree's not as old as it looks. Maybe it was a small tree back then.

Do they really grow that fast?

I've no idea. I doubt it.

Beyond the cedar, directly in front of us now, there's a drive and some cars and a low gabled cottage on the left and, to the right, the old garden wall and a curl of smoke – someone's having a bonfire. A glimpse of a man.

Oh God. Julia touches my arm. Are we going to have to say something?

The man hasn't seen us. He's walking in the other direction.

I hesitate.

Shall we just go and knock on the door?

Do we dare?

I dare if you dare. I mean at least you are a real Yelloly. You have every reason to be here.

But it's you who's writing about Mary!

But even if we wanted to change our minds, we couldn't. Already there are faces at the window. Small white faces. Kids? Still clutching your paintings, we knock on the door.

Two women, one of them wiping her hands on a tea towel, look a bit startled when we say the name Yelloly. They wave at the bonfire man, who's walking towards us in his wellington boots. They take the paintings from us and study them

147

carefully, wordlessly, and we ask if they know that Woodton Hall once stood here.

They're still staring as I continue to explain.

I'm Julie and I'm trying to write about it. But this is Julia, and she's a real Yelloly.

The women and the man all look at each other for about three seconds, then they start to laugh.

You'd better come in, says the first woman. Yes, we know all about the old Hall and the Yellolys. It's just – well, this may take some time.

Elaine and Steve Hill have Sunday lunch all laid on the table – a low-beamed kitchen, an Aga, checked tablecloth, glasses, dishes, mats. The friend is helping and there are teenagers around, sloping in and out in their socks.

Oh dear, I say. You're just about to have lunch.

We've come at a terrible time, says Julia.

Not at all, Elaine says. This is exciting!

We follow her through a dim corridor into a dark and elegant wooden-floored dining room.

What a beautiful room, says Julia and we stare around us while Elaine bends down to the low sideboard and pulls out box files, piles of papers, spreads them on the table.

This is all that's left of the Hall, Woodton Hall, this bit where we live, she says. We did this place up ourselves, from scratch. It was quite derelict. We think it was the stables or the servants' quarters or whatever.

This room was definitely stables, says Steve, who has taken off his wellingtons and padded in. Just there where you're standing was a kind of a byre. And there was a great big pile of manure the very first time we walked in here.

All right, Steve, thanks very much, laughs Elaine.

148

You mean you put down this floor? says Julia. But it looks so original.

Steve looks pleased.

Now take off your coats, sit down, he says, and I slip my coat off and sit next to Julia, who's already settled herself at the dining table.

Cup of tea anyone? offers Steve and Elaine's friend, who has just popped her head round the door. Julia and I look at each other.

This is so kind of you, says Julia. But aren't we keeping you from your lunch?

Lunch can wait, says Elaine firmly.

We say that in that case we'd love a cup of tea.

This is turning out to be the strangest day, I tell Steve.

It's so lucky, Julia adds, that we came and knocked, because you see we so almost didn't –

Oh but you shouldn't have hesitated! Steve says and he beams at us. Now, which one's Julie and which one's Julia?

We tell him.

And are you sisters?

We laugh.

We actually only just met this afternoon.

Now Steve and Elaine look at each other. You're not serious? You two have only just met?

About half an hour ago. It's quite funny, isn't it? says Julia.

And I look out of the window at that view which is straight out of your album – the hazy greens and greys of Woodton, the ragged, windblown skies – and I think, Yes, it's funny.

Elaine puts some more documents on the table. A view of Woodton, 1842, Dilapidated.

It was pulled down soon after that, she says. You do know about the curse?

Julia and I flick a look at each other. The tea arrives and is put down on the table.

What curse?

Ah well, you should get in touch with this man Patrick Baron Suckling, Steve says. It was nothing to do with the Yellolys really. It was the Sucklings, so he knows all about it. And they – what was his daughter called? Wait a minute, it'll come. He lives in Spain but she's in Norwich, I think. Or she was. Here you go – Caroline. Caroline Suckling.

Suckling. Your sister Anna married the Revd Robert Suckling. A descendant of theirs, then. I write down the names and phone numbers.

There was this family called Fellowes – lived at Shottisham Castle. Still do, some of them. An amazing place not far away, you should go. And sometime I don't know when – 17-something, certainly, there was a row over a woman and he – Fellowes, I think – kicked a Suckling down the steps of Woodton Hall. And he put a curse on the place and said he wouldn't rest till it was pulled down, brick by brick.

And this was before the Yellolys came?

Oh yes, goodness, long before. And every Suckling started to die after that. They died young, all the men did anyway.

What a horrible story, Julia says.

Elaine and Steve say they need to go and eat lunch now, but we're very welcome to sit and drink our tea and look at the documents.

Take your time, says Elaine. It's no trouble at all.

And if you've got time, after lunch I'll show you round if you like, Steve says. I can show you exactly where the walls of the Hall stood.

Left alone, Julia and I start sifting through the papers on the table.

I wonder if the Yellolys knew about the curse, says Julia. I mean they were fine when they came to Woodton, weren't they – and then they all started dying.

I tell her this had crossed my mind too.

I ask her if it feels strange, to be a Yelloly sitting here in the very house – or the stables anyway – after all this time.

She sips her tea, thinks about it.

Not really. Because you see I'm just me really. I mean the past, it's interesting, I'm very interested in it, but at the end of the day, it's not what I am. It's just the past, isn't it?

As the sun gets low and the light turns silvery, Steve takes us on a walk right around the edges of his land, pointing out the depressions in the earth – now tangles of bramble and thicket – where the foundations of your home once stood.

It's amazing that you can still see them so clearly, says Julia.

Oh, they're very obvious when you know what you're looking for.

It's so much bigger than I'd pictured it, I say.

Oh yes, look – he indicates the sweep with his arms – you can tell, it was a vast pile.

And we all stop for a moment and take in everything that's around us. And just like before there's that sudden odd quality to the air – a strange skittering lightness and a sense of grandeur, or height? – that makes me feel I can almost sense the Hall still standing there around me.

It's a funny old place, says Steve, it's got this – atmosphere.

I nod because that's exactly what I'm thinking.

We walk on, the dog sniffing eagerly, then tearing off to chase a scent, while Julia lags slightly behind taking photos.

My Dad will want to see, she says.

Steve tells us that the road used to run right up here, between the Hall and the church. But the original owner, Alfred Inigo Suckling – the man who rented the Hall to the Yellolys – didn't like it being so close to his property.

So he had it moved – ha! – just like that, right down there, to where it is now. You could in those days, if you were rich. You could do anything if you had the money and the clout.

We walk through mud and leaves. In the middle of all these trees there's no wind whatsoever. Though the sun has gone, the sky's still smudged with brightness.

I ask Steve how they came to live here and he says they saw an ad in the *Eastern Daily Press*.

And how long did it take to do it up? asks Julia.

Five years. Us living in a mobile home with the three kids. It's my life's work really. Not much fun sometimes in the mobile home either.

I bet it wasn't, says Julia.

Must be an amazing place for the kids to grow up, though, I say, reminded for a moment of Joanne Sandelson's kids and the mad white puppy in the earthworks at Narborough.

Yeah. Yeah, it is. Ah, now here's the well – look.

The original well?

Yup.

He pulls a cover off the side and we look down. I can see nothing, just a long drop into darkness. But Julia leans in and takes a photo and shows me – it shows up perfectly on her camera. Pale brickwork going round and round, down and down. A glimmer of something shining at the bottom.

It still has water in it?

Oh yes. The Yellolys would have used this well. Their servants would have, anyway.

We walk back up to the house past stagnant ponds, petrified trees. The air is so still.

I ask Steve what he does for a living.

Teacher, design and technology. In Bungay.

He asks Julia what she does.

Computer analyst, she says, making a face.

And she's a serious athlete as well, I tell him. She competes in triathlons.

The very last thing Steve shows us is the Yelloly coach house – still intact – where the primrose-coloured Yelloly coach would have been kept. He shows us the little alcoves in the wall where the coach lanterns would have been placed and I hold my fingers there for a second on the rough old brick.

And beyond the coach house is the walled garden – he tells us proudly how he's been repairing the walls gradually all by himself, a bit at a time – a painstaking process, exhausting at times, but quite satisfying all the same. Little piles of pink bricks waiting to be slotted back into a several-century-old wall.

Before we leave, we go back up to the house to say goodbye to Elaine. She gives me a phone number.

Monica Churchill, she says. She used to be the church warden. She might well know where your poor Yelloly girl was buried.

It's almost dark now – the kind of creeping gloom that turns black as soon as you go inside and turn on a light. In the kitchen, the table's empty except for a couple of place mats and the dishwasher's on. The corridor's dark and the TV flickers in the sitting room and two teenagers loll on the sofa. A girl, and a boy in a hoodie – half-watching TV, half-strumming a guitar.

Oh, my kids play the guitar, I say. My eldest's got one just like that, I think.

Electric? says Steve and the boy looks up, half-interested. Yeah, it's a bit of an earful, isn't it?

It is if you use an amp, I say.

And Steve folds his arms and lets out a big sigh and for the first time I think I detect a flicker of stress in his eyes.

Oh my God, he says. Just tell me about it!

The court said we were to visit our father every other weekend and more time to be agreed between them in the holidays. I didn't know how this would be agreed as he refused to speak to our mother except through a solicitor.

The first time he came to pick us up – it must have been September – we hadn't seen him for about three weeks, not since our mother left. I was looking forward to seeing him and to seeing our old house again (I'd lain awake so many nights trying to remember every single square foot of it) but I was also terrified. It was like being picked up by a stranger.

But I knew this was silly because he was our daddy and we'd only been on holiday with him a few weeks ago. Swimming in the sea, eating sandwiches, watching the little portable black-and-white TV he always brought with him in the hotel bedroom.

He picked us up. His car. Clean beige upholstery and cigarettes. The full ashtray which always made me cough. I don't remember what we said to each other after all that time, but I know we stopped on the way home to get some frozen food.

There's nothing in the house any more, he said. You'll see how different it is.

★　　★　　★

Our boy's attendance at school is getting patchier and patchier. Many days now he doesn't even pretend he's going to get up in the morning, doesn't even waste time talking about it.

In some ways this is a relief. It means I don't have to go up there, trying to rouse him, seeing his pale face surrounded by half-eaten plates of food and mouldy glasses, crumpled Kleenex and old underpants. It also means we don't have to suffer his destructive and chaotic presence tipping everyone off balance at breakfast.

Most days we get an automated message from the school-attendance line, informing us that he isn't there and asking us to give a reason.

And I tell the truth.

We don't have a reason, I explain to the school answerphone. We think he ought to be there. We passionately feel he needs to be put on the spot, told what his options are. We've suggested his teachers threaten to expel him. But they haven't, so we really don't know what we can do.

I say these words – or something like them – several times a week. Some days I feel assertive and honest and resigned as I say them. Other days I just feel miserable.

He doesn't go to school because he knows he can get away with not going. He doesn't go to school because he's forgotten all about why he was going in the first place. He doesn't go to school, we are realising now with a sinking, tearing certainty, because he absolutely and definitely can't stop smoking cannabis.

When we challenge him about this, when we try to talk about skunk, he laughs at us.

I don't buy skunk any more, he says. Do you think I'm crazy or something? The guy I buy from, he's a really good guy. He goes out of his way to make sure it's not skunk.

But you used to smoke skunk?

Used to, yes. But this is mersh. Much weaker, OK?

But how do you know?

He rolls his eyes.

Because I trust the guy, OK? He doesn't want to fuck people's brains about with skunk, does he?

Doesn't he?

If he gets chucked out, says his father, he's out of here. I mean it. That's it. He's pushing eighteen and if he's not in education, well, I don't know if I can live like this much longer.

He says it partly to himself, to hear what it sounds like, and partly to me, to see what I'll say. I don't say anything.

Meanwhile our boy's routine doesn't waver. On days he goes to school, he gets up about ten and leaves after a shower and a bit of shouting. The relief in the house is palpable. The silence. The lack of tension. The quality of the air actually seems to change.

On days when he doesn't, he gets up at around two and maintains what feels to us like a steady and carefully judged campaign of aggression and belligerence. It's not that any of the individual things he does – stumbling around half-dressed, swearing and yawning and scratching himself, making a pot of coffee and enjoying it on the lawn, smoking a joint and playing his guitar wearing nothing but a pair of boxers – are so very extraordinary or intolerable in a teenager. More that he makes it quite clear that all of this is non-negotiable. That we have no say in how things will be in our home. The noise, the mess, the fury – we have no choice but to put up with it. In fact, if we complain, he seems to go out of his way to make sure the volume increases.

Sometimes, trying to work, I lean out of the window and beg him to stop singing. Just for a bit.

I just need half an hour, I tell him. Half an hour of peace so I can think.

He squints up at me as if he's forgotten who I am.

One more song, he says. And he turns straight back to his guitar because it's not a question. If I continue to object, or if I decide to go down there, he'll start one of his rants where he follows me round the house, shouting at me and asking for money. And if he does this, then I can say goodbye to work for a couple of hours or more.

I shut the window. I'm hot. I try to work. His voice continues. I push my fists in my eyes, hold back the tears.

If we ask him to clear up the mess he's made, he replies that he'll live as he sees fit.

As you see fit?

He grins.

Look, his father says as mildly as I've ever heard him talk to anyone, while you're standing there waiting for the kettle to boil, couldn't you just unload the dishwasher? Or wash up the pan you used for the sauce?

His son tells him to fuck off and stop being such a megalomaniac control freak.

That's a bit of a tautology, suggests his father. And all I'm asking is that you behave like a member of this family.

This isn't a fucking family, says his son, who loves to try and make out that we are – and always have been – supremely dysfunctional in all sorts of fundamental ways that do not relate to or involve him.

And some days I think he is right. Some days I wonder, What did we do to our child? What exactly was it? What toxic concoction of qualities did we two parents somehow bring to this young family of ours, to cause such a disastrous thing to happen?

And then I look at the photo I have on my desk of him fast asleep in his father's arms when he was just a few weeks old. A young, soft-faced man in an old brown jersey, eyes full of love. And a tiny baby boy, eyes tight shut, fists clenched, white shawl carefully folded around him by that same young man, who moved me so much when he asked the midwives to show him how to swaddle an infant properly.

In May 1829, your sister Sarah takes a trip to London with your mother and Harriet. They call on various friends – the Rowlatts, the Wrights, the Lears, the Dobsons and the Marcets. Frank Marcet is a celebrated surgeon, who belongs to the same clubs and sits on the same committees as your father. Your family and his are firm friends.

They go to the Bazaar in Soho Square, where they probably buy hats, gloves, handkerchiefs, shawls and lace, as well as some drawing and painting materials. Then they go to a watercolour exhibition. They drive around Hyde Park, go out to dinner and to the theatre, and attend a fitting of a new gown that's being made up for your mother. They go to the opera in Covent Garden:

> We were in Lady Holland's private Box which Mrs Marcet had for that even. Our party consisted of our 3 selves, Mr and Mrs Frank Marcet & Sophy Marcet and Mr J. Prevost joined us at the Play. Mrs M was not well enough to go. We saw some very pretty baby linen which they were going to send to Geneva for Mrs M's baby, and for Mrs de la Rive.

They go to Crouch End, from where they take a pleasant walk to Shepherd's Cob Fields, and on the Sunday, as always, they go to church. They eat bride cake at a Mrs L's and then go on to an exhibition at Somerset House where they particularly admire pictures of the Duchess of Richmond by Sir T.E. Lawrence. Sarah is struck by the fact that Lawrence's pictures fetch up to 600 guineas each.

They go to Bond Street to admire statues of Tam O'Shanter and Souter John, done by a Scotch stonemason. And then on to the Spanish Bazaar in the Hanover Square rooms, which they find rather crowded:

> All the lady Patronesses were ladies of quality, Countesses etc etc. We saw there Lady Morley who was much better looking than we expected, Lady Anson also and Lady Ann Coke. It was a very gay scene indeed, a great many fashionable people, buyers and sellers. The gentlemen seemed very niggardly inclined and were complaining of everything being so immensely dear.

On another night your father, who has now joined the party, takes your sisters to see the celebrated opera singer María Malibran García:

> The music is extremely fine, Mad Malibran is a most graceful actress and very interesting looking woman. An act was performed from 'Il Barbiere', Rossini; Mad Sontag who sang an aria divinely and looked most sweetly. A short ballet merely a divertissement.

The next morning they all get up at half past four and set off by telegraph coach for Carrow Abbey.

Your sister's journal of this trip sits on my desk by my computer, among the other papers and journals lifted from the box. And I'm flicking through it for the fourth or fifth time when I notice what I never noticed before. Right at the very back of the book, hidden on the inside-back page long after the journal has ended, a note, scratched in the faintest pencil. It takes me a while to decipher:

You must come too (to Epsom). Stay here and then I shall have the pleasure of talking to you. You've been forgetting how happy I am between [?] too. I'll do everything you tell me whatever I do. Ah, you are all perfection, I do not require any change. Take my [?] and [?] to each [illegible initials]. Come to find us to say goodbye. How long do you love [?] . . .

The writing is so faint, so almost not there, that there are a few words I just can't make out, words I have to give up on. What does it mean? And I can't quite tell if it's your sister's handwriting, the same as the journal, or whether it was written by someone else.

The only thing I'm sure about is this: almost two hundred years ago, under a card table, during a lengthy opera, or on the crowded edges of a bazaar, these words were hastily scribbled by one person for another to see: *Ah, you are all perfection.*

I'm looking at a secret two-hundred-year-old love note.

Our old house – our father's house – was different. We didn't live there any more. It wasn't the same. There were sad patches on the wall where pictures had been, dusty dents in the carpet where furniture had gone. The fridge was empty and the toilet bowl had a rusty ring. There was fluff on the carpet and a dead spider in the plughole of the bath.

Downstairs, though, there was a bigger TV and a brand-new thing, a video recorder. He showed us how you could be in the middle of watching a programme and make the people freeze. *The Sale of the Century, New Faces.* You could make them all go backwards and start again. When he showed us, we laughed and laughed and said: Do it again, so he did it again. For a while it felt like we had our old fun daddy back.

There was more whisky than there used to be and there were all the same old ashtrays, including the one where you pressed the button and it went around and the ash fell down, but they'd just been emptied not wiped. And he had another new toy, an electric organ (he had a talent which was that he could play any instrument by ear without music). He played it for us, hands all flat on the keys and cigarette held in the side of his mouth. When he played, his eyes went dreamy and his face turned into someone else's face and something about the electric texture of the music made me feel a bit sick.

Upstairs our rooms were sad and cold and all our ornaments were gone. Just fluff and dead flies on the shelves where our glass animals had been.

Well, they're gone because your mother took them, he said and we couldn't really argue with that. He said he wasn't replacing anything she'd taken. He said we couldn't really expect to benefit from being the children of divorcees.

I never asked her to go, he reminded us as he shook another cigarette out of its packet, and we felt sorry for him all over again.

He said it wasn't really worth turning the radiators on, now we, his own daughters, weren't living here.

But just for the weekend?

He shook his head.

They wouldn't get hot in time. And by the way, he said, he'd rather we didn't call that other house, our mother's house – the house where she was living in sin with That Man

– home. This was still our home, this empty cold place with nothing on the walls.

OK, we said.

We listened to our father and we tried to be sympathetic. Maybe we were sympathetic. It wasn't his fault, after all, if he was a bit upset. I thought I'd be a bit upset too if I had my whole life taken away like that, in the space of one August night.

Even the dog, as he pointed out in a voice so angry it was almost a whisper. He told us he was asking our mother for the value of half of the dog: £8. The dog had cost 16 and so he was asking for 8.

I call a branch of Narcotics Anonymous that meets in Bloomsbury once a week. It's the only one in Europe that's specifically for under-twenty-fives.

The leader tells me it's fine for our boy just to turn up. Or he can call and speak to him first if he prefers. I tell him that the boy in question doesn't believe he has a problem and is unlikely to call. I just wanted to be able to let him know what was available.

Just give him the information, the leader says. You're doing the right thing. This way you're equipping him, so that when he's ready he can make the choice himself.

My darling,
Please read this letter from your interfering mother who loves you so much.

I could be wrong (please forgive me if I am) but I still very very strongly feel/sense that you are smoking too much cannabis. I don't care how much you're smoking – whether every week, every weekend or every day.

Whatever. I just have this hunch that everything (I mean school AND everything else, your music, your relationships, your sense of fun, everything!!) would go much more how you want it to go if you were able to stop.

Wait! Don't tear this up! Hear me out . . . please. I do know that feeling of wanting to get OUT of your head (you won't believe me but I've been there and used other things to get there). But why not try staying INSIDE your head for a while? It's maybe not as scary or boring a place as you think. Your head is fascinating. You're turning it to mush with drugs. You know this and it's scary.

No, don't tear this up! Just read it, OK?

A NICE NORMAL guy called R. runs the only Narcotics Anonymous meeting in the whole of Europe for young(er) people. They meet every Friday in Bloomsbury. You can just turn up. The people are aged mostly between twenty and twenty-five though some are younger and the point is that though a few of them have moved on to heroin, most HAVE NOT. Most are just doing WAY more cannabis than they want to be doing. Plus (R. says) usually a bit of coke. Like you, in fact.

The reason they've (finally) given in and come to the meeting is they've tried very hard to smoke less but have failed. This scares them. R. says it does a person's head in when they're quite strong and intelligent and therefore presume they'll be able to kick something when they want to . . . then they decide they DO want and find they can't.

I very very much want you to try going to a meeting. All right, I can't make you. So you can:

a) Tear this piece of paper up (no, please don't!).

b) Refuse to go because you're sick-of-me-interfering-in-your-life-and-I've-got-it-all-wrong, but AT LEAST fold the piece of paper up and keep it in your pocket for when you change your mind.

c) Go to a meeting with ME next Friday 19th and I buy you dinner afterwards.

d) Go to a meeting on your OWN next Friday 19th – and meet me for dinner afterwards . . .

Or just call R. on this number. He says you can call him at any time if you want to find out more. You can say I gave you the number or you don't have to. Just say you got his number from Narcotics Anonymous. He gets called all the time, it's what he does. He sounds really nice. Intelligent, sense of humour, kind of normal.

The thing is, I know we went on last year about you going into rehab but I think that wasn't quite it. I don't think you need rehab. But I think you need a reason (and some help) to quit something that you thought you enjoyed but is in fact taking over your life. I think you know this. These meetings (and NA itself) have only been running this long because they work. Most people decide to quit and do quit and get happy, get clean.

You can go to just one meeting or you can go when you feel like it or you can go every Friday. But it's worth a try. I don't see what you have to lose . . .

That letter. I spend time on it. I write it so carefully, choosing every word with the very best intentions. But reading it back now I wince as I see how badly I got it wrong. It's far too long, for a start, and it's trying much too hard. A boy can smell a mother's anxiety a mile off and this letter stinks.

I don't know if he ever really read it. But I do at least know that he took option b.

Because months later, clearing out the flat he's just been evicted from, the same flat where he abandons his cat, I find the letter – its once-sharp creases fuzzy with age, folded and zipped into his old jacket pocket.

Caroline Baron returns my call.

Oh I'm sorry, I tell her, I thought your name was Suckling.

No, it's Baron. Used to be Baron Suckling, I think, a long time ago, but at some point the Suckling bit was dropped.

I explain what I'm writing about.

Oh well, it's my father you need to talk to, she says. He knows everything. All I know, you see, is just what he's told me. He lives half the year in Tenerife but he's back soon. I can give you his email.

I thank her and say I'll contact him.

We're about to say goodbye when she adds: Did you know, by the way, that the curse continues? Yes, well, it's supposed to be the eldest male in the family and it always skips a generation but, twenty years ago when my cousin David died of a brain tumour, my father thought, Ah.

Your brother Sam's journals, kept while he's living in London and Ipswich, supposedly studying the law, but in fact putting far more energy into having a good time, are more revealing than Sarah's.

Sam always has plenty to say, doesn't he? He's lively, vociferous, likeably curious, a little bit full of himself, perhaps. You wouldn't exactly call him quiet and bookish – he never seems to opt for an evening in when he could go out. But he does like reading and seems to get through many of the notable volumes of the day (Anne Grey, Hallam, Preston, Blackstone, Allemagne), gobbling them in late-night bursts, or else at breakfast.

Sam is sociable. Very interested in women – quick to notice pretty ones, inclined to complain about ugly ones. He enjoys eating and drinking and smoking his pipe. He is, he happily informs us, 5ft 10½ in his boots and weighs 11st 6lbs. Quite bulky, then.

He has plenty of friends and, so it seems, no shortage of invitations to dinner and to the theatre and opera. He spends a lot of his London time following up contacts of his father's – people who are not always in or available when he calls. But this doesn't seem to throw him. He's affable, persistent, an all-round good chap, easily amused – even if the jokes he cracks in his journal are maybe not always quite as funny as he thinks they are. His landlady doesn't seem to find him all that amusing either – especially not his lateness, his rowdiness and his off-hand manner. But at least when she gives him a jolly good talking-to he's sufficiently stung to record it in his journal.

He always reports very solemnly on the weather.

And he's a good correspondent – regularly writing individual letters to all of you – mother, father, sisters, brothers, even you, Mary. But he seems to allow himself to be dragged back to Woodton only on sufferance, always slightly cross with himself for staying for longer than he intended. The comfortable lure of home.

I'm not sure how you feel about him as a brother, but from here he looks like a young man full of energy and optimism and good humour, keen to make his way in the world, keen for independence. Deep down, though, perhaps it's dawning on him that he's neither as bright and hard-working as his distinguished and successful father, nor as artistic and engaging as his mother and sisters. I wonder how he copes with this.

In his journal, your brother describes a freezing, wet Ipswich February – the February of 1838. We know he discusses world affairs over pipes and ale and, skates slung over his shoulder, walks down to test the ice at Mill Pond, sometimes getting his feet wet. We know he eats partridge and gets his hair cut and stands on Waterloo Bridge to get a good view of the traffic passing up and down the river to Greenwich.

And I've no idea what was happening to you that February, no idea whether you were sick already and, if so, how sick. I don't know if you stayed in bed, coughing and gasping under your chilly sheets, or else were brought to lie on a couch in the drawing room. I don't know if you were well enough to sew frills on to sleeves and paint and draw and even venture down the icy church path to gather snowdrops.

But I hold this journal of Sam's in my hands right now and it makes my heart lurch to think that, sitting up after a smoke and a jug of ale to write it, he was almost certainly in the very room in Ipswich where, less than six months later, you would come to die.

I take a train west, on a boiling hot late-spring day, to visit a rehab centre that the addiction counsellor has told us is the best in the country for young people. Not the slickest or the most expensive, but the one with the highest success rate, simple as that.

Kids agree to go, thinking they're there for six weeks, she tells us. But they end up staying six months. That's why it works.

We are nowhere near getting our boy to agree to go anywhere. He is still, just as he always has been, absolutely in denial about the seriousness of his drug use. But it seems to me that we need to know about this place. His father and I talked to him last year about the possibility of rehab. But back then we had only the vaguest sense of what we were talking about. Now I want to have a clear and practical picture of it in my head so that, when the time comes, I can say: OK, here you are, this is where you're going.

The person who gets on that train on a sunny summer morning and goes there doesn't feel like me. The person who is shown around the clean, friendly, but shabby and no-nonsense house where our boy would live is not a mother. I don't know who she is, not really. She is a lost person, a person in waiting, a person who would really sympathise with the poor mother to whom this is all happening.

How must it feel, to need to send your child to a place like this.

But downstairs, lunch is cooking and it smells OK. Plastic beakers of weak orange squash are lined up on the counter. A placid young man is laying the table.

Everyone has jobs, says the warm young woman who shows me round. It's very important that everyone pulls their weight, everyone belongs.

Upstairs, the rooms are neat and warm but – she explains – possessions from home are not encouraged. No photographs from home. No personal stereos and so on. This place is all about a fresh start. Facing yourself without props, without the means to escape back into yourself. Escaping the desire to self-medicate.

All of this makes total sense to me whilst I'm being shown around, but later, on the train home, those bleak and tidy rooms with their immaculate single beds make my heart speed up and I have to suck a mint to calm me down.

She shows me the room where people are waiting for a group therapy session. You can hardly see the faces for the fug of smoke.

Three addicts kindly agree to speak to me. We are put together in a sunny attic room at the top of the house. They face me, intent, serious-eyed, anxious to be truthful, anxious to help, to tell their stories. They are all so young. They all began with cannabis. With skunk. They ask me do I realise how incredibly, dangerously powerful it is? Yes, I say, I do. And as I tell my story, they nod their heads and look at their shoes.

It's all so fucking familiar, one of them says.

All of them stole from their families, all of them lied, all were in denial, some for years. None of them hit their mums, though, no way. There's a sharp, shocked intake of breath when I tell them that this is what my boy did.

All three are currently in recovery, but all of their faces are wan and spent, their eyes haunted. Hands and bitten fingers moving ceaselessly. As we shake hands and say goodbye, they deal the final blow. All three of them have been in rehab many times.

Many times?

You manage to stay clean for a while, sometimes even a year or so, and then you relapse.

But – you still come back?

You just have to start all over again and hope that this will be it, this will be the time, one of them says with a shrug.

UNTITLED

Saw three unloved in wait for ride,
one played prompt the rest replied,
but oh this chat it was not for free,
he said, 'You'll worship only me.'
Two sisters trapped by circumstance,
they followed his uneven dance,
but then their play went rather foul,
his hand slipped and in return,
she slapped him round his broken brow.
He stood unfazed, t'was just a game,
and one that he had often played,
'You do that again and I'll have you,'
and he stood up straight and he was tall.
The two stared back with certainty,
they knew the script repeats, you see.

6

CARROW ABBEY IN Norwich, where you live before you come to Woodton – where, as well as painting your Picture History album, you squeeze lemons to make lemon sponge and listen to Ellen practise her music – well, that place no longer exists.

Or at least that's what the woman at the Norwich tourist office tells me. There are a few ruins left, yes, she thinks so, but nothing else. In fact, somewhat confusingly, she is pretty certain the Abbey itself was pulled down by Henry VIII during the dissolution of the monasteries. Which would actually make it rather impossible for my Yellolys to have lived there at all. And yet, there's a clear painting of Carrow Abbey in your album: two long, low houses joined together, with a roof and chimneys. More like a house than an abbey, certainly. But the caption, written in your wobbly, little girl's hand, says *Carrow Abbey near Norwich*. I'm baffled.

Then I discover an intriguing website – over three thousand photographs of old Norwich taken by a man called George Plunkett (1913–2006) during the 1930s and '40s. And typing Carrow into the search box straight away brings me a clutch of black-and-white pictures of the ruined Abbey. One of them, labelled *The Prioress's House*, is incredibly similar, if not identical to, the house you painted. It looks Tudor, possibly even older. Dark and intricate brickwork, mullioned windows, tall chimneys and elaborate stone lintels over the main door, where the thick, twisted trunk of a wisteria curls.

In front is a smooth area of grass and, on the path next to it, a couple of dark-suited men in trilby hats are frozen on the edge of that pre- or post-war lawn. It's an atmospheric photograph, somehow both glamorous and austere, taken more than a hundred years after your time at Carrow. Different people, different clothes, but the same house, surely? Is this where you lived? I try holding the photograph up against your painting, but the number of windows don't quite match up.

Desperate to solve this puzzle, I email Jonathan Plunkett, son of George and the one who runs the website now, to ask him if he knows anything at all about Carrow Abbey. He says he can tell me that the pictures were taken on 16 May 1940 when his father went around Carrow's ruins on an archaeological excursion. He's very happy to email some good copies of the pictures to me, but he's sorry to say he doesn't have any more information on the Abbey or what happened to the Prioress's House. Personally, he's never come across the place.

Meanwhile, among the paintings in the Yelloly box, I find something I'd only glanced at before. A tiny sketch done on a piece of white card with an embossed surround. A pencil sketch, very fine, very perfect: *Carrow Abbey near Norwich by S.B. Yelloly October 1828*. Done by Sarah, your sister.

It's a bit more accurate than yours. When I hold it up and compare it to the photo taken by George Plunkett in May 1940, I see that it's identical in every way. Every single door, window and chimney matches up. Only the men in their trilbies, absorbed by their archaeological excursion, are missing.

This is the place, then. This is definitely the house you lived in. But it can't possibly still exist or else surely the lady at the tourist office would have known about it? Such a grand and striking old Tudor house is just not going to drop off the tourist map. I assume that most likely it was bombed and destroyed in the war.

Then, on the Internet, I discover an article from the *Eastern Daily Press* written just this summer:

> As factory complexes go, the Carrow Works, which is home to both soft-drinks producer Robinson's and the separately owned Colman's mustards and sauces business, must rank as one of the most unusual. The sprawling Norwich site includes part of a Grade 1 listed abbey . . . the view from the staff canteen is unusual – the ruins of Carrow Abbey, which dates back to 1146 and was demolished on the order of Henry VIII. Just the Prioress's lodging was spared and the Grade 1 listed building, once home to the Colman family, is now hired out as a conference facility as well as being used for meetings and training by both Robinson's and Colman's staff.

The Prioress's lodging. It was spared. It's a conference centre. I get on the phone to the PR people at Robinson's.

One Saturday afternoon, our boy wants his usual three o'clock shower but there's no hot water in the children's bathroom so he asks if he can use ours. He asks quite politely and as usual we're so absurdly grateful when he speaks to us in a nice voice that we say yes, of course, go ahead, take as long as you want. He takes his towel and heads up to our room.

He's been up there five minutes or so when I suddenly remember there was money in his father's trousers. At least two 20s, maybe more, stuffed in the pocket of his old cords and flung down on the bedroom chair.

His father often has money in his trouser pockets but we never leave cash out these days when our boy's around. Not even pound coins for parking. Over the past year he has stolen so much from us, regularly dipping into my handbag or his father's wallet whenever he could. Now I always lock my bag away when I have to leave it for more than a few minutes. And if we go out for the evening, we lock both our studies and our bedroom. And yes we are appalled at being forced to do this. Even more appalled that it's so quickly become a way of life. When our boy was out of the house, the relief at being able to leave doors open was a strange kind of heaven.

The shower is running. I run up to our room to check the money. The trouser pockets are empty except for a scrunched handkerchief. Both notes gone. Two 20s. Forty quid.

Hey, I call through the closed bathroom door. Have you taken some money from Dad's trousers?

What? he shouts through the heavy din of water.

I said, have you taken some money?

Of course I fucking haven't! he shouts. How dare you fucking well accuse me? Now fucking well leave me in peace, will you?

There's no lock on our bathroom door, never has been. So I do what I've never done to any of my children and would not dream of doing, not since they hit puberty anyway – I push open the door and walk right in there. I don't look at him, I don't look at the blur of his long body in the steam. Instead I just grab his clothes off the bathroom floor.

Hey, where the fuck're you going with those?

I shut the bathroom door again and sit down in the bedroom chair. In his jacket pocket, two £20 notes. He took the money first, pocketed it, then got on calmly with using our shower. Something about the order of that makes me feel sick.

It's a warm day and the air is noticeably still when I finally walk up the wide, hard drive to what must be the Carrow Works. Because the traffic is so slow, the taxi ends up dropping me off so I can walk the last bit, but I take a wrong turning and instead find myself at a place called Carrow House – confusing but clearly not right. A receptionist for Norfolk Social Services, Mars bar wrapper on desk, phone cradled between shoulder and ear, points me back up to the roundabout: left and left again, you can't miss it – and suddenly it's obvious I'm entering an industrial site, even if it is a leafy one. The air smells of the country but there are security barriers everywhere.

At the first barrier I tell the man behind the glass that I'm here to see Jeremy Howard.

He frowns at his clipboard.

What company do you work for?

None. I'm just – myself.

Aha, a lady who is herself!

He gives me a badge and hands me a large plastic-covered information sheet with full security instructions: no smoking, no drugs, no alcohol on site. And an emergency number to dial.

Emergency?

Yeah, so if Jeremy suddenly keels over or whatever, you dial this number, OK?

OK, I say, deciding not to mention that I don't have a mobile phone.

All right. He leans out of his kiosk to watch me clip on my badge. Now if you head towards the *No Entry* sign over there and go right across the road, you'll see a fifteenth-century building with a glass extension right in front of you. Walk straight towards it and Jeremy should be waiting for you at the entrance.

Fifteenth-century building, I think. This is it, then.

And I walk past trees and up a drive edged by lawn and, in a second or two, right there in front of me is the house you lived in when you were eight years old. This is where you were when you painted the album I looked at in the bookshop in Mayfair.

I stop and just look for a moment. It really looks no different at all from George Plunkett's 1940 photo, an effect only heightened by the fuzzy warmth of the air and the strange lack of people. There's no one at the entrance – in fact no human being in sight anywhere. But the main door is standing wide open, so I walk right in. And find myself in an old and creaky wooden hallway with a wide wooden staircase twisting up to the right.

No one to go up the best stairs whilst cleaning.

The air pulses with silence. Late-afternoon sun slants down through the stained-glass window at the top of the stairs. Arranged around the big fireplace are several glass cases containing photos and archives about Colman's Mustard. Opposite them, hilariously out of place, a few lone bottles of Robinson's squash.

I look around me. There's got to be somebody here. A reception area or something. Where am I supposed to go?

Hello?

Silence.

I go out on to the gravel again, back into the sunshine. A youngish man is walking towards me. Smiling, but somehow reticent. He has on a bottle-green factory coat and fluorescent waistcoat. He shakes my hand and I apologise for being a bit late and explain about the wrong turning. An easy mistake, he says.

He asks if I'd like to see inside or do the grounds first. The grounds, I decide. But he says first he'll show me a little display they've got about the history of the place. I follow him through into a massive modern glass structure which has been somehow welded on to the side of the Abbey. An extension?

Yeah, he laughs when I comment on it. Stuck on to a Grade 1 listed building. You'd never be able to do it now. But you could get away with that sort of thing in the '60s.

The glass structure somehow turns a corner and becomes the staff canteen – which must be the one referred to in the article I found on the Internet. I ask him how many people Robinson's employs.

Five hundred staff, thirty-five acres the site is altogether. Some of it has river frontage which is quite nice.

And how long have you worked here?

Oh, only eighteen months or so.

And are you from around here? I say, hoping he won't think I'm interviewing him too much.

He laughs.

No! Can't you tell? I'm from the north-east.

I apologise to him for being so bad at accents.

I actually used to be at our Beckton plant in East London, he says.

It must be a lot nicer here.

Oh yes, it's a much slower pace of life. It's good. I've got a two-year-old child, you see.

Two is a lovely age, I say.

We're now standing in a rather featureless meeting room, which looks over the grounds. The same smooth lawns that I recognise from the photo, half in sun, half in shadow. Now and then a small, toppling mound of stones suggesting a ruin.

Jeremy shows me the meeting-room walls, where a well-meaning but sparse exhibition has been mounted. Yet more sepia Colman photographs and laboriously typed captions, curling at the edges. It has the dutiful tone of a display that no one ever looks at. Jeremy says that, when Henry VIII dissolved the monasteries, the Priory itself was pulled down and only the Prioress's House survived.

Because a relative of Anne Boleyn's wanted it, he says.

Ah.

And it's supposed to be haunted, he adds, unable to stop himself checking my face for a reaction.

Seriously?

Well, there's one room, the Prioress's bedroom, we call it, which – well, I don't know, it depends what you believe really. Just, a lot of people have felt something in there, that's all.

Really? I say, trying not to look too interested. What kind of thing?

Well, only about a year ago, one of our sales people was last out of a meeting and a woman pushed past him to get into the room and he said: Oh, excuse me! and turned round, and there was no one there. Depends if you believe in ghosts really, he adds, checking my face again. I'm not sure if I do.

I tell him I'm not sure I do either.

But will you show me the room?

Sure. We'll go there in a minute. After we've done outside.

We wander across the lawn, past pale pink shrub roses and towards a wilder bit where paths have been mown between the nettles and trees. A squirrel dashes past and a blackbird lifts itself into the air.

I think of the journal your mother made you all keep when she was away. *Have you walked five times round the garden before breakfast? Sarah, Jane, Harriet, Sophy each signs: 'Yes.'*

Five times would have been a lot of walking.

Jeremy points out a tree, bigger and wider and older than all the rest.

It's – I'll remember the name in a minute, he says. Anyway, whatever it's called, it's the second largest of its type in Britain, apparently. I suppose it would have been there in your girl's time, wouldn't it?

I suppose it would, I agree, gazing at the enormous fat trunk. Perfect for hiding behind. A pale wrist brushing the bark. Your slim shape almost hidden. One single curl of hair giving you away as you can't resist peeping round.

Weeping beech! Jeremy says. That's it. I knew it was weeping something.

It's beautiful, I say.

Yeah, it's quite something, isn't it?

And I glance back towards the Abbey for a moment and notice that, apart from the big glass 1960s-built box where the canteen is, the view I'm looking at is no different at all to the one your sister Sarah drew in her pencil sketch.

Inside the house, the dark wood panelling has been re-stored, giving the heartlessly opaque feel of reproduction furniture. Thick, teal-coloured carpets add to the confer-ence-hotel feeling. Jeremy takes me through several ground-floor rooms with cavernous stone fireplaces and mullioned windows. Most of them are also equipped with easels for flip charts, as well as kettles and shiny white cups and small blond baskets containing catering packs of sugar and milk.

I follow him upstairs, where we emerge into a long dark corridor full of shadows. Lots of rooms leading off, rows of dark doors all tightly shut.

Your parents moved here from Finsbury Square in London with nine small children. Ellen, the baby, was born here. Was she born in one of these rooms? The yowl of a newborn zinging through this thick dark air. Quick footsteps on the wooden stairs. The sigh of a door opening and closing and the crying stops. A startled gulp. The hypnotic relief of a child sucking. What can it be like, giving birth for the tenth time?

I take a couple of steps. The floorboards creak. I step back. They creak again.

They're all meeting rooms now, says Jeremy. But I suppose they were bedrooms or whatever back then.

Do you know how many there are?

He hesitates.

Well, there's fourteen meeting rooms that we use. But it's not just us who use them. We hire them out to other companies too, you see.

And which one's the room you were telling me about?

He smiles.

We'll come to that.

It's fifteenth-century, then, is it, this place? I ask him.

Some of it's older. Some of it dates back to 11-something, I think.

Dutifully, he takes me in and out of the rooms. Each one is more or less the same. Each one, just as downstairs, filled with conference-style chairs and tables, flip charts, screens, and the small baskets of sugar and milk. I'm grateful for how patient he's being. I wonder what he thinks I'm looking for. I wonder what I am looking for.

Monday, Tuesday etc. To walk for an hour and a half after breakfast, at the expiration of that time, the school bell to be rung, everyone to come in and go to lessons in the following manner . . .

I hope I'm not taking up too much of your time, I say.

He smiles.

Oh no, not at all.

In one room, I walk over to a window and put my hands on the rough stone sill and look out. Down on the lawn, in what feels like another world, two foxes are playing on the lawn in the sunshine. Grappling, cuffing, rolling over and over.

Hey, now you see that door over there in the corner, says Jeremy, indicating the one to my right. Go and open it, and then look down.

I do as he says. The door opens on to a small dark space, with a steep, twisty stone staircase leading straight downwards. A fairy-tale staircase. A thick tasselled rope hangs across it, indicating it's out of bounds.

Oh, I say, where does it go?

Just down. Downstairs, I mean.

What was it for?

No one to go up the best stairs whilst cleaning.

He shrugs.

Just another staircase, I suppose. Now open the next door and I think we can go through. You can get to this next room via two different doors.

I try the door but it won't give.

Oh, sorry, it must be locked, says Jeremy, and he leads me back on to the dark landing and along the corridor, so we can enter the next room by a narrow door which is at the very end of the corridor.

This is it, he says.

The haunted one?

He nods. The Prioress's bedroom.

And who was she, the Prioress?

I don't really know.

We're standing in a long low room – larger than the other bedrooms – with another large stone fireplace. A long table in the centre, surrounded by chairs – and yet more sachets of sugar and milk. I walk across to the window, conscious of Jeremy behind me, staying by the door. I look out. The lawn's empty now, almost in shadow. The foxes have gone.

So was it just about where you're standing? I ask him.

What?

The ghost.

He glances behind him.

I suppose so, yes.

And did he say anything about what she was like?

I don't know. Dark clothes, I remember that. And that she pushed past quite rudely. That was about it, I think.

And so – I mean, are people scared to go in here?

Jeremy smiles.

I don't know. Yeah, I suppose people do tend to avoid going in on their own. I know the cleaners will only go in in the morning.

I'll show you one more thing, he says.

And he takes me up another smaller and much shabbier flight of stairs – unused, dirty, paint peeling – and unlocks a small door at the top. We find ourselves in a huge, derelict attic, seven or eight large rooms, wallpaper from the 1950s or '60s falling off the walls. Lemon yellow and mauve. Flowers. Patterns.

What an amazing space, I say, looking around me. It's a whole flat – big enough for someone to live here.

Someone did, Jeremy says. I think one of the last Colman ladies lived here till she died.

I think about this. I'd completely forgotten for a moment that this place belonged to the Colmans. Colman's Mustard. The Colmans lived here after you all left for Woodton.

I think there were several of them, Jeremy says, several sisters. The last of them didn't die that long ago.

Really? I try to imagine how it would have felt to live entirely alone at the top of this ancient building. And no one's going to do anything with it now?

We walk from room to room, our footsteps and our voices echoing oddly. It feels like a space that's grown unused to life. Disturbed and set on edge by our presence.

Too expensive, Jeremy says. Because of it being listed and so on. You have to use exactly the right kind of wallpaper and all that rubbish. It just wouldn't pay, I suppose.

He locks the little door behind us again and we go back down the narrow stairs. Back to the dark corridor leading to the Prioress's bedroom.

Jeremy glances at his watch.

I don't know what you want to do now, but you're more than welcome to have a little wander round on your own for a bit – if you want to soak up the atmosphere. I can leave you to it if you'd like to do that.

I hesitate. In my original polite, pleading email to the Robinson's PR people, this is exactly what I asked for. To have a look around, preferably on my own.

I'd seen myself wandering through placid sun-filled rooms, thinking about you, sensing your long-ago presence. If they'd said I would have to be accompanied at all times, I would have been disappointed.

I glance down the corridor. The sun's gone in completely. Every scrap of light has been sucked away, turned to shadow. The blackness beckons.

You know, I say, that's really nice of you but I think I've seen enough. You've given me such a lovely tour and I've certainly got a sense of the place. I think I've got exactly what I came for.

I thought it would be a bit boring and sad when we visited our father in that big empty house where there was nothing much to do except make people freeze on the TV, but I did at least think he would want to see us.

But he was so angry with our mother that he found it hard to be friendly, even to us, his kids. From the first weekend we went to see him, he'd sit us down and talk to us about all the things our mother had done. He'd sit there and smoke and tell us about all the terrible things as if they were actually our fault. I was twelve and my sisters were ten and eight and we wanted to dress up or make a den or go out and play with our friends in the village, but for at least some of the weekend we had to sit and listen to everything that had gone wrong with his marriage and his life.

He told us how he'd been taken for a ride by our mother, how she'd stolen half his property and how the man she was living with, the man who later became our stepfather, was *a long streak of piss*. Our future stepfather had two sons about our age who we got on quite well with, but we had to promise our father that, if they came round, we would not speak to them or look at them. If they came in the room, he said, we must look away.

OK, we said.

There were so many rules. More and more rules – he was piling them up so hard my throat ached. And the more rules there were, the more things it was possible for us to do wrong if we stopped concentrating for even a second. And if we forgot the rules, it would really hurt him. If we called our house *home* by mistake, for instance, he shuddered visibly and shut his eyes. It felt bad, to give our daddy pain like that, especially when he had already been through so much, but sometimes it was just so hard to avoid.

He told us a lot of grown-up things, things I didn't really mind hearing but which I worried weren't quite suitable for my sisters. One time, he got out the affidavit for the divorce and made us read bits of it out loud. I don't remember what it said but I remember it felt odd to see my littlest sister, who was only eight, having solicitor's language explained to her like that, and some of it was about sex and I didn't think he should have been making her read it.

I'd always been an anxious child, but those weekends made me more and more jumpy and sad. I'd stand in the hall with my bag when it was nearly time for him to collect us, and have to take deep breaths. And as soon as we were in his car, I was alert to him – smiling and trying to laugh at his jokes and judge his mood. Sometimes he was fine, he was the old, friendly, lovely daddy. Other times, though, you could see that something had happened – maybe Mum's solicitor had said something to his solicitor, or else he had discovered some new thing about our lives that upset him – and then I'd have to navigate his mood, taking a deep breath as we went over the bumps.

At least six months before the day we tell our boy to leave our home for the last time, he gets a girl pregnant. We find out about this because the girl's mother calls late one night, upset and certain, she tells me, that our son is the father.

My son. The father.

She tells me her daughter is upset because our son hasn't been that nice to her recently. She needs to stay calm because she's really very hard to control when she's stressed out. So if you could just have a word with him and ask him to speak to her a bit more nicely, you know?

With a strong feeling that I somehow need to talk her down, keep her calm, I tell her I'll do that.

She can't have it, she goes on. She's got to do something about it. She's too young to have it. She's only sixteen years old, you see.

Oh yes, I say, I mean no. Oh my God, this is terrible – I am so sorry.

I'm trying hard to think, but the woman's stopping me. She's still talking. Her voice never stops.

Please talk to her. She won't listen to me.

Of course I want to help, I say. But I don't know her very well. Will she really listen to me?

Oh yes. She likes you. You're a nice lady. She's said that lots of times.

I had met this girl once, about ten months earlier. Now this girl tells our boy that she's going to have his baby. To spite him. Because he spoke rudely to her. Because he hasn't been very nice. Because he was nasty and said he wanted to split up, when she had thought he was her boyfriend and they were still together, she says she intends to ruin his life for ever.

We make him sit down and talk to us properly. We try to make him understand what a very serious situation this is.

This isn't a game. A life has been started. We absolutely have to talk this girl into a pregnancy test and, if necessary, a termination. Dad and I are willing to pay so that it can be quick, but surely you see that we can only do it if we have her trust?

The boy looks unconcerned.

She just wants attention, he says. She doesn't even know what she's saying half the time. She's really warped, you know.

I'm not interested in her motives, I tell him. That's not relevant. Letting her have this baby is not an option.

He looks at me as if I'm mad.

But what am I supposed to do about it?

I stare at my boy – the boy we would support through anything, any accident, any problem, but who right now seems so totally unwilling to accept any responsibility whatsoever for his actions.

All we are asking you to do – the only thing! – is be nice to her. Be kind, be gentle. Don't say anything inflammatory. And if you can't stop yourself doing that, then stay away from her. We'll do the rest.

He looks at the floor, swallows.

I'm not putting myself out for that crazy person.

My heart bangs in my throat.

His father stands up.

For goodness' sake, this is your mess! You did this! Don't you at least see that?

You've simply got to start taking some responsibility here, I tell him.

That night the boy deliberately walks off with her mobile phone. We discover this because she rings us in the early morning, sobbing, threatening to send the police round.

I go up to his room and pull the duvet off him.

Why? Why did you do such a bloody stupid thing?

He blinks at me and it's clear he knows exactly what I'm talking about.

Because she bloody well pissed me off, that's why.

Where is it? Where's the phone?

She won't send the police round, says the boy. He pulls the blankets over his head.

His father is furious.

Are you completely bloody crazy? Your mother's about to go round there and try to do the supremely difficult thing of persuading this poor girl into a pregnancy test, so we can check she really is pregnant before we try to talk her into a termination, and you're busy stealing her phone because – what? – because she *annoyed* you?

A dark look crosses the boy's face.

I don't know why you're bothering to get involved, he says. She may not even be pregnant. And even if she is, she's done so many drugs, isn't there a good chance she'd miscarry?

Early that Saturday morning, having failed to persuade our son to give up the phone, I drive to the house in Brixton where I'm told the girl spent the night, where she often spends the night. A house full of half-asleep teenagers. Windows dark with plants. A smell of ashtrays.

Have you brought her phone back? a yawning boy asks me.

No, but I'm working on it.

She's really fucking annoyed about it, you know.

I know. I'll get it back to her.

Someone goes off to fetch the girl as I stand there in the hall in my jeans and dark linen coat, clutching my car keys and feeling somehow sinister. The Angel of Death.

She trips down the stairs, smiling and yawning. Slept-on hair, slim body wrapped in acid-bright clubbing gear.

Hi, she says, pulling down her stretchy skirt and adjusting her bra straps with a little smile.

I tell her I want to take her to Marie Stopes for a pregnancy test. I tell her – as gently as I can – that she hasn't got to cope with this mess all alone, that I'm going to help her sort it out. I tell her I'm truly sorry that my son has behaved so uncaringly.

She gazes at me.

OK, she says.

I'm really sorry I haven't got your phone, I add, but I'll find it and bring it to you later this afternoon, OK?

OK, she says again and then she asks if she can just go and get her shoes.

Of course, I tell her, surprised, because I expected more of a fight.

(She can go either way, the boy has told me, really calm one moment and completely fucking out of it the next.)

She reappears a moment later with a pair of shiny red high heels, hopping from foot to foot as she tugs them on.

I feel a bit funny going along in these, she says, laughing. Last night's gear, but they're all I've got.

The test is positive. The girl looks suddenly small. She's only sixteen. I realise I never even asked if she'd had breakfast.

We book a termination for first thing Monday morning – the earliest possible appointment. It's private but we don't dare wait for an NHS appointment. Her mood could change at any time.

I fill in some forms. At every moment I keep expecting her to change her mind. To throw a tantrum, to walk out. But she doesn't. The termination will cost more than £700. The girl is shocked at the price. She thanks me for paying.

Don't be silly, I tell her. All I want is for you to be OK.

It's not true. It's not all I want. All I want is for this to be over before she has time to change her mind.

After that, because it feels too cold just to drop her back, I take her to Café Rouge and insist she eats something nice. She orders a Diet Coke and a chicken baguette with chips but leaves most of it, pulling out the cucumber first and piling it on the side of her plate.

She asks me what happens in a termination. I try to answer in a way that's honest but reassuring. But when I start talking about uteruses and eggs and placentas, the drinking straw falls from between her lips and her eyes widen. Has no one ever talked to her about sex before?

We tell the boy the termination's booked and we beg him to stay away from her all weekend. We just can't risk him getting into an argument with her. But he refuses. He says it's not convenient for him. That he needs to go to a party that night which she may well be at. We plead with him to miss the party. It's just not worth the risk of getting into an argument with her. What can be more important than this?

This termination is costing £700, I tell him. And as I say it, my voice sounds different – dirtier, harsher. Has it really come to this?

He shrugs and says it's not his fault that she's half-crazy. He's not going to let that get in the way of his social life.

I was going to take the girl to the termination, but in the end someone she knows better kindly steps in and offers to take my place. Relieved, I sit all morning and watch the clock.

It's not until I get the call to say it's all over and the girl is fine that I feel it: a surge of dark, dark mourning for what just occurred. The termination of what was almost certainly my embryo grandchild. I also feel incredibly tired.

CARELESS

It would be careless not to say,
my heart has gone astray,
and now it flies to you.

When I'm around you.

So I teeter on the brink,
of saying what I think,
as your eyes meet mine.

But the words won't come.

We'd flit and we'd flirt,
but it never used to hurt,
now you leave me dazzled.

Confused and all unravelled.

So I'm lost in smiles,
whilst I keep my thoughts disguised,
and away from you.

It can't go on.

7

Dear Mrs Myerson,
Yes, I know all about the Sucklings and Yellolys at Woodton. My great-grandmother was Fanny Jane, daughter of Alfred Inigo Suckling. Do come and see me on my return. Where do you live?
Patrick Baron

Dear Mrs Myerson,
Yes, my watercolours of the interiors of Woodton Hall are painted by Yelloly. Will contact in May. My eldest daughter went to St Felix.
Regards, Patrick, Frank, Nelson, Baron Suckling (full name but not used)

Dear Mrs Myerson,
I am at sea on the Arcadia and will not be home next week. Will ring you when I am. Have the paintings of Woodton Hall on my stairs.
Regards, Pat Baron

THE DOOR TO Patrick Baron's Norwich apartment has a Suckling coat of arms on it. It's standing wide open as I come out of the slightly juddery lift at the top of a smart modern block in the city centre.

Hello, hello, how are you? How do you do?

A tall, well-groomed man shakes my hand. Elegantly dressed and, I would guess, quite a bit older than he looks. We stand diffidently for a moment or two in the dim carpeted hallway – a crowd of silver-framed family photos gleaming from the gloom – before he ushers me forwards and shuts the door.

Straight away I catch a glimpse through into the sitting room – enormous panoramic windows.

Hey, I say, what a view.

He walks me through and over to the window.

Yes, yes, isn't it? Look, you can see right over Norwich from here.

I gaze out over the pale rooftops.

I love being high up, I tell him, lucky you. And you live in the Canary Islands too?

Yes, half the year there, half here.

What a great life.

He laughs.

Well, yes, yes, it is, oh yes.

And you really are a direct descendant of Lord Nelson?

That's right, yes. Absolutely. Nelson's mother, you see, she was a Suckling.

And so – what do you do?

Did. Merchant Navy. Retired now, of course.

The apartment's immaculate – gleaming surfaces, polished wood and silver and glass, all reflecting back at each other. Lots of heavy dark old furniture, coffee tables and vases. In the little kitchen at the end, a youngish woman with glamorous hair is making coffee. I try to decide whether she's his wife.

Patrick introduces us and she shakes my hand, smiling, but I don't catch her name and before I can ask her again she's vanished, leaving us a tray on the dining-room table.

You want to see the pictures?

Walking stiffly with his stick, Patrick leads me out of the dining room and back into the hall where a smooth flight of carpeted stairs leads down to another floor.

There you go, he says and he turns on some lights so I can see better.

Eight large framed watercolour paintings hang on the landing and stairs walls.

Oh! I say, I didn't think they'd be so big!

He leans forward.

Hmm. Pretty large, yes.

As well as being double or maybe three times the size of any Yelloly paintings I've yet come across, they're also somehow different in style. Unexpectedly lucid, smooth and highly coloured. Very deftly executed, the detail is incredible.

The first is of the now very familiar view of the exterior of Woodton Hall standing just behind the church. I don't think I've ever seen it so close up. I count the windows – fourteen of them, with five chimneys on top. A great big impressive pile of a place. Beneath darkening skies, inky with rain, sheep and cows graze in the field in front. I could almost put my finger on the path which now leads up to Steve and Elaine Hill's house.

Recognise it? Patrick asks me, holding on to the banister, watching my face and smiling.

I do, I tell him, of course I do. I was there just a few weeks ago.

The other seven paintings are interiors of the Hall as I've never yet quite seen it. Immediate, specific, well lit. Intimate, too. In one or two of the pictures, All Saints Church tower can be glimpsed, grey as a shadow, through the windows.

They're alive with furniture – elegant tables and chairs, paintings, statues, vases, mirrors. Two birds in a cage. A guitar laid down on a chair as if someone had just that second stopped playing it. Even if there were no people in the pictures, you would sense them. These are rooms where life is going on, has just been going on.

But there are people. In almost every picture there are young women – two, three or four. Yelloly girls. But which one is which? Which one is you?

Do you have any idea who did them? I ask Patrick.

He waves his hand.

Oh, please, take them off the wall, if you like. I seem to remember there's something written on the backs.

Very carefully, I take each one down and turn it over. The pictures aren't dated, but each says *Done by the Yellolys while they lived at Woodton.* One of them says it's by your sister Anna.

They really do all look like they were done by the same person, I tell him as I replace each one on the hook and take the next. So I suppose if one says *Anna*, then it probably means she did them all. And I suppose it would explain why you have them too – handed down the Suckling line, I mean.

He nods.

Ah. It would, yes, it would.

But what's really amazing for me, I tell him, is to see so many of the Yelloly girls.

Several of the pictures feature two dark-haired girls with centre-parted hair and ringlets. In another painting a much smaller girl – could it be Ellen, who was only eleven when you moved to Woodton? – plays with a dog, making it sit up and beg.

In a drawing room, two dark-haired girls sit at tables opposite each other. One looks as if she is writing, the other – because you can see the splodges on the paper – painting. Dresses that look like they would rustle if the girls stood up. Long, curled ringlets hanging down over their ears. The girl in the foreground wears dark drop earrings, and both girls' feet are propped on tiny footstools as they lean intently into their work.

In the portrait of your sister Sarah that Tony Yelloly showed me, the one that reminds me of Julia, she's definitely dark-haired. But the pencil sketch of you that I found in the trunk, the one done after your death, the one without a face, suggests a girl with fair, even blonde, hair. Are none of these girls you, then?

In another picture, what look like the same two girls are joined by a third. Here the guitar – is it a guitar? – is picked up and played, while another girl works at something large – it could be a painting but looks more like a screen or tapestry, balanced on the back of a chair. The third girl crosses the room with a small pot or vase of flowers. Through one window you can see the church, and through the other – sash flung wide open – the fields loom warm and delicious. A breathless summer's day.

In a high-ceilinged bedroom, a fire crackles in the large stone hearth, and the four-poster bed has a heavy ornate canopy fringed with tassels. Rich rugs – maybe Indian or Persian? – and bare floorboards. A washstand with pitcher and bowl. An older woman, wearing a bonnet and shawl, is getting something out of a small trunk which is leaning on two chairs pushed together.

Another lady – also older and bonneted – carries a garment in her arms. Is this your mother? Her slim feet are in dark pumps with a criss-cross strap like ballet shoes. Her cool, placid face looks both purposeful and ever so slightly tired. Some kind of a heavy stole or scarf hangs round her neck, almost to her feet. In the far-left corner of the room, a door stands tantalisingly open to a room beyond.

Or, in a sunny breakfast room a table is laid for a meal – white linen and ten place settings. Silver coffee pots and buns, and a jar of what look a lot like sweet peas in the centre. A woman in a frilly bonnet stands at the open door looking out on the blowy Norfolk countryside – is she calling people in to eat? – whilst two younger girls chat at the table. Chat about what?

The paintings offer up so many clues that I ought to be satisfied. So why, instead of feeling invited in, do I somehow feel excluded, pushed out?

I want to walk right in there and smell the coffee, the flowers, feel the Norfolk breeze from the open window on my cheek, the well-beaten rugs under my feet. I want to sit you all down and make you stay and answer all my questions:

So where's Sam? Is he in Ipswich now? And Nick and John, where are they? What year is it? Who's the girl playing the guitar? Do you all play? Is the small girl with the dog Ellen? And can you tell me which of you is Mary?

Silence.

Mary? Are you there?

Nothing.

Silence again. The sound of a door closing.

A note on the back of one of the pictures says that the large cabinet in the breakfast room between the windows – a huge, dark piece of furniture with very distinctive carving and glass doors – was later at Barsham Rectory, where your sister Anna and her husband lived.

If it was at Barsham, I say to Patrick, then is there any chance it could still be in the Suckling family – in your family, I mean?

Oh yes, he says, indicating with his stick. Lots of the furniture in this apartment came originally from Barsham.

I look around me and suddenly see the place – this modern apartment in the centre of Norwich with its polished, dark tables and chairs – in a whole new light. Your furniture. The pieces that stood in your home, in your life.

Oh certainly. Nearly all of the bigger pieces. And the chairs. I know a lot of the chairs came from Barsham.

He says he's never looked all that closely at the furniture in the pictures, but now he leads me into a little study off the landing. Against the wall stands a grand sort of cabinet.

Could this be it? he says.

I take a breath. It's the one in the picture.

It belonged to my grandfather, he tells me. That's all I know really.

I put a finger on its gleaming polished surface. The wood is cool and hard.

Patrick says he has a spare set of black-and-white photographs of the paintings that I'm welcome to take away with me.

But he also gives me something else: some folded sheets of yellowing paper, well preserved and neatly drawn out in brown (or was it once black?) ink – ruled lines and careful annotations, measurements in feet and inches. It's a set of plans for Woodton Hall – ground floor, first floor, attics, and the gardener's cottage. Each floor plan is precisely measured and shows stairs, doors and the position of windows, fireplaces and even cupboards. For instance, I'm able to read – because someone has added it on in pencil – that the schoolroom is 21 feet square and *Mrs Y's* room 10 feet square.

But even if it weren't for that dead giveaway, that *Mrs Y*, I'd still be able to guess that these were Yelloly plans. Because on the large plan of the ground floor, that same pencil person has been unable to resist doodling a neat but romantic little sketch of the front of the Hall, perspective perfect, with its thirteen windows and the curling flourish of a nearby tree. The style is instantly recognisable. A Yelloly tree.

And I think that's all. But it's only when I get back to London that, inspecting the photographs of the paintings, I notice something else. That in your sister Anna's picture of the grand sweeping staircase and entrance hall at Woodton, there's something I'd managed to miss completely when I looked at it on Patrick Baron's landing.

As well as the half-dozen or so oil portraits hung above the stairs, a dark grandfather clock, two chairs, a table and a sort of cartwheel lying on the floor, there's a statue, clad in a suit of armour and brandishing a sword. It's about three-quarter life-size.

It's the precise object that led me to Tony and Bryony Yelloly: the oak carving of Oliver Cromwell that they donated to the Cromwell House Museum in Ely in December 2003.

The secondary school we want our children to go to is a partially selective comprehensive. We look around and fall in love with its atmosphere of contained excitement, energetic and engaged teachers, alert-looking pupils and buildings ablaze with Virginia creeper.

We feel it would be the right place for all three of them, but more than anything that our boy will feel at home here. It's the kind of school where you don't stand out for being interested. And he's always interested.

But you have to sit a test to get in, and the verbal- and non-verbal-reasoning questions are the kinds of things our boy has never come across. Neither have we. Without some preparation, he won't stand a chance. So we buy the papers and, for a few weeks, we practise. Every day after school he walks round to the flat where I write, and together we spend an hour or so going over the methods and then doing timed tests.

We don't make him do this without an incentive – he gets extra time on his PlayStation as well as a rise in pocket money. But the truth is that, once we've fallen into the routine of it, we both find ourselves quite enjoying these sessions together. Me timing him with the stopwatch and marking him while he tots up how much money or PlayStation time he's earned.

Sometimes I'll have a snack all ready waiting for him when he arrives. Other times, after we've worked really hard for an hour, I take him out to the café down the road for a muffin and a chocolate milkshake. And one time there's a massive thunderstorm while we're in there – bursts of thunder and lightning across the rooftops of Lavender Hill. Rain so heavy that we have to wait in a shop doorway before we can even make a dash the few yards back to the flat. We're so wet we have to dry ourselves with towels.

And for a long time afterwards, he'll ask me if I remember the time with the milkshake and the thunderstorm and us getting so soaked. And I'll laugh and say weren't those days fun and weren't you great, working so hard to get into your school.

When we open the letter offering him a place (which means his siblings will get in too) I burst into tears. The children stare at me.

That night, to celebrate, we take our boy out to a posh Italian restaurant, just him and us. He wears a sunshine-yellow cotton shirt bought specially that afternoon at Peter Jones, because he doesn't have a single smart thing to wear. He looks so grown-up in the shirt. Almost eleven and on the edge of a whole new phase of his life.

And he eats spaghetti, because he always eats spaghetti – white food, boy's food – and then, trying so very hard to be adventurous, instead of ice cream he orders his very first tiramisu. Will he like it?

If you don't, I'll eat it, his father says.

We wait. And he says it's the very best pudding he's ever had in his whole life. In fact from now on he's never going to order anything else ever again. And his father and I can't stop laughing as we try to picture it – this great long line of tiramisus, stretching on into infinity, waiting to be eaten by our boy.

But six years after that, I do something I never dreamed I'd do, something more painful than almost anything I've done in my life. I call his tutor, his nice, supportive, warm-faced tutor, and I tell her that, although our son's education has always been the thing we care most passionately about, we no longer mind whether he gets any A levels or not. All we want is for him to learn that, when school says there will be consequences, they mean it. We think it's time they excluded him.

I never thought I'd feel this, or have to say it, I tell her. Please believe me when I tell you it's the hardest thing for me, having to sit here and say this to you. But his father and I would really prefer that you expelled him. This is no longer just about education. We're seriously worried about the kind of person he's turning into. I care more now that he changes and sees the need to stop taking drugs. I want him to have a happy life. I want him to learn to be a good man, and, you know, A levels have started to seem a small thing next to that. And we don't think he's attending enough to get any anyway.

His tutor sounds a little taken aback. But she seems to listen and, at the end, she thanks me for talking to her so frankly.

When I put the phone down, tears are standing in my eyes.

I think she understood, I tell his father later, I really do. I think she knew I meant it, that I couldn't possibly have said all those things if I didn't.

And we wait for them to tell him the bad news. No more chances.

That night he walks in whistling and tells us he's been given one more chance. He demands we give him a beer.

Not on a school night, says his father, no way.

Stop telling me how to live my life, he says. I'll have a beer if I feel like one.

He's standing near the fridge and we are by the cooker. I feel suddenly like I'm not there at all. As if I'm looking down on the three of us from above.

Carefully, I put down the wooden spoon I am using to stir the soup. Calmly turn off the ring.

On what basis have they given you another chance? I ask him.

He shrugs. He's still looking at the fridge.

As long as I go in, they won't exclude me, he says.

But they want a hundred per cent attendance?

I dunno. I suppose.

And do you intend to give them that?

He grins. I'll see how it goes, won't I? They can't tell me how to live my life any more than you can.

His father and I look at each other.

That's it, I say, we say. We can't do this any more. We're sorry. You're going to have to find somewhere else to live.

He stares at us. It's an old refrain but not one he was expecting tonight.

But I'm at school, he says. This is my education we're talking about.

You hardly ever go to school and you've just implied that nothing's changed. You don't plan to start attending properly now.

He smirks, but I notice he doesn't disagree. His father is silent, his head in his hands.

But – what am I meant to do? How am I supposed to go to school if I can't live at home?

You'll find a way, I tell him, surprised at how calm I sound, how powerful I feel. Honestly, you're a strong and healthy young man, you're extremely bright, creative and clever. You have so many resources available to you. Dad and I love you so very much and I used to be so worried for you, but I'm not any more. I'm actually more worried about Dad and me. Look at us. Look at him. We're exhausted. We can't do this any more. We need some time just to live. And I think you need to go out into the world and find your way. Really, I think you'll do fine.

He stares at me and I try to work out why this moment feels different from all the other moments. And then I know. It's the first time I've managed to ask him to leave without crying.

But a few nights (or is it weeks?) after that, I come across (or do I seek it out?) his little yellow cotton shirt, the one I decided to keep for ever because he'd worn it on that special night of tiramisu, the night that seems to be from some other mother's lifetime but was actually only six short years ago – in a drawer downstairs. And I sob.

I sob until my head hurts and my clothes are wet. I sob until I can hardly breathe. I sob so hard that the dog backs away, alarmed. And then I fold the shirt carefully and put it back in the drawer, wash my face, put on a clean T-shirt and go and make supper for my other children.

When Daddy collects us for the weekend, one of the rules is he won't come into our house. He won't even walk up our drive. In fact he can't even look at the house, so he draws up a little way down the road and so, from about ten minutes before he's due, we have to be standing there, waiting at the window, looking out for him.

What would happen if we didn't see him, or if we forgot to look? Sometimes I think he would just light another cigarette and drive away, thinking, Oh well, that's that then.

One time we're all waiting there on a Friday night with our bags and there's a phone call – he always gets someone else to phone – to say he's not coming, he can't come, he has too much work on this weekend. The relief as I unpack my bag, putting my pyjamas back under my pillow, is massive, joyous, a feeling of holiday.

Another time, we're at his house and it's Saturday night and suddenly he looks angry and says we should pack up our things, he's taking us home.

I blush very hard even though I've done nothing wrong, and I go and pack. My sisters pack. We don't say anything, we just pack. And we have the hamster with us that weekend, so we pack him up too, put him in the hall by our bags, where, because it's quite dark in the hall, he starts going round and round on his wheel, oblivious to our father's mood.

Our father says it was actually the hamster that made him suspicious. He suspects our mother's gone away, gone off on some kind of a holiday, a dirty weekend. He doesn't see why, after all she's put him through, he should provide childcare. So he's going to call her bluff, send us home.

We wait as he picks up the phone and lets our home number ring and ring. He wants to see if she's there. Ring, ring, we can hear it ringing. What if she's out, what if she's gone to the cinema or something? And if she has gone away, what then? Will he make us go back and stay in an empty house?

We wait in the hall, watching his face. My heart bangs in my chest.

In the end, she picks up. I hear her voice. Straight away he puts the phone down, flinching at the sound, and for a moment no one says anything, standing there in that dark hall. Just the creak, creak, creak of our hamster's wheel.

I go to the Principal Families Division at Holborn and, starting with your grandfather Samuel Tyssen's will, I look up Tyssen after Tyssen – a century and a half of Tyssens – until finally, an hour later, I find a Michael John Tyssen of East Sussex who died in April 1990. Michael John. A direct descendant of yours.

His will tells me he left everything to his wife Frances Joan. And she died ten years after him, with probate granted to Mary Elizabeth Sanders-Hewett, née Tyssen. Their daughter. A female Tyssen. An address is given.

Back at home, I ring Directory Enquiries and am immediately given a phone number. I dial it and, getting an answerphone, leave a brief message explaining about my book, and asking if this Mary Sanders-Hewett might possibly be related to the Tyssens who married into the Yelloly family.

Only an hour or so later, I find a message on my answerphone from a friend of Mrs Sanders-Hewett, who says she's house-sitting for her while they're away in New Zealand.

They're back in a couple of weeks, she says, and she'll be absolutely delighted to talk to you, I think. She'll find this very interesting indeed. What I mean is (a little laugh), that's right, you've got the right family.

This time – almost a year to the day since the first time we asked him to leave – we don't change the locks. This time we want to do it nicely. We tell him he has two weeks to find other accommodation, to make arrangements. We will lend him the deposit, the first month's rent. And we add that we'll even extend the time if he needs us to – we don't want to put him on the streets. But in return, he must not steal from us, threaten us, or intimidate us. We insist that he behaves sociably in the house.

He tells us we are insane. That we always have been. He threatens to carry out some damage to our property or to us. When we ask him not to threaten us, he tells us he means it.

I'll take a knife and stab you through the heart, he mutters at me during one conversation and for a moment I'm confused. I know he doesn't mean it. But if I heard someone say that to someone else, I also know I'd take it very seriously.

His father does take it seriously.

In that case, he says, forget it. Forget everything we've offered. Just leave. I mean it. Just go right now.

So he goes.

But not straight away. First he goes downstairs to the basement and plugs in his amp and plays the guitar loud enough to make our teeth hurt. And when his father turns off the electricity at the mains, and silence throbs through the house, he swears and kicks at a couple of doors, before he goes.

But he does. He goes. We are both surprised to get off so lightly. We ask him to please leave his key and he does. Just like that. I can't decide if this is less or more painful than the day we sat on the stairs and watched the locksmith slide a new slab of metal into the front door.

His father puts an arm around me, pulls me to him, gives me a hug. I'm too empty to cry.

I can't bear his threats. But as soon as he's defeated, I can't bear that either.

I go over and watch through the window as he disappears down the street. His brown jacket. One canvas bag. That slightly lopsided walk I know so well. But I don't make myself watch him turn the final corner. Before he goes out of sight, I move away.

I'm tired of punishing myself. I'm really bored of it.

So is his cat. Straight away, like a wife who has got used to being dumped, then taken back then dumped again, she goes back to sleeping on our bed.

Mary Sanders-Hewett is back from New Zealand and apologises for having taken so long to ring me. She explains that her daughter just ran in the London Marathon and the Docklands Light Railway broke down and it was a nightmare because it was so humid and when they got back they were all just so shattered and, anyway –

But this is all very exciting! I don't know if you realise that I'm the very last Tyssen?

Seriously?

Mary Tyssen was my maiden name. It's a bit sad, isn't it? None of us were male, so that was that. But we called our eldest son Sam, and one of our boys has Tyssen as a middle name, poor thing!

I tell her I'm in touch with the Yellolys, and Julia is actually the last Yelloly too.

How incredible, she says. All these different branches of the same family who know nothing about each other.

She tells me she has a portrait of Samuel Tyssen.

A huge oil painting. It's on the upstairs landing – outside my daughter's room. She's always hated it. She says the eyes follow her! Oh, and there's something else. I've got a wonderful two-volume book about the Tyssens and Yellolys called *A Forgotten Past*.

For a moment I'm thrown.

Two volumes? But – you mean by Florence Suckling?

That's the one.

But – well, that's very funny because I've got a copy of that too, but it's only the one volume.

Oh well, mine is definitely two volumes. They've been in my family for ever. They're bound in red leather and, well, fascinating, but kind of slightly cobbled together.

How do you mean, cobbled together? I ask her, allowing myself the faintest flicker of excitement.

Oh well, you see there are lots of different typefaces and even some handwritten bits. Photos stuck in too.

Photos?

Oh yes. Black-and-white, of course. Quite a few of them.

Of people?

A few of people, yes, but also, as far as I can remember, of various family treasures, bits and pieces, jewellery and so on.

Relics.

But, I say, as my heart speeds up, so you mean yours isn't printed? You're saying it's not like mine, which is a published book?

Um – no, not really. It's more like a scrapbook kind of thing.

I tell her it sounds like the original manuscript of Florence Suckling's book.

It might be. It's hard to describe – you'll just have to come here and have a look at it, won't you?

Our boy has nowhere to go, so he moves in with his grandmother for a bit. His grandmother who lives alone in a modern block on the river at Vauxhall, and who has always loved him, ever since the day she first held him on her shoulder and walked him up and down her cream-carpeted corridor while he screamed and screamed.

Her first grandchild. She was widowed for a few years, and had nursed her husband through a long final illness. When our boy was born, she suddenly got younger. I had always liked my shy, elegant Australian mother-in-law. But the practical, loving, unconditional help she offered me with all my babies sealed our friendship and made me love her.

And even though there are six grandchildren now, our boy is still the first. She seems to let him walk all over her in a way she lets no one else. And he in return seems to tolerate her endless fussing with a patience he shows no one else except (sometimes) his cat.

At three years old, he sat in his navy-striped dungarees at the little red plastic table she bought specially from the Early Learning Centre and crayoned pictures which she stuck to her fridge. At ten or eleven, he weeded her flowerbeds. At fourteen he showed her (again and again, with extreme patience) how to use a computer. At fifteen he programmed her video recorder.

But now he's aimless and angry and she's tired. Too used to living alone, more and more inflexible by the day, she frets

209

about doors opening and closing, mess, the sound of the TV, anything in fact. And he does nothing but open and close doors, turn on the TV and make noise and mess. They love each other, but they're hardly well suited. She warns us that it can only be a temporary arrangement. She doesn't think she can have him and *all his stuff* there for all that long.

Her son tells her she shouldn't be having him there at all.

You're padding his corners – making it so he doesn't have to face up to the reality of who he is, what he's done – don't you see that? He has to be forced to face up to reality.

Oh well, it's all very well for you to say that. But what do you expect me to do? Send him away? Please don't ask me to put him out on the streets.

It's his own choice. He has a perfectly good home with us but he chooses not to live in it like a decent human being.

Oh well, all that's between you and him. All I said was I'd have him here for a short while, until he finds somewhere to stay.

All right, but make sure you hide your purse. You're not still keeping your pension in that absurd place in the kitchen, are you?

Don't worry, I won't do that.

And don't leave valuable jewellery lying around.

Oh, he wouldn't take my jewellery.

Mummy, he's a drug addict. He wants cash. He'll take anything and justify it later. I don't know how to make you wake up to this.

Oh goodness, there's nothing wrong with that boy. You're so intolerant. You're always shouting at him, that's the real problem. He's told me so.

A pause. A deep breath.

All right, forget that. Just tell me this: is he going to school?

Ooh, yes. He went yesterday. He hasn't gone in today though because he's got quite a sore throat. But I phoned the school and told them, so that's all right.

But you mean to say he's been in every day except today?

Not quite every day.

How many days has he been in?

I'm losing track a bit but I do know he's been in at least once this week.

But, Mummy, it's Friday!

I know that our boy needs to bottom out now. I know he needs to be thrown out of school, to run out of money, to be cold and hungry, to be forced perhaps to live rough and maybe be in some kind of physical danger, in order to make him understand for once and for all that he has a serious problem with cannabis and we can only help him if he acknowledges this and agrees to accept that help.

But I am just so relieved that, for the moment at least, he's sleeping on Granny's sofa bed.

His father and I lie in bed, him reading a novel, me flicking through an old Sunday magazine, looking at clothes I don't want to buy and food I will never find the energy to eat, let alone prepare.

I wasn't going to tell you this, he says, but I bumped into Janice the other day. She told me that Charlie has just got a place at Oxford.

To do what?

English, I think she said.

I lower my paper. Charlie's a year older than our boy, but, back when they were babies, they were friends for a while, pushed together by the parents but well matched all the same.

Both obsessed with *Thunderbirds*, both naughty, bright, sweet, advanced for their age.

And she told me about some of the others, too. Remember Danny? Sarah's boy? He's doing VSO and going to Manchester next year. And his sister's already in her first year reading Russian somewhere.

I think about this. All of these kids, all of our babies, our toddlers. One summer we all went away together, rented a house. And back then all our problems were exactly the same: how to get them off to sleep, how to relax about the pond at the bottom of the garden, how many cartoons to let them watch on a Saturday morning.

That's great, I tell him, and then after a pause: What do you mean you weren't going to tell me?

He stares ahead and sighs.

I don't know. Just – I suppose I thought it might be hard to hear.

I think about this.

It is hard to hear, but that doesn't mean I don't want to hear it.

He sighs again.

OK. Good.

He takes up his book.

The church clock strikes eleven. I put the paper down, sort out my pillows, turn off my light. His father continues to read. As the last strike of the clock sounds, the room slides back into silence.

I miss him so much, I say after a moment or two, even though I know this is absolutely the wrong time of night to start something like this.

His father says nothing.

I wish I could talk to him right now.

I shut my eyes, open them again. Still his father says

nothing. But what exactly do I want him to say? OK, ring him then. Or, I wish I could too?

I'm just so – oh I'm missing him, I say again, feeling a tear sting my nose.

His father puts his finger in the book, turns to me.

But, look, would you be feeling like this if he was, say, away on his gap year? he asks me.

For a second or two, I'm confused. I see a strong tanned boy in a T-shirt picking grapes. Or standing by a truck in the middle of a desert somewhere. He looks happy. He doesn't look like my son.

No, I say.

Well, then.

He goes back to his book.

He goes back to his book. But the other day, when I was doing the same thing – picking away at the keenest, rawest part of the wound much too late at night and after one too many glasses of wine – I accused him of not caring enough.

I didn't put it exactly like that. But after I'd described to him as meticulously as I could some aspect or other of the pure, lurching grief I'd been experiencing, I turned to him and said: But I don't think you feel it like that at all, do you?

And he was silent for a quick moment. And then he told me how when he went alone to Lord's the other day to watch the Test match, he could hardly bear to look at all the other fathers coming in with their seventeen- or eighteen-year-old sons. He felt so jealous and lonely and sad that it almost broke his heart.

It took every ounce of strength I had not to burst into tears right there in the pavilion, he said.

I reached for his hand and held it tight.

★   ★   ★

Driving us back from somewhere late at night, driving along quite a fast road, not a motorway, but driving quite fast because there's hardly any traffic, the boy's father notices I keep on bracing my foot against the floor and am having to concentrate on not putting my hand out to touch the dashboard.

What is it? he says glancing sideways as I grasp the door handle. What's the matter with you?

Nothing's the matter, I'm OK. Could you drive a tiny bit slower, please?

I'm not even doing 60.

I know. It's just –

He flicks another look at me. Tries to smile.

Come on, he says. Relax. I mean it. You've got to stop this. We're not going to crash. What is it exactly that you're worried about?

What is it? What am I worried about? Where is it coming from, this feeling of being so exposed to – harm?

The air is dark. Thick. Everything moving backwards so fast. Everything moving past us. The road swallowed up before I can register it.

I just feel I'd rather be in the back, I tell him, but even as I say it I'm half laughing, because I know how ludicrous it sounds.

In the back?

Yeah. It just feels kind of safer. It's like I want to have something between me and the point of impact.

He laughs too and then he stops.

Impact? What sort of impact exactly are you expecting?

I have no answer to that.

I finally get myself to a Families Anonymous meeting. I don't ever manage to find one for myself. Instead I end up going to the same one that the boy's father has been going to all these months, except that he's decided to take a break for now.

Wednesday evening, seven o'clock, birds singing outside. An easy drive, but I park the car reluctantly. I don't want to go. I'm only going because I just can't find a reason not to go any longer.

We sit around a table, not that many of us, just seven or eight, men and women, the warmth palpable. I'm the youngest there, the most obviously nervous, the newest. The one finding it hardest to reach out. Which surprises me, because I always thought of myself as someone who could do just that. But then I used to think of myself as lots of things.

We go around the table introducing ourselves.

When it's my turn, I tell them the barest facts. Our boy's age. His choice of drug. That he's not living with us any more.

Silence.

So I hear myself telling them that he got a girl pregnant. That he stole from us. That he gave his younger siblings skunk. That he hit me. (Always a gasp when I admit this to anyone.) I tell them that I'm not sure where he is right now but I hope he's OK. That I love him deeply. Deeply.

It's just, I say, my voice wobbling, it's just that I miss him so much.

When I feel the tears start to come, I stop. Bite my lip till it hurts. Wait for the next person to speak.

But it doesn't work. These people are unembarrassed. They're used to listening – making space for people to talk, however long it takes. And the silence goes on long enough to make a tear slip down my cheek.

Mary Sanders-Hewett has blonde bobbed hair, a red car and a yellow handbag. This is how she said I would recognise her in

215

Kettering Station car park. And she drives fast. Not dangerously fast, and not fast enough that any normal person would
notice, but it takes all my energy not to put my hand out to
grip the dashboard.

I took the train here. I haven't driven anywhere out of
London in months.

And it's a warm, windy day and in the car, one hand all the
same discreetly holding on to the edge of my seat, I keep on
sneaking glances at her pretty face with its straight, slender
nose and fine, fair features.

Here I am, sitting in a fast car next to the very last Tyssen.
Your mother's family. Energetic, creative, distinguished – and
fast.

Mary pulls in on a slope next to their wisteria-covered
cottage and jerks on the handbrake and we climb out, squinting
in the sunshine. Then into the cool, flower-scented darkness of
the hall, where two large collies hurl themselves at our legs.

There there, down, down, calm down, both of you!

Mary hushes but they keep on going. She explains which is
the older one and which the younger and which one came
first. I make a fuss of both. They don't exactly calm down. I
follow them all through into the long, low sitting room –
carpets and cushions and an even headier flower-petal smell.

On a low polished table, two red-bound volumes are
waiting. My eyes go straight to them.

Here you go, says Mary. And she hands them to me then
perches at the front of an armchair to my left, holding one of
the dogs against her legs and patting it.

I open what I quickly realise is the original manuscript of
Florence Suckling's book. A manuscript containing all the
visual elements – photographs and even little paintings – that
were omitted from the published version.

Is it what you were hoping for? asks Mary with a smile.

It's – oh it's incredible, is all I can say.

Some of the pictures I recognise as being simply photographs of the original drawings in Tony Yelloly's box. Others are of objects I'm looking at for the first time. A great deal of jewellery, minutely captioned. And objects from your home. A photograph of a china christening bowl, for instance – chipped and with a large crack in it. *Last used to baptise Constance Suckling*, notes the caption. I know that Constance was another of your sister Anna's daughters. Another of your nieces, had you lived.

There's so much in here, I tell Mary. Even without looking through properly, I can tell there's so much in here.

I read through some of the text. Part of it very familiar – exactly the words I've already read in Florence's book. Other parts absolutely fresh.

She must have edited it for publication, I tell Mary. Cut stuff out.

So there's stuff in there you haven't read?

Lots! My God, I'm going to have to read the whole thing. And she smiles.

Her two dogs are nudging at my legs as I struggle to ask her: I don't suppose – I mean, is there any chance you'd let me borrow these for a week or two? If I brought them straight back afterwards?

She takes a breath and looks uncomfortable.

Oh dear. It's just – well, they're so very precious to me. I look at them all the time. They're irreplaceable.

A thud of disappointment as I tell her I quite understand, of course I do. I quite understand, I tell her again. It's a big thing to ask and I'm sure I'd feel exactly the same if they were mine – please don't worry.

Oh dear, Mary says again, I'm so sorry.

I ask her whether in that case it would be OK for me to come back some other time and perhaps spend a morning alone with the books, making notes. I'd probably only need an hour or so.

She beams.

Of course, I don't have any problem with that!

She tells me she's about to go away on holiday. I tell her not to worry as I'm off to Yale next week to see some other Yelloly sketchbooks. I tell her about them and she looks interested.

You're going specially?

I have to really, don't I? Anyway, the kids are pleased. We're taking our two youngest for a half-term treat.

We make a date for me to come back in three weeks' time.

Before I leave, she shows me the portrait of your grandfather Samuel Tyssen on the landing – a grand and portly gentleman in a blue silk waistcoat and powdered wig.

This is the one your daughter doesn't like?

She laughs.

It's the eyes. Just look at him. You can see what she means, can't you?

I haven't spoken to our boy in almost a month but he still has his phone – his phone which we are continuing to pay for at the moment on the basis that he promises to answer it if we call him. His father doesn't think we should call him.

You're not doing him any favours. Let him come to us. He really has to get to a place where he realises how much he needs us.

Missing him badly, I call him.

Yes?

There's a lot of noise in the background.

Hi, darling. How are you? Are you OK?

Sorry, but this is not a good time.

He hangs up. I redial and get his voicemail.

Next day he calls me. Just the sound of his voice makes me go still inside.

Look, Mum, what you've got to understand is it's fucking difficult to talk to you when there are a couple of idiots hanging around me just waiting to steal my phone, OK?

Sorry, I say, I didn't realise. How are you?

(A little pause.)

I'm OK.

Are you still at Granny's?

Sometimes.

Are you going to school?

(Another pause.)

Mostly. Yeah. (His voice is softening by the second.)

And – well, how are things?

OK.

And – do you want to know how Kitty is?

(A little sigh.)

How's Kitty?

She's fine. She's OK. To be honest, I think she's missing you a bit.

Yeah, well.

Well, would you like to come over and have a meal sometime, see Kitty?

No thanks, I don't think so.

Then how about we meet up and I buy you a coffee or a meal?

He hesitates again.

We could go to Tootsie's. (He used to love Tootsie's. The vegetarian burger with extra goat's cheese and barbecue sauce on the fries.)

It's not a good time right now, Mum. Maybe some other time, OK?

And he hangs up, and I don't know whether I feel better or worse for having spoken to him. I don't tell his father I called him.

The day I drove to Croydon to buy his kitten was 30 January 1995, the day before his sixth birthday. He had wanted a kitten for ages but we begged him not to get his hopes up because it was the wrong time of year. Kittens are difficult to find in January.

But after hours spent with the *Yellow Pages*, I finally tracked down a pet shop in Croydon that had a litter.

Mainly black, one or two black-and-white, said the man. And there's one that's got white paws and bib and a white tummy.

Is it a girl?

Yeah. That one's female.

I asked him if he could possibly hold on to her till I got there. I got in the car and hurried to Croydon.

I still remember the precise texture of that January day. The bright cold sunshine, the horrible old white Citroën we had back then, Michelle Shocked and k.d. lang on the stereo.

The pet shop was on the grey main road, between a party shop and a kebab shop. The kittens – six or seven of them – were all squashed together in one big cage. The one I'd reserved happened to be the liveliest. She was the one who was playing the most, rolling over and over and smacking the one next to her. I knew from the books that this was a good sign. The man picked her up and put her in my hands and she mewed at me but didn't struggle.

I'll take her, I said.

All the way back to Clapham, she mewed and mewed. Every time we stopped at a traffic light, I poked my fingers in the box and tried to talk to her, but nothing would console her. But, once we got her in the spare room where we were hiding her for the night, she relaxed, had a drink and started washing.

That's good, said the boy's father, who knew about cats. That means she feels at home. Oh look at her – he's going to be over the moon, isn't he?

Over the moon didn't begin to describe it.

All that evening, the last evening ever of being only five, the boy had a frozen, terrified look on his face. A kind of fearful joy. I knew what he was feeling. I knew that he suspected that he might just be getting a kitten, but was afraid to let himself hope even for one tiny second. We'd told him not to get his hopes up. And back then, he was such a good boy, he always did as he was told. The effort of not hoping was almost unbearable.

In the morning we put the kitten in a cardboard box with a bright yellow ribbon tied around it. And when he opened it and saw her small black face looking up at him, he couldn't speak at all for a few moments.

And he couldn't decide whether to call her Hoover, or Fluffy, or Scrap. Because he had a shortlist of about ten names. But in the end he plumped for Kitty because he thought it suited her best.

But she began her life as Hoover and, though I thought that only lasted a day or two, maybe it was longer. Because when, a few months after our boy has finally left us, I happen to be going through Clapham and stop at a vet's on Lavender Hill – a vet we haven't been to in years and years – to buy some worming tablets for our dog, the assistant asks me if we're on their records.

Only from years ago, I tell her. We've moved house since. She frowns and scrolls down on the computer.

1995? Would that be it? A cat called Hoover? First injections?

Goodness, yes, I say. That was a very long time ago.

And I pay for the tablets and leave the surgery and walk out into the sunshine. And as I walk, a long-ago memory of a small boy struggling along the pavement with the basket containing his kitten – determined to manage it because no one else is allowed to carry her – comes into my head. I make myself think about something else.

SPIRITS

My fingers curled,
round an open bottle of
thought. Sat here
I still choke
on the liar's retort:
'I sip mine to keep
my spirits high.'

8

GRAND CENTRAL STATION, New York. A hot, damp summer's morning. People rushing, coffees and papers in their hands. I queue up and buy a return to New Haven in Connecticut.

On the commuter train, a large red-faced man in a string vest rolls around, taking up at least two seats, sighing, snoring, muttering. Now and then someone moves to get away from him.

As we pass through Hartford with its rows of pretty clapboard houses, more and more people get off at each stop. The day gets hotter. I wonder if String Vest is going as far as New Haven. Might I even be left alone with him? But two stops later, he wakes and leaves the train, wobbling down the steps and sitting straight down on the platform with his head between his knees. We rattle off again. Relief.

Outside the cosmopolitan comfort of Manhattan, America turns back into America: a raw, tired place, dusty and poor and fractious. At New Haven Station, I need the loo but, as I hesitate at the entrance to the women's toilets, a young black woman with teary eyes grabs at my clothes and tries to follow me in, demanding $2.

Please leave me alone.

Just give me the $2!

I turn and walk quickly away and back into the station and she spits, calling me a cunt. The last person to call me that was my son. She's still standing there, cursing and crying, as I get in a cab to go to Yale.

The Yale Center for British Art is on a very long, tree-lined street, dotted with depressing and pointless shops selling expensive things that no one needs. Perfumed candles to make your eyes water. Bath bombs. Marbled paper. Flower-patterned garden forks and trowels for people who will never touch soil. On the other side of the street, men in vests slump in the park, drinking and dozing on the dying yellow grass.

I reach the building which houses the Paul Mellon Collection and check in and head straight for the über-smart stainless-steel loos. Washing my hands, my face in the mirror looks exactly as I feel: incredulous. It just seems so impossible that this cool, blond building in the middle of America could contain anything of Woodton – anything that you or your family ever touched.

But it does. I sit at a table in the hushed, air-conditioned library and a pale and humourless young man with a face as transparent as his glasses carries them over just as carefully as if they were someone else's babies – a small pile of your sketchbooks.

For a moment, blinking at me, he almost seems unwilling to hand them over, and I want to laugh and ask him to explain his claim on them. Has he scrambled over the church wall at Woodton with your great-great-great-niece? Does he have your mother's crocheted purse at home in his study? Has he stood on the rooftops at Narborough and seen the whole of Norfolk spread out before him?

He shows me how to handle the books and gives me a special purpose-made rest, demonstrating how to lay them on it so as not to crack the spines. For a moment I think he's also going to ask to see if my hands are clean. I think of Tony and Bryony's dining table strewn with history, as well as crumbs and peas and glasses of apple juice.

As I open the first sketchbook – and am plunged straight back to the mauve and brown skies of Woodton, the familiar dark sweep of the Norfolk land – the librarian's still standing there.

Do you know how the books ended up at Yale? I ask, hoping he'll go away if I take the lead.

He licks his lips. I'm sorry. I have no knowledge of that.

Well, I say, I'd love to know.

He looks at me doubtfully. Then he gives me some slips of paper to mark the pages, telling me I can make a note of any pages I might like to have photographed and then I can place an order. Then he installs himself behind the nearby counter and, hands folded, watches me like an exam invigilator.

The first sketchbook, the smallest, is done for your sister Harriet – a batch of pictures signed by Sophy and Sarah. A man called Harris stands stiffly, holding a pitchfork and wearing grey breeches, cobalt stockings and a tall hat. The date is 9 July 1839 – you were no longer alive by then. *Harris.* Could he have been employed by your father? I know I've come across that name already in the past few months.

Another sketch shows *old Mrs Smith* in her dark bonnet with a pink ribbon, pink shawl, blue shoes, holding a basket. Another servant? And then the *Kingswood vegetable woman* in her brightly patterned clothes and *Miss Atkins*, who makes more than one appearance.

An interior of a lace maker's room shows a small girl gazing intently up at an elderly woman. The careful detail in this picture – the criss-cross leaded windowpanes, the pair of candlesticks on the mantelpiece, the warming pan on the wall – take me straight back to a scene in your album – the same people, the same room. The same potted geranium on the sill.

Two figures on a little filigree card are inscribed *to Harriet Jan 18th 1845 from her affectionate mother.* Another, *For Sam,* shows the back view of a young woman in a red cape and blue dress with a dark bonnet.

Finally, there's a picture of a pretty, blown-about young woman in a big green check coat and dark bonnet with white ruffles around the face. The scarf at her neck is daffodil yellow and her brown dress seems to be covered with a white apron or pinafore. Behind her, the sea is a watery pale blue. The picture's labelled *Harriet at Hastings* – by her mother. Harriet has dark hair and rosy cheeks, a sharp, thoughtful face. Your sister.

The last sketchbook is the most interesting. A bigger brown book with dull red corners, quite different in style and tone to any of your family's work I've seen so far. This is Jane's book. Your sister Jane Davison Yelloly who died of smallpox at the age of thirty. One day before you. Buried with you.

These paintings are far more abstract and careless and wild than anything you or your other sisters or mother ever did. They seem to indicate what I've somehow sensed all along: that Jane was different from the rest of you. Less placid, less pretty, more difficult to deal with, cleverer, perhaps.

Many pictures are copied from an artist called J.J. Burns Esq. And there are some competently executed waterfalls *after Turner.* But the best are recognisably straight from real Yelloly life.

The curious effect of snow seen at Carrow Abbey Nov 16th 1831 – is a startling scene of white ground against cold and heavy grey skies. In the foreground a large tree with a few coppery leaves still clinging to its dark branches. Could it be the weeping beech that Jeremy Howard showed me?

Effect at sunset March 15th 1833 as seen from the window at Woodton Hall, drawn March 16th 1833 from recollection shows a hot pink-jelly sun sliding behind the barest black trunks of winter trees. And next to it, someone – your mother? – has written *Excellent!* in pencil.

Yes, I think, it is.

Finally, *Twilight with Venus the evening star seen from Woodton Hall March* 1833 shows that small moment between dusk and darkness when only the upper part of the sky is still washed with light. You're out walking through fields to-wards home and it's still just about light. But as soon as you get indoors and light the lamps, the windowpanes are black with night.

And *Bedingham and Woodton Halfway Oak after its fall July 10th 1837.* An enormous tree lies on the ground by the hedge, a small wooden gate inviting us forward on the right. What happened? Was there a storm and did the tree fall and did you girls all rush out to sketch it? Did you go too? Standing there gazing solemnly on a dark yellow morning, the light sour and calm after the storm of the night before.

And then July 1837. A date it's impossible to ignore. Jane the painter – alert and energetic, physically robust, generous and intense with her brush – didn't know she had less than a year to live.

I look up. The young man has left his desk.

Outside, the Connecticut sun is baking the drunks in the park, but here in the library I suddenly feel myself right back where I started: driving into Woodton on that bleak, cold February day as the light died.

Our boy remains homeless, sleeping on people's sofas and floors, sometimes arriving at his granny's in the middle of the night and causing her to ring us the next morning in tears.

It's not that I don't want him here, it's just that, when I wake him in the morning, he doesn't even try to get up.

The weeks roll by. We have sporadic contact with him. Or at least, I call him and sometimes he answers and sometimes he doesn't. Then he calls round and asks to speak to us. He tells us he wants to get a flat. He's looked into it and he's eligible for Educational Maintenance Allowance because he's still at school, and Housing Benefit as well if he can just get someone to let him rent a flat. But he can't rent a flat without a deposit and a guarantor. Would we be prepared to lend him a deposit and guarantee him?

Would we?

His father actually seems to be thinking about it. I'm surprised.

How will he ever face up to his problems, I say, if we go and underwrite him in a nice cushy flat?

It's difficult, his father says, frowning as he attempts to sort out his thoughts. But if, as he says, he doesn't in fact have a problem with drugs – if there's even the tiniest chance that this is true – then we should probably try this.

But he does have a problem with drugs, I say. We know he does.

His father sighs. I understand the sigh: we both continually move back and forwards between the absolute sinking certainty that our son is addicted and a faint, glimmering hope that he maybe is not.

I know, I know. But all the same, I just wonder – should we at least give him one chance to show us he can live normally?

So we can at least say we did?

Exactly. Though of course if, as we still suspect, he's smoking all the time, well then, it's absolutely the wrong thing to do.

It'll just delay his recovery.

Meanwhile the boy – who assumes he'll talk us into it in the end – gets on with hunting for a flat. He puts a lot of energy into this – so much energy that he barely goes to school for two weeks. When I confront him about this, he tells me it's OK. The teachers are sympathetic to his problem.

How the fuck am I meant to concentrate on schoolwork when I have nowhere to live?

And if you got this flat, you'd start working?

He looks at me as if I'm quite mad.

Of course I would! You think I don't want to get some fucking A levels?

We're still hesitating about helping him, still weighing up the pros and cons – still trying to balance our love and concern and the strong impulse to put a roof over his head against the tougher course of action which we suspect is the more responsible one – when the mother of one of his friends, one of the boys he's known since primary school, rings me.

We used to be sort of friends too, this mother and I. We often chatted while we waited to pick the boys up from one activity or other. Our boys both struggled, briefly, with learning to read (and we supported each other) and then, to our relief, they both took off, excelling at English. They did drama classes after school together, cricket practice on a Sunday. We shared lifts.

As they got older, the boys drifted apart and so did we. But I continued to run into her at parents' evenings and she was always friendly. Now our sons seem to be seeing each other again – her own boy is working hard at school, possibly planning a gap year in the US before university.

It's been years since she's had reason to ring me. I can hear the nerves in her voice as she apologises for cold-calling like this but, well, it's been keeping her awake at night. She has to ask: why are we allowing our boy to be homeless like this?

You're going to think I'm such an interfering old cow, she says.

I tell her nonsense, of course I don't. Then I take a breath and try to explain that we're struggling with the concept of tough love – so neat in theory, so hard to carry out in practice – but we have a feeling that for him, now, it's the only way. I hesitate for a moment as I consider telling her more about the ways in which our lives have unravelled over the past year. But I don't really know her any more and it doesn't feel right, so I decide not.

I hear her draw breath.

But he can't carry on living like this! she says, her voice a little tighter now as she senses that I'm not going to give way. You're his mother, Julie, for goodness' sake – I mean, we used to be friends and I know you care about him, but don't you want him to have a roof over his head?

Of course I do, I say.

He's told Luke he wants to get a flat share but that you're refusing to support him. Wouldn't you rather he was living in a flat than sleeping on people's floors?

I try to breathe, even though my heart is thumping in my chest. Why is it so stressful to have another mother, even a mother you used to like, tell you how to care for your child?

I want him to have a roof over his head, I say again. And I don't want him to live like this. In fact, I can hardly bear it. I love him so much –

Well, I have to say you have a strange way of showing it!

But no, since you ask, I don't think he should be living in a flat. He's still at school – in theory anyway, though he's barely attending. His father and I think he should be living at home.

I hear her thinking about this.

All right, but he doesn't get on with you, does he? Luke says you're always fighting. That's not exactly his fault. OK, I'm not saying it's easy. I'm sure he's not easy. But some teenagers go through rough patches. And I don't want to get into the rights and wrongs as it's none of my business, but don't you think, however he's behaved, he deserves at least one chance to live properly?

I take a breath.

I would give anything to have him live properly, I tell her, wishing my voice would stop trembling, but he's addicted to cannabis. I don't suppose he's told Luke that. We seriously believe he has a problem with the drug. He can't stop smoking. He can barely go a day without a joint. And he's chaotic. He's not in control of what he does. We don't believe he'd keep up the rent on a flat, because any money he gets just goes on drugs.

Drugs! the woman scoffs. Oh come on. It's perfectly normal at their age to smoke a bit of dope. Luke had some friends round just the other night –

It's not a bit of dope, I say again, feeling my anger rising. It's skunk. For two or three years, he's been smoking skunk. Do you know about skunk? It's nothing like the stuff we all smoked at university.

Now she wavers.

Of course I know about skunk. But I'm sure that's not what they're smoking. Luke says they'd never buy it.

How does he know what he's buying? I mutter.

She ignores me.

Anyway, even if he smokes a bit too often, what on earth makes you think he's addicted?

Because his personality has changed completely. You remember what he was like at seven or eight? That bright, happy boy –

But all teenagers –

Because every aspect of his daily life has ground to a halt. Because he hardly goes to school –

But what do you expect when he hasn't got anywhere to live?

He wasn't going to school when he was living here. Day after day he refused to go, or went back to bed even after we begged him to get in the car, I tell her quietly and for a moment this stops her.

Look, please, I say. Forget whether he's an addict or not. Maybe addict is a difficult word. All I know is he needs to stop smoking cannabis and we just can't help him till he does.

I'm finding this really upsetting, she says. I lay awake last night wondering what I could do and I only rang to offer support but it sounds like you just don't want things to improve for him. I just can't understand where you're coming from. Whatever you think he may or may not have done, he's still your son.

I'm sorry I can't tell you the things you want to hear, I say, but she's not there any more. She's hung up on me.

I discover I am shaking. *He's still your son.*

I look at the boy's father, who is staring out of the window with a bleak face, one hand on the radiator, the other on his cheek.

Why does it feel so traumatic to have someone accuse you of not loving your child enough? I ask him.

He says nothing.

I do actually think she means well, I tell him as brightly as I can. I mean, I wanted to kill her, but I do actually think she genuinely believes she's acting for the best, doing the right thing.

She doesn't mean well at all. She's an enabler, he says, real fury in his voice. She may not know that's what she is, but she is. At best she's ignorant and utterly misguided, utterly wrong. If she's letting her own kids smoke skunk, then she's just giving up on them.

Not everyone who smokes gets addicted, I remind him, wondering at the same time why I'm bothering to defend someone who has just accused me of not caring about my child.

I sit down on the bedroom floor, my arms on my knees. We are both silent for a while. Kitty comes in, her tail held tall. She pushes against me but I don't stroke her. Then I relent and I do.

But – so – what do you think? Should we try and do this? I ask him.

I don't know. What do you think?

What do you think?

He sighs a very long sigh.

We do. We do it. We do it because we can't bear the alternative, which is not to have done it. But that doesn't mean we have any faith it will work.

But we don't do it without some conditions. Conditions which, quite surprisingly, the boy agrees to.

We'll lend him the deposit and act as guarantors on a flat. But in exchange he has to attend a Narcotics Anonymous meeting every Friday – the same young people's one that I told him about months ago, the details of which (though I don't know it then) are still scrunched in his jacket pocket.

On top of this, he has to do a weekly drugs test for us. If he fails to be clean, then it's all over (though actually, of course, it's not, because we're stuck with the flat for six months either way and he knows it). But if he stays clean, then great – we'll happily renew on the flat after six months.

The boy seems very happy. In some ways almost his old self – reliable and chirpy and calm. He seems to think what we hoped he'd think – that staying clean is a small price to pay in exchange for having somewhere to live.

I've been wanting to cut down anyway, he tells me brightly. It won't be hard. I often don't smoke for two or three days at a time, you know.

Two or three days isn't very long, I point out – with a faint sense of déjà vu because haven't we debated this exact point before? But even so I allow myself to feel a quick, sweet rush of hope.

Maybe he isn't addicted after all, his father says. Maybe he can just stop once he has a reason to.

We both agree: we'd give absolutely anything to have his friend's mother proved right.

A few days later, the boy tells us he's found the perfect flat, and someone to share it with – a nineteen-year-old boy with a mop of ginger hair who we've met a couple of times when they've turned up on our doorstep together.

Isn't he the one who always looks a bit stoned? his father asks, attempting to sound more humorous than anxious.

The boy looks shocked and says this is nonsense. Ginger has never touched drugs in his life.

Sitting in a café and working out the finer details of the rental deal with us, Ginger confirms this.

Yeah, I'm allergic. I've tried smoking weed but I can't really do any of that stuff. It really so totally freaks me out.

He blinks and offers to pay for his tea.

Oh no, don't worry, I say. This is on us.

For a while, everything feels good. We see quite a bit of the boy as we help him move stuff into his flat and some days we almost begin to feel like his parents again. I offer him sheets, pillows, towels.

Don't give him any of the good stuff, his father begins to say, then checks himself.

And that's it – that's as close as he gets to saying he doesn't have faith. Because we both feel it, even though we don't dare mention or discuss it: an incredible, swooping sense of hope.

The first urine test is clean and the boy goes to the meeting. He tells us later that it's ridiculous, that he has nothing whatsoever in common with the fucked-up junkies in there. But, I remind his father, at least he went, and at least he stayed.

The second urine test he's very late for, but at least it's clean, although by the time he's done it there's no time left to go into the meeting. His father, who has driven through a Friday-night rush hour to meet him there, comes home feeling cheated.

OK, but he's always been a bit unreliable, I point out. A terrible time-keeper, even in the old days. It doesn't necessarily mean anything.

Yes, but he has a deal with us. It's part of the deal.

OK, but isn't it just so great that the tests are clean?

The third urine test he doesn't show up for at all. When he doesn't call us and his mobile is switched off, I start to worry.

Oh dear, this is bad, I do hope he's OK, I tell his father, who just smiles a grim little smile.

An hour later he rings to say he's at a police station because he was picked up for trying to *help himself* to some bed sheets in a shop.

You mean shoplifting?

He laughs.

Well, if you insist on putting it like that. But it's OK, the guy doesn't want to press charges.

But – I gave you sheets –!

One lousy sheet?

Don't give him the good stuff.

Oh come on, Mum, you know I do these things. I've never tried to hide it from you. You know what my life is like.

By now our boy has been in his flat three weeks. By the fourth week, there have been so many complaints from neighbours about noise, disruptive behaviour and fighting in the street outside – Fighting in the street?! Oh, just a little disagreement that broke out between me and Ginger – that both Lambeth Council and the police are involved. The primary school whose playground the house happens to back on to also alleges that Ginger appeared naked at the kitchen window one lunchtime and fired a water pistol at the kids. We're speechless.

Is it true? we ask our boy. Is it really possible that he did such a thing?

He shrugs.

Oh, those police, they're so fucking over the top. I don't know if he did it or not, but if he did it was just a bit of fun, that's all.

He did it, his father sighs, eyes on the floor.

And they say he called your downstairs neighbour a cunt and yelled at her that he hoped she got breast cancer, I continue. Please, please at least tell me that's not true.

Our boy chuckles.

That woman downstairs is so fucking crazy. She so totally hates us.

And have you said anything to her?

Hey, don't look at me. You've no idea how hard I try – I'm the fucking peacemaker around here.

By the fifth week, the boy and his flatmate are evicted. We're told by the (very reasonable and communicative and, we think, remarkably patient) landlord that, if they don't move out by the Monday, we'll be liable for another month's rent. Which of course doesn't bother the boy, who, it turns out, has already left town.

He calls me from the train.

Hey, Mum.

I've been calling and calling you. Where are you?

On a train to Sheffield. Just had to get out of town for a while. The whole thing of the flat and all that, it was doing my head in. And there's this girl I met –

But – my head is spinning – you can't just go. Today is Friday and you know bloody well that we've got to move all your stuff out by Monday –

Yeah, well, I was going mad in there. What the fuck was I supposed to do? And anyway this girl –

Who?

238

We only met a week ago, but it's pretty serious and she's in Sheffield. Look, Mum, sorry, I've got to go, but I'll call you, OK?

But –

Next time I try his phone, it's off again.

That's when I rescue his cat.

Saturday morning we spend in pouring south London rain, stuffing his things into black bin bags and driving them back to our house. The things we only drove there less than six weeks ago. It takes two trips with a full car.

Even though we'd worried he might not, Ginger does at least turn up to deal with his stuff, accompanied – bafflingly, surreally – by the girl. The girl I last saw when I sat with her in Café Rouge as she picked at her chips and I attempted to describe what it would be like when my embryo grandchild was sucked out of her.

She has on high-heeled boots, brand new and unscuffed, and a powder-pink dress with a matching zip-up jacket and she is as smilingly polite as ever.

I go back to Mary Sanders-Hewett's house in Northampton-shire on a dark wet pouring day in late July.

The two red leather-bound books are waiting for me on the dining table. She makes me coffee and chats to me from the kitchen while the two collies bump around my chair, sneezing.

Then she leaves me to it.

First I look at the photographs – endless dark Victorian photographs of mostly Tyssen relics. Jewellery and silverware, purses and knives, needle cases, buckles, thimbles, bracelets. All of them carefully arranged for the camera and caught – still and hard and cold.

I feel I ought to be interested – because most of this at some point belonged to your family, some of the items possibly even belonged to you – but it's relentless stuff. The true deadness of old lives when all that's left is pot and plate. I realise that a real historian, a proper biographical researcher, might find significance and interest in each and every one. But they're not what I'm after. What am I after? Some emotion? Some clue that you really did once exist? A flavour of your face, your breath, your hair?

The collie who has settled at my feet heaves a sigh.

There are some small paintings similar to all those I've seen before. Interiors of rooms which may or may not be Woodton. Not as clear or vivid as the ones that hang on Patrick Baron's landing.

And there's a nice little watercolour of a house in Epping Forest. I know about this house. In 1813, a couple of years before you are born, your older brothers and sisters are struck down by a bout of whooping cough, and your parents whisk them all away to Epping. Out of London, away from the germs.

But they recover from the whooping cough only to contract measles and, somewhere in the middle of all that, Nick is born – Nick, who is so poorly for the first part of his life that they have to wait six months before baptising him. Poor Nick, whose existence begins pretty much exactly as it ends. Three months after that, in the August, your sister Anna is born, there in that same pretty watercolour house. Then they all return, parents and eight children, back to Finsbury Square, where you come into the world. Ellen, as we know, is born at Carrow.

It's dark in the dining room. Squalls of chilly summer rain batter the window. One of the dogs has gone, but the one that settled under my chair is now snoring quietly. I carry on reading Florence's hand-typed text. Though much of it is identical or similar to my published version, now and then something stands right out. An extra sentence or paragraph. A little footnote. Pieces of information which, for whatever reason, were edited out of the published book.

Some enticing detail, too. Describing the house in Finsbury Square where your parents begin married life and where you are born, Florence notes that:

> They finished this house at great expense. The family bedstead where most of the children were born cost £100 and Mrs Suckling (Anna) was born in it at Walthamstow in Essex and her daughter Constance was also born in it at Cavendish Hall 1849. It was hung with chocolate-coloured chintz that cost 7s 6d a yard.

Chocolate-coloured chintz. You are conceived and born into a bed hung with chocolate-coloured chintz. Your newborn eyes struggling to focus on cocoa-coloured drapes, rich brown fabric swathes.

She goes on:

> The drawing-room chairs were black, elaborately gilded, they cost 72s apiece and were sold by Mrs Severne at Cavendish Hall. A mahogany bookcase with drawers under it was bought at Seddon's, and it is represented in one of the bedrooms at Woodton (sketched in water-colour by Anna).
>
> The front of the bookcase is lined with yellow. This was left to Mrs Suckling by her mother and sent to Barsham. She also had from her mother 2 inlaid card

tables that were bought at Seddon's for the Yelloly wedding, the table belonging to this set was left at Cavendish for Mrs Severne.

If the bookcase ended up at Barsham then it's very likely it's now one of the pieces in Patrick Baron's apartment.

I read on. Now and then names jump out at me. William Harris is one. Harris. It's the name I wondered about at Yale. And now I remember why I knew it, because here it is, on the little card written to your brother, *Uncle Sam*, from some unknown nephew or niece. The original is in the Yelloly box but here it is again, reproduced:

I have got the toothache and couldn't eat no dinner hardly. I am very sorry that I didn't say goodbye and I'll ask him where he was that I didn't say goodbye. Which station did you stop at and how did you find your chicken and grandmamma's horses and how is Harris and please how is Phyllis and Vilet and I forget the others and how is Aunt Sarah's room . . .

How is Harris. In the Yale picture, Harris, with his blue breeches and pitchfork, looks a lot like a farm labourer. But he must be more than that – he must be known to your family in some more personal way, if the young letter writer enquires after his health. In the next paragraph, I get my answer:

William Harris was the old Yelloly coachman and he survived beyond and into the days when young Sucklings delighted to play hide-and-seek in the old disused chariot.

The old disused chariot. Fun and games and hide-and-seek in the old primrose Yelloly coach. I think of the coach house Steve Hill showed us with its little alcoves in the brick wall where the lanterns were put. And then I think of something else. If Harris is the old and trusted family coachman, then does he do that terrible midsummer's drive to Ipswich to collect your grieving sister? Is it Harris – faithful servant, patient with you all when you are children – who is trusted with the task of bringing your poor body back to Woodton for burial?

I've imagined that drive, that journey several times, but suddenly I can't imagine it any more. It's gone. I can't see it. It was easier when I had less detail. This is why I can't get close to you, Mary. The more I know, the less I seem to see.

Another name: *Sarah Rhodes.* I haven't come across that name anywhere before but it turns out she is your nurse, another trusted servant, and she dies at Carrow. There's a tablet to her memory in Trowse Church:

Sacred to the memory of Mrs Sarah Rhodes
Who died at Carrow Abbey on 6 April 1831
After a long and severe illness in the 65th year of her life
Much and sincerely lamented, she was for many years the respected and faithful nurse in the family of Dr and Mrs Yelloly of Carrow Abbey.
Their ten children whom she nursed with the greatest care and affection have erected this stone as a tribute of their regard.

1831. I think back to the entry I read in your mother's pocket almanac for that year:

Accept oh Lord my humble thanks for all thy mercies particularly for preserving to me my dearest husband and children, though Thou has pleased to call away one of our household, yet let me acknowledge thy wonderful goodness in suffering 24 years to pass over without visiting our house with death!!

Twenty-four years – that's a reference to your parents' wedding in 1806. Snow Hill. The twenty-two-year-old Sarah, alone in the world but full of hope. Not alone any more.

Twenty-four years without death. And then, 1831. The year your nurse dies at Carrow is the same year that you all pack up and move to Woodton. Over the next eleven years your mother will lose four of her children, and then her husband. I wonder if she ever looks back on that year, and the move to Woodton, as the beginning of the end. The beginning of her loss. Her losses. I think I would.

And what about you children? Are you sorry to leave Carrow? Do you miss those pretty lawns, those ancient ruins, that enormous fat blazing tree? Or are you relieved not to have to creep along those shadowy corridors any more? Are you glad to quit those dark and creaky rooms, which will one day in the faraway future contain flip charts and sales teams? And have you seen the ghost who pushes her way into the Prioress's bedroom? Or does she only start making her presence felt later, when you're gone? In which case, who is she?

And then I come across something else – a sliver of emotional detail about your parents, which is so surprising it makes me sit up. Something that was cut from the published book:

Sarah had a lover who was loved in return, but his suit was rejected by a Guardian. Dr Yelloly, a friend of Sir Joseph Banks and an ardent admirer of Miss Tyssen, had been rejected by her but was chivalrous enough to say to her:

Madam,

If I can forward your suit in any way, you have only to command me . . . If your surprise is called forth at the address of one who has had the honour of an acquaintance with you of some years standing, let not your anger be raised at presumption, nor your displeasure construe the intrusion into an impertinence. The subject on which I am about to address you has for a length of time been the source of much anxiety to my mind, the disclosure may perhaps put an end to hopes with which I have long flattered myself, but can never erase the sentiments of respectful regard I entertain towards you. Since your [. . .] you can be no stranger to my [. . .] and if you think me worthy of my attention and one to whose care you would with safety confide your future prospects it shall be the present pride and chief pleasure of my life to contribute to your happiness.

The many amiable qualities I am convinced you possess, among which politeness of manners and sweetness of disposition must be conspicuous to everyone who has the pleasure of your acquaintance, induce me to hope, whatever may be your opinion of the step I have taken, you will indulge me so far as to favour me with an answer. You will not be displeased I trust at my subscribing myself with very great esteem and respect,
Your faithful and devoted servant,
J. Yelloly

I am holding my breath. This is not what I imagined. Your mother's reply is shown beneath it:

Sir,

Allow me to express the high sense I entertain of the honour you have conferred on me, of which I am fully sensible, though I have not at present any wish or intention of changing my situation in life, pardon me if I add that it appears to me that our acquaintance has been too short, or in any degree not sufficient to develop the temper or habits of either of us, which are so essential to be fully known before a subject like the present be properly considered. This reason will, I flatter myself, be deemed a sufficient apology for my declining the honour he has done me. I trust too much candour to do me so great injustice as to construe my conduct on this occasion into the slightest mark of disrespect. I earnestly hope that this occurrence may and will be buried in oblivion and never in the smallest degree interrupt that sociability and harmony which for my part I shall always be happy to maintain and which the close connection between our families renders so desirable.

I remain with great respect,

S. Tyssen

PS A brother who has ever been accustomed to share my confidence is the only one that has the smallest idea of what has passed and I feel not in the least hesitation in giving my word that he will continue to preserve the most absolute silence on the subject.

Maybe I shouldn't be amazed at this, but I am. The sense I have of your parents' relationship, of their meeting and eventual union, is so – solid. Because of the purse, I suppose. That one small knitted purse – a lifetime of romance! – has coloured my whole view of your parents' marriage.

But it isn't like that at all. It doesn't happen that way – the two orphans meeting, the sudden swift recognition, the uncomplicated comfort of making a home, a family. No. Your mother turns your father down. She loves someone else.

She loves a man who is considered unsuitable and who she is somehow prevented from marrying. Who is it she loves? What happens to him? Where does he go?

And, though she thinks of John Yelloly as a friend, maybe even a dear friend – *one who has had the honour of an acquaintance with you of some years standing* – she cannot consider him as a husband, a lover. And she tells him this, quite bluntly, confiding at the same time in your Uncle Sam. Sam, I don't know what to do. I've had this letter from John Yelloly. I don't know what he means by it. I can't possibly marry him!

How is she feeling when she writes that letter? Does she hate to disappoint him, to hurt him? Or is she so deep in love with the other man, the Someone Else, that she hardly cares? Hot tears cried into her pillow at night. That tearing feeling in her chest.

She'll get over it, say the guardians. Maybe Sir Joseph Banks tries to talk her round – Banks, who has a vested interest in promoting Yelloly's cause. Banks, who, like Yelloly, is a scientist, a botanist, famous throughout the country ever since as a young man he went on Captain Cook's first voyage. Banks, who by this time is old and suffering badly from gout and has to be wheeled around in a chair.

What exactly is wrong with the Someone Else? Why is he so unsuitable?

247

And anyway, does she get over it? How long before she changes her mind enough to make the little purse for John, hoping it might rekindle something?

And meanwhile your poor father. How deflated he must feel. *The honour you have conferred on me . . . buried in oblivion.* I can be your friend, but never your wife. Friendship. A word that's full of good intent, but devastating if you love someone and want them to love you.

But the text goes on:

His devotion to her interests and unselfishness won her in the end. Many years afterwards, she gathered her sons about her and said, 'I married your father because he was an honourable man,' and gave them a homily in manly honour.

An honourable man. Manly honour. Well, it could mean anything. It might be true – there's nothing wrong with honour. Or it could be the thing you tell yourself, the story you weave to make it all OK. And most of the time, the story works. It's more or less true, so it works its careful, reasonable magic. Until you glance out of the window one day at a smudged sky and your heart just implodes with loneliness.

Mary Sanders-Hewett's dog breathes a long, hard sigh against my foot.

The published version of *A Forgotten Past* quotes at some length from a letter written to Florence by a Mrs Jane Coulcher, who was a friend of your family.

In it, she talks about going over to Carrow Abbey and seeing your older sisters all looking so pretty in their white muslin dresses with coloured sashes. Their lovely complexions.

She's a bit judgemental about your brother John, saying that, when he went up to Cambridge, he was a rather uninteresting young man. Though she hurries to add that, in later life, he became a charming-looking old man. Like everyone else, Jane Coulcher is full of praise for your mother – so highly educated, such a charming Shakespeare reader and accomplished artist, but who also makes a point of teaching her daughters ornamental cookery.

In her letter, Mrs Coulcher also writes this:

His [. . .] first call at Woodton (when he was staying with his grandmother Mrs Fox who lived at Woodton Old Hall) on a later occasion, and the walk in the woods, and the engagement. Dear beautiful Sophy was engaged to Mr Groome, afterwards, Archdeacon Groome. Sophy's and Harriet's engagements were I think the two first to the two clergymen, brothers Groome, sons of Mr Groome, Rector of Monk Soham and Earl Soham in Suffolk. They were college friends of John and were introduced to them at Carrow. Sophy remained engaged and with very warm affection on both sides until her death at Dawlish.

Next to those words *Sophy's and Harriet's engagements*, there's an asterisk and a revealing footnote that was left out of the published version:

*Harriet's engagement to John Groome, brother to Robert. During the course of this engagement his affections passed to Sarah, and Harriet released him, but Sarah never allowed any approaches to be made to her. The sisters never spoke of it to each other.

I think about this and I feel for your sister Harriet, but it also makes me wonder about Sarah. If John Groome decides that he loves her, then does she really not return his affection, or is she simply denying her own feelings for her sister's sake? Can she really be so noble? And is it really worth it? Is this why she doesn't marry until so late in her life?

Florence goes on to add that, although Sarah was frequently sought in marriage and *loved one suitor of early life* she saw in him only *vacillation and weakness* and her common sense asserted itself. She decided their union would not rise to her ideal of married life.

Is this suitor John Groome, then? John Groome who treats her sister Harriet badly and whom Sarah can't help judging as bad husband material as a result?

Either way, the mention of Robert Suckling's visit to Woodton and his subsequent engagement to your sister Anna, that all makes sense to me.

Until I see that, here in the original manuscript, the text is subtly, shockingly different:

> The sisters used to tell us about their different engagements, especially I remember Mr Suckling's first call at Woodton on a later occasion, and the walk in the woods, and the engagement. Poor Mary! But her engagement did not come off in a marriage and she died not long after.

Poor Mary. Poor Mary! *Her engagement did not come off in a marriage.* We know that Anna and Robert get engaged, but is there another engagement first? Are you the one who Robert proposes to on that famous first walk in the woods? Is it possible that he fell in love with you first?

In the dark room, with the dog at my feet, my fingertips are cold.

She died not long after. Is it even possible that you were engaged to be married to Robert Suckling when you died?

Going back to the published version, I now see what I'd managed to miss. A chronological clue that has actually been there all along.

In the winter of 1838/1839, still mourning the loss of you and Jane in the summer, the family travels to Dawlish, where they are to watch poor Sophy slip away. A month or so later, in the spring, returning to Woodton, your sister is *sought in marriage by the eldest son of the owner of Woodton, Robert Alfred Suckling.*

I see now that this bit of chronology – something I paid no attention to when I first read the book – is very important. In that spring, Suckling proposes and Anna says yes. But by then you have been nine months dead. A respectable amount of time has passed. What seems likely now is that he proposed to you the spring before, the spring of 1838, months before you died. Is this what really happened? Is it possible that, whatever Suckling eventually feels for your sister Anna, however happy their eventual marriage, does she – and everyone else – have to live with the knowledge that he loved you first?

Mary comes in. Mary Sanders-Hewett.

So how are you doing? Are you OK in here? Hey, have you got enough light?

I lift my head and the room swims into view.

So how's it going? Is it any use? Are you finding anything?

I tell her I'm finding out a great deal.

She smiles.

Brilliant. I'll leave you to it, then. God, though, look at how dark it's got. You wouldn't know it was July, would you?

She flicks on the light for me and fuzzy electric light floods the page. I thank her. And am sucked straight back to Woodton.

It makes perfect sense, of course, that Florence chooses to leave all of this out of the published book. I keep forgetting, she has an agenda of her own.

Your sister Anna marries Robert Suckling, and they have a son called Thomas – Captain Thomas Suckling, Florence's future husband. But what if they don't marry, what then? What if Suckling marries someone else – you, for instance?

In the end, what it boils down to is this: you need to die in order for Thomas Suckling to be born. Life is like that, a series of domino knocks, a rattle of consequences. And why should Florence Suckling, family historian par excellence, bother admitting what a close call it was? How this so very nearly did not happen. How her long marriage to Captain Thomas Suckling owes its entire life and existence to the long-ago death of a twenty-one-year-old girl.

Actually, it's worse than that. It's bigger. Because, you know, if you hadn't died on that terrible summer night in Ipswich in 1838, if you had lived and married and had babies, then the whole Baron-Suckling history might have taken a different turn.

You, not Anna, would have been Mrs R.A.J. Suckling, mistress of Barsham. It would be your furniture, not Anna's, crowding Patrick Baron's Norwich apartment. Except, of course, there would never even have been a Norwich apartment at all. Because, if you had lived, Patrick Baron and his daughters would never have been born.

So there you are. It's easy. Florence only has to omit a dozen or so words – hardly a crime – in order to obliterate this inconvenient love affair. Your only love affair.

And who's it going to harm, after all, if the girl in question is long dead? If a person dies so young, so unrealised, then does it really matter what people write about her? Who's going to care about that person's right to an emotionally honest biography?

Your only love affair. That's what I just said. But going back to Jane Coulcher's unedited letter, there's more, and my heart stops all over again:

> Mary Yelloly and Charles Tyssen were said to be attached to each other, but Mary in pique engaged herself to Mr Brown. This was broken off.

You and Charles? Your cousin Charles? Charles who inherited Narborough whenever it was, and built a watermill there but, as far as I know, never married? You and Charles, one of the cousins you grew up and ran around with at Narborough, playing and shouting in the earthworks and – perhaps? – looking out over Norfolk from that secret attic door on the rooftops?

Did you love him, then?

And if so, who was this Mr Brown and what was the pique all about? I've only just got used to the possibility of your being engaged to Robert Suckling. How many lovers did you have?

The fair-haired girl sitting on the wall, swinging her legs and eating apples, has faded and a new one has taken her place: serious-eyed, delicious, ready for anything.

Ready to be loved. Or to love. Ready to be happy or sad, uncertain, excited, seduced, desired. Ready for the thrill of being wanted. Certainly nowhere near ready to die.

It's almost lunchtime and the rain has just about stopped when I come to the last revelation in this unedited manuscript. Or, OK, maybe not quite a revelation – more a quick sketch of Yelloly life lived on after your death. Maybe that's the reason it moves me so much – because you had no part to play in these months. Because you just weren't there any more.

It's another Yelloly journal, or extracts from one anyway, dated May–December 1839. It doesn't say who wrote it, but because you, Jane and Nick are all dead and everyone else seems to get a mention, it has to be Harriet.

These are strange days, sunny and bleak by turn. Poor Sophy is often quite unwell, but her fiancé the ever-devoted Robert Groome calls often to take her out for drives, or else to sit with her. Plenty of friends seem to call either to dine or play games.

There's battledore and shuttlecock outdoors, or in the big oak room on rainy days. Your mother takes painting lessons. It turns warm. A woman is killed in a thunderstorm at Bungay. And a second thunderstorm demolishes two sheep. Your sister makes a solemn note of this.

There's sadness too. Sadness about you:

In the evening we went to the church to see the Tablet to the memory of my two dearest sisters, Jane and Mary, and to weep over their graves and that of my dearest brother Nicholas; though we trust they are now in perfect happiness through our Lord and Saviour Jesus Christ.

254

Weep over their graves. But which graves and where are they exactly?

Meanwhile, Miss Lucy Suckling and her brother Robert start calling. Yes, that's the same Robert – the Robert who may have loved you first. Does he still think of you like that, I wonder? Has he cried about you, does he still mourn? Or has he moved on?

I have to tell you that he and his sister seem to find all sorts of excuses to call at Woodton. First they stop by to varnish some pictures. Then Robert begins a drawing of the *curious picture* over the oak-room chimney piece. He begins, which of course means he must keep on returning, if he hopes to finish it, that is.

On another occasion he stops by to read *The Siege of Corinth*. Or, he and his sister come and walk in the woods and everyone sits down to tell stories. I assume that *everyone* includes your sister Anna.

One day, Lucy Suckling comes over alone and has a long and serious talk with your mother about her family's affairs. She and Robert have had a *blow-up* with their father at Barsham. This makes some sense because the Revd Alfred Inigo Fox Suckling was a notorious spendthrift who almost ruined his family. It's only your father's later sensible handling of Anna's marriage contract that saves the Sucklings from complete ruin.

The next day, though, Robert calls at Woodton to sit under a tree and finish reading *The Lady of the Lake*.

After that, it all happens quite swiftly:

12th, Robert Suckling called; a very rainy day. He stayed in oak room and afterwards played battledore and shuttle-cock with Anna in the Hall. Robert Groome left us, and I sat with dear Sophy in the drawing room after he was gone.

13th, Robert Suckling came into the front of the house and looked at Papa cutting laurels. Anna and I were dressing to dine out at Mr Howe's with Papa and Mama.

14th, Tony and Robert Suckling called, also Mr Howes. After luncheon Robert and Anna, Sarah and I walked in ·the Shrubbery, when the announcement took place between R. Suckling and Anna. I trust God's Blessing will attend their engagement and that they may be very happy. He had a communication with Mama on his return, and in the evening with dear Papa, when he came to drink tea, and seemed the happiest of mortals.

I wonder what they say to each other, Robert Suckling and your father, as he snips away at the laurels? Do Anna and Harriet, upstairs dressing, snatch furtive glances out of an upstairs window, fully aware of what must be going on down there? Two men standing on the gravel, heads bent, earnestly talking. Are there embraces in that upstairs room, laughter, tears of happiness?

And what about your father? What does he really feel? Pride, excitement, or a touch of sadness? Is his joy for Anna eclipsed, however briefly, by his memories of your own all too brief love for this man, by the still raw fact of your young death?

The summer is full of joy, it must be. But November finds them all at Dawlish with the now severely ill Sophy. Meanwhile, Anna gets measles. Ellen also becomes unwell. And then there's a long break in the journal when Harriet herself succumbs to fever.

She gets better. So does Anna. So, for the moment, does Ellen. But on 10 December:

Dearest Sophy confined to her bed and very ill, the Clergyman came and administered the Sacrament to us all. She got into the water bed but did not like it. Robert Groome arrived, saw her for a moment, I went down for the first time since my illness. Sophy better – continues improving.

The journal ends here, but I don't really need any more. I know what happens next. Sophy doesn't continue improving. This is it. She dies a month later on 11 January. Just six months after you.

What's a *water bed*? Is it a normal thing in those days – used to prevent bed sores, perhaps? Or is it somehow associated with death? What's wrong with it, exactly? Why doesn't she like it?

She got into the water bed but did not like it. Why is it that those words fill me with such particular dread? Why do they seem to bring home more vividly than almost anything I've read so far the panic and confusion and terror of a young woman's final illness, the terrible, yawning momentum of loss?

Before I leave, Mary and I go to the pub across the road for lunch. Ten minutes later, her husband Paul joins us. The rain has stopped now and the trees are dripping. The air has the slightly chocolate smell of wet summer leaves.

Mary and I order fish and a glass of wine and Paul has the pie (I always have the pie!). They tell me that their son Sam Tyssen Sanders-Hewett has just got engaged. And we talk about all the Yelloly and Tyssen treasures that have been lost.

I tell them how I read in the manuscripts that your sister Anna's jewels – the Yelloly-Tyssen family jewels – were in her handbag, on their way to the mender's, when it was stolen at Cheltenham Railway Station, never to be recovered.

And Mary laughs, and then Paul tells me how the manuscripts themselves were almost lost in a flood at her parents' house in Sussex ten or fifteen years ago.

Yes, Mary says. He drove down there to rescue everything and I said to Paul, whatever you do, for God's sake get the books!

They were in a cabinet in the sitting room, Paul says. Fortunately high enough up to be unharmed. But it was a close thing. A few more inches of water and that would have been that.

A few more inches of water.

Your romantic and emotional history was nearly obliterated by a bossy Victorian historian with an agenda of her own in 1898. And a hundred years or so later, a Sussex flood almost finished off the job.

ROMANCE

How brilliant this life is,
with all its ways to wander.
New people to meet,
new problems to ponder.

In a million dusty years,
a new pair of shoes,
will scuff this sidewalk,
breathe in and rapture

perhaps pick up a pen
and capture.
Do all the things I did,
when I was confused.

Suffer at the hands of idiots,
ripped up and abused,
but still smile when
love comes round the corner.

Still see the girl with ivory eyes,
and need her, want her.

Never ever know where to begin,
dream till your head is all in a spin,
think wishful of all the things
you could have been,
but still know that whatever becomes
you'll never give in

Till it's Romance that's won.

9

OUR BOY HAS finally dropped out of school. Or at least, he does not actually drop. It is more that one day the strings of absences just join up together and become an absence so long, so extended that the school informs him that, unless he turns up on a certain day just to speak to them, he will no longer have his place.

He's dropped out of school but he still has his phone. It's the only thing he does have. I call him about every four or five days. Sometimes he answers and sometimes not. Sometimes he says he's busy and hasn't got time to talk. Other times he seems never to want to hang up.

Every time his phone goes straight to voicemail, or else rings and rings and there's no answer, I worry. I see him lying in a dark alley somewhere, frightened and alone, unable to move or call for help.

His father says that's ridiculous. He says he's no more or less likely to come to harm than any other eighteen-year-old boy. Less, probably, because he's smart, streetwise, strong and actually incredibly healthy.

Yes, I think, but the trouble is, in the life that our boy now leads – not going to school, not living in any fixed place, not having anywhere, in fact, where he regularly has to be – it would just be so easy for him to slip from view. Who would notice if he didn't drop by? Who would think anything of it if they didn't see him for a week or two?

I can't keep this idea in my head for long without starting to feel sick.

Then he finds a room in a house in Brixton. A man from Sierra Leone has a room to let. And the rent is cheap and his Benefit should cover it. The only problem is that, when he was evicted from the last flat, he never bothered informing the Benefit Office, even though we begged him to.

You're committing fraud if you don't tell them.

Well, what the fuck am I meant to do?

Tell them!

But my phone's out of charge.

Then go round there. Go today.

I can't go today. I've only just got up.

He never went. And we stopped asking him to.

But now at least he has an address again. I ask if I can come and see his new place. I could bring him some bedding.

Not quite yet, Mum. Let me get settled first, OK?

A week passes. Then another week. I call him one evening around eight and feel relief when he answers. I can hear noises in the background.

I'm on a train, he says.

A train where?

Just, you know, back to Streatham.

Not Brixton?

On my way to Brixton, yeah.

Overground?

Yeah.

It's easier for him to fare-dodge on the overground trains, I think.

He sounds tired. I ask him what he's been doing and he launches into another long, muddled story about how the Housing Benefit people have lost all his details. How first they told him he was eligible for back payment of Benefit and how then *some stupid fucker* lost the piece of paper and said he wasn't. And now they're changing their minds all over again. But they still can't say when they'll pay him or how much.

Well, you did a really stupid thing, didn't you, I tell him. When you didn't let them know you'd been evicted from the flat.

The words are hard. The words are true. But I know that my voice is soft.

But, he says, the phone reception cutting in and out, what the fuck did they expect? Have you any idea how hard it is, trying to manage your life when you've got nowhere to live?

I decide to move on.

So how're you paying your rent?

Well, at the moment, to be precise, I'm not.

But – doesn't your landlord mind?

He says nothing.

OK, but – so how are you managing? How are you eating? I'm not.

His voice is bleak.

Then please at least come home and let me cook you a meal. You can always come here for food, you know that.

OK, he says. Thanks.

We both know he won't come.

There are apple trees in our father's orchard. Plum trees too and damsons. When we lived there properly, we used to pick them and eat them, even cook with the apples. Now, though, no one touches them, they lie rotting on the ground, wasps crawling in and out of the ragged brown holes.

One weekend I think what a waste and how nice it would be to take some apples home and make a crumble. So I get a plastic bag and collect the best of the apples off the ground. I think about asking Daddy if it's OK to take them home – he doesn't want them, after all – but then I realise that it would be very hard to ask this question without using the word *home*. So I decide it's easier just to leave the bag of apples at the front of the house – outside the front door – and then, when our mother comes to collect us, I can pick it up at the last moment and take it without him knowing. It doesn't seem like a bad thing to do, more a diplomatic one.

I leave the bag there and go and do some other things.

But later, hours later, I see that the bag has gone and I flush. My knees go shaky and my ears feel hot. Has he found it and removed it? Is he angry? Does he think I was trying to steal from him?

Inside, he's watching TV. I offer to make him a cup of tea and he accepts. I bring him the tea, strong but milky the way he likes it, and he thanks me but says nothing else. Carries on watching his programme, smoking his cigarette. What should I do? Should I say something? I decide not.

An hour later, I check and the bag's still gone. Maybe it wasn't him after all. Maybe someone else took it. Maybe it was stolen. Whatever the explanation, I feel deep worry and another feeling too, a feeling I can't remember having felt before. It's shame. A strange and complicated sort of shame.

In the British Library, I find two books. One, *Two Suffolk Friends, Being Recollections of Robert Hindes Groome and Edward*

Fitzgerald, written by his son Francis Hindes Groome in 1895.

The other, *A Short Memoir of the Revd Robert Alfred Suckling* by Isaac Williams, Fellow of Trinity College Oxford, published in 1859.

I do have a copy of a portrait of Robert Suckling, from the National Portrait Gallery archives. It shows a weak-faced young man with annoying hair. An anxious little frown. Exactly my idea of a Victorian country parson.

I got him wrong. He's nothing like that at all.

He's born in 1818, eldest son of the Suckling family and heir to Woodton. He goes to sea at thirteen and remains a sailor till 1839 – the year he gets engaged to your sister. He then gives up a promising naval career (he is, after all, directly descended from Lord Nelson) because he feels so strongly called to the Church. His experiences in the Navy are tough. The ship is struck by yellow fever:

20 Jan 1838

I have had the fever and am now convalescent. What has not happened in the short time elapsed since I was taken ill? I have been at death's door and calmly said to myself, death is approaching. It has no horrors for me. I fear not that I could have no hope. It appears to me a dream, I cannot imagine how I could have been so indifferent, so hardened; but I find it is the nature of the disease; all are so. We are on our way to the Island of Ascension. The ship is a perfect pesthouse. Our decks are covered with the sick. We have only 5 men as well. We are becalmed on the Line. It is horrible; nothing but the groans of the sick and the ravings of the dying are to be heard. I have been in this state. I do not feel thankful that I am preserved; I ought to do and I strive . . .

I do not feel thankful that I am preserved. It is in this state of mind that the twenty-one-year-old Robert Suckling returns to Woodton to visit his grandmother Mrs Fox. This is what he's just been going through when you meet him. He has only just left the pesthouse.

And, judging by the dates, your walk in the woods together must take place just after the episodes described above. Terrible, life-changing episodes, experiences that cannot easily be let go.

You are both so young, both just twenty-one. What do you talk about as you crunch over the bracken, the hardened ground? Does he tell you honestly about the things he's seen, the dangers he's faced? Does he know that you're ill? Does he return to sea, in love with you and engaged, only to return to find himself bound to an invalid who will not last the summer? The green shoots of spring are all around you. Love is good. Do you even ever see each other again?

In 1839, months after your death, Robert retires from the Navy to study for the Church and that same year, because of the crisis brought on by his father's spending, he agrees to *cut off the entail of the Woodton property.* Woodton Hall is sold and falls into the hands of the Fellowes – who immediately pull it down. Brick by brick. The Suckling Curse.

In fact, it's only thanks to your own father's calm clear-thinking that the Sucklings retain any property at all. Once Robert is engaged to your sister, Dr Yelloly is so firm about the marriage settlements that he more or less rescues the family from ruin.

Your sister and Robert are married on 22 April 1840 and live happily at Barsham – modest compared to the grandeur of Woodton – with their six children, who include Florence Suckling's future husband Thomas.

Robert's death comes suddenly. He's just taken Holy Communion at church on All Saints' Day, when he suffers *with some attack of internal inflammation.* For two days he writhes in agony on the floor, and then he dies. He's just thirty-three. Your sister is a widow for the rest of her life.

The book about your sister Sophy's fiancé Robert Groome gives only the baldest details of his life.

Born in Framlingham in 1810, second son of the Revd John Hindes Groome, ex-Fellow of Pembroke, Cambridge, Rector of Earl Soham and Monk Soham. He goes to Norwich School, where he meets your brothers John and Sam. Then up to Cambridge, before being ordained as a curate in 1833. He is friends with many writers and thinkers of his time. In 1845 he succeeds his father as Rector of Earl Soham and Monk Soham and later becomes Archdeacon of Suffolk.

Yes, yes, I think, but come on, when are we going to get to the bit about Sophy? Instead we pass straight through the 1830s, before coming to this:

On 1st February 1843 he married my mother, Mary Jackson (1815–93), the youngest daughter of Revd James Jackson, Rector of Swanage.

I've been naive. Just like Florence Suckling, this biographer has an agenda of his own. What interest of his could it possibly serve to mention his father's youthful love affair with a girl who died? Why bring up any adventures, romantic or otherwise, that might threaten the smooth, uncluttered line that leads to his own birth?

What about Robert, though? How do things really work out for him? Does he love Mary Jackson with a mature intensity that shows his earlier romance up for exactly what it was: a youthful passion, never really tested, always doomed to come to nothing?

Or does he spend the rest of his life in the grip of a compromise, trapped in a perfectly adequate and fruitful marriage that nevertheless never rouses in him a tenth of the excitement and longing that he felt for your sister?

A few pages later, I find the closest thing I'm likely to get to an answer: an old photograph of Robert – the first and only one I've ever seen.

He's standing near a pond on the Grass Walk. A tall, lean, dark-faced man in late middle age, wearing a long black coat, bowler hat and tense, rather humourless expression. He could be an undertaker.

Robert Groome. I scrutinise him – his face, his long feet in their shiny shoes, the long shadow that he casts – but what exactly am I looking for? Just a clue, I suppose. Just any flicker of something in that face that suggests he was the same eager young man who once wrote all those sweet love poems to a Yelloly girl.

A woman, someone I was briefly quite good friends with a long time ago, has been killed in a car crash. Late at night, in Devon, her car sped off the road and into a field. Because she used to be on TV, her death makes the papers. Otherwise I doubt I would even have known. I'm surprised, even a little embarrassed, at how upset I am. I haven't thought about her in years. What right do I have to cry?

Our boy and her boy were best friends at primary school. They made friends in reception on the very first day, aged five. And it turned out she lived just around the corner from us, a single parent – her child's father had always refused to have anything to do with him, she said. So we started sharing the school walk, taking it in turns to take and collect the boys.

I liked her. She wasn't someone I would necessarily have been best friends with, but she had the kind of energy that swept you in, lifted your spirits. When I went to that flat – a big sunny upstairs maisonette – she was always making pancakes or painting a wall or about to order a bed or a wardrobe and dying to show me the catalogue and hear what I thought.

In the evening when she came by to collect her boy, she'd sometimes stop for a glass of wine, breathless with news of her day, and we'd sit in the warm chaos of our kitchen while the children – ecstatic at gaining an unasked-for reprieve – went on playing. One night she came round and, eyes shining, told me she was pregnant. The baby's father was married to someone else, she said, but it was fine. He was being so supportive, so generous. And she seemed to mean it. She kept her loneliness so tightly under wraps that at the time it never really occurred to me to wonder if she was just being brave.

And when the baby – another boy – came, I visited her in her big white bed in the private hospital where, surrounded by flowers and cards, she asked if I'd be his godmother. I hesitated – I'd only known her a few months. But saying no felt difficult, so I said yes.

I saw my friend and her baby several times in those newborn days. I know I took him presents and I think I tried hard to believe in my role as his godmother. I can still see his round blond head, can still remember his soft clean weight on my lap.

And then we changed schools and she moved away – where? To the West Country? I can't even remember – and I never saw her again. Just like that. I don't even remember how hard we tried to stay in touch, or if we tried at all. I know I felt a little guilty about the godmother thing, but I consoled myself with the indisputable fact that the promised christening had never taken place – or at least, not with me as godmother it hadn't.

Her car skidded off the road at 10.20 p.m. I think it was a Friday. She was alone. She was pronounced dead at the scene.

I try to remember what she was like. All I get are flashes of her energy. The bounce of her dark, shoulder-length hair. Some kind of puffa jacket she wore. And I think of her two boys, the big boy who must be our boy's age now, and the smaller one who was so very nearly my godson.

Do you think he got another godmother? I ask the boy's father. Do you think I ought to try and make contact?

He looks at me as if I'm mad.

After all this time, that would be entirely the wrong thing to do, he says.

He's right, of course. And it takes me longer than maybe it should to see what this is really all about. That it's not about her at all, but about me. Me and my boy. Like just about everything else these days, every trail, every thought, every tangle of feeling leads straight back to him. My craving for what he was, for what we had.

Because, when I think about my friend, what I see most clearly isn't us, but them. Not her, but him. Our two boys. And the sheer, uncomplicated happiness of those days when, yelling and bumping around together, they'd beg to be allowed *just one more half-hour, pleeease!* before we'd peel them apart and, laughing, take them home.

I remember one time when our boy was a baby, about four or five months old, and he cried so much he made me cry too.

It was hopeless. His father was away working abroad and so I was alone and he cried and cried. Nothing I could do would make him stop. And I was twenty-nine and a new mother and all alone and it was a hot, light May evening similar to the evening eighteen years in the future when he would turn around and hit me so hard. But right now he was tiny and he was crying and I just didn't know what to do.

I fed him, I changed him, I burped him, I soothed him, and he screamed and screamed. I put him on the bed. He screamed. I picked him back up off the bed. He screamed on my shoulder, great gusty sobs that shuddered through his whole small body. I kissed his face and held him right out in front of me and tried to make him look at me, but only his mouth was open. Eyes tight shut, his whole face given over to screaming. I felt like shaking him but I didn't. Instead I began to sob.

And at that moment, his grandmother, my mother-in-law, happened to ring. Hearing the screaming and also the tears in my voice, she took command.

All right, she said, now listen to me. You're going to do exactly as I say.

OK.

First, you're going to put down the phone. Then, while I wait on the other end, you're going to pick up the baby and you're going to walk very calmly to his room and put him down in his cot. Then you're going to shut the door and come back here and sit on the bed and pick up the phone again. Do you think you can manage that?

Still crying, I told her I thought I could.

The screaming continued while I put down the phone and did as I was told. It continued and then it slowed down and almost stopped. Then it started up again, then it almost stopped again. I held the phone to my ear and used the other hand to grab a bunch of tissues and dab at my eyes.

All right?

Yes. Thanks.

Has he stopped?

Not quite.

Now, when you say goodbye to me, you're going to go and run a nice deep bath and pour yourself a glass of wine. Then you're going to get in that bath and – even if he's still crying – you're going to try really hard to drink the wine and take some deep breaths and wait for him to stop. Because he will stop, you know. He'll fall asleep. He's exhausted, the little monkey. But you know something, so are you. You're shattered. And you need rest as much as he does. And I'll tell you something else that's worth remembering. No baby ever died of crying.

The boy agrees to have lunch with me. Or, to be accurate, he agrees to let me buy him food.

Having got that far, I call him throughout the day to try and arrange it but his phone's always off. So I send him a text. Then another.

Don't chase him too hard, his father warns.

In the end, at about four-thirty, he calls me.

Can you call me back? he says.

I dial. It's an 0208 number. I think I recognise it as Brixton or Streatham.

Where are you? I ask him.

Oh, just somewhere.

Are you OK? I've been trying to get you all day.

Yeah. Sorry. Phone's not charged.

You sound tired.

I've only just woken up.

But it's almost five.

Yeah well. I didn't get to sleep till late.

Why? What were you doing?

I was all over the place. Look, Mum, I wondered if I could ask you a favour?

Sure, I say a little cautiously. What is it?

But I only want a yes-or-no answer. I don't want any of your negotiations, OK?

What's the favour? I say again, as his father looks up from reading the paper and starts to shake his head.

He explains that he's behind with his rent. Because the Benefit Office owe him such a backlog. He has literally no money.

Are you managing to eat? I ask him straight away.

Yeah yeah, but you see it's not very fair on my landlord. So I wondered whether as a gesture of good faith you and Dad could just give him a cheque for £500. He wouldn't cash it, of course. I just think it would make him feel more secure, that's all.

I pause. I ask him whether the landlord knows he somehow managed to afford a £200 ticket for the Reading Festival only a few weeks ago.

That's hardly relevant.

I'm not sure your landlord would agree with that. I think it's actually very relevant indeed, since it's what you've spent your Benefit on.

Oh come on!

And anyway there's really no such thing as a cheque that someone doesn't cash. What I mean is, he would almost certainly cash it and I wouldn't blame him, not if you owe him rent. And remember, I continue, that you already owe us more than £1,000 in rent from the flat you were evicted from. We're not even counting the cost of the termination –

Oh for fuck's sake, Mum –

No, don't you see – if you'd just try and start paying a little of that back – just £1 per week would do, as a gesture of good faith – then we'd be able to lend you more.

I just can't believe you won't fucking well help me –

You have no idea, I say softly, how much we want to help you.

Well, I said I wanted a yes-or-no answer, he reminds me angrily.

I'm afraid it's a no, then.

I ask if we can arrange lunch tomorrow. He says he doesn't know what he's doing yet, that he'll have to see.

Anyway, he adds, I'm not sure it's a good idea. I've been getting pretty wasted in the day.

Wasted on what?

You know on what.

You mean cannabis?

You know I do a lot of other drugs too. For God's sake, Mum. Don't pretend you don't know that.

And he hangs up, leaving me bruised.

When I tell his father about this, he smiles, a long sad smile.

Oh darling, but don't you see what he was doing?

What?

Don't you realise he did it on purpose?

He did?

Of course he did. He knows how that would make you feel, to hear that about drugs. And you refused to give him money, and so he punished you. He knows exactly how to make you hurt.

★   ★   ★

274

We go out to dinner at the house of good friends, people we haven't seen in a while. Everyone stays too late, everyone drinks too much. It's past one o'clock and no one's even begun to call taxis and more wine is poured and I think, This is good. We hardly ever have fun like this any more. We've let ourselves get much too sad lately. We should say yes to things like this more often.

And then one of the guests, a sharp, attractive woman with fair hair, whose job is something to do with theatre in education, asks if our eldest has applied to university yet.

I try to do what we always do with strangers. Tell just enough of the truth not to have to tell a lie, then move on.

Actually, the boy's father often doesn't even do this much. Often he's all for saying nothing, or even lying if necessary. What's the point? he says. Why should we let this become the narrative of our lives?

He's right, of course. All he wants is some time off. But I find it very hard to lie successfully.

He's dropped out of school, I hear myself telling her. And he's not living with us at the moment. He has quite a big problem with cannabis.

The table goes quiet. I realise how what I just said sounds.

Just cannabis? someone says, as they always do. And I can feel it starting. That's not so bad then, someone else will say. It's a phase they all go through, another will add. All well meant. Intending to reassure. Instead:

Does their school have a drugs problem? someone asks me and I think for a moment.

Not really, no. There are drugs, yes, obviously, as in all secondary schools, but I wouldn't call it a problem.

Oh come on, says the theatre woman, I know that school. I've done some work there. It's full of drugs –

Oh no, I reply, I really don't think so. And anyway that's not where he started smoking –

It was some kids from a public school, a boarding school, actually, his father tells them with a bitter little laugh. People he hooked up with in the holidays.

But the woman insists she has good reason to believe the school does have a significant drugs problem.

But surely no more than any other London secondary school? I hear myself protest.

Oh, yes, I would say so.

And my heart sinks and I can't work out why. Does she think she's somehow doing us a favour, shifting the blame on to the school? I think of the calm, hard-working, sedate and thoughtful place we've been sending our children for the past few years. Then I remember the blank, well-meaning faces of the teachers as we tried to tell them how worried we were about our child. I push that thought from my mind as a hard lump of panic rises in my throat.

I just don't think we can blame the school in this, I say and I throw a beseeching look at the boy's father, who, to my dismay, chucks it straight back.

And I see that he's listening hard to what the woman is saying now and, arms folded, frowning and nodding. How can he do this? I hear him telling her he thinks she may be right. Maybe the school has had a role to play.

But, I begin to say, it's not the old-style cannabis but skunk we're talking about.

Oh yes, someone agrees. That stuff is lethal.

Lethal, yes. Suddenly I feel so tired.

And maybe she notices the expression on my face, because now she's telling me that her own children are younger, admittedly, they haven't hit that age yet.

So you see, she continues, her eyes alive and ready for more, this is all very interesting to me.

Go away, I think.

She waits for me to say something.

I'm finding this quite hard to talk about right now, I tell her. I'm sorry, but I can't tell you how stressful and sad all of it has been for us. There's so much other stuff – stuff that you don't even know.

The whole table is silent and the boy's father is looking at me. The look is the equivalent of a kick on the shin.

I'm sorry, I say.

And I pick up a napkin and put it to my eyes because for some reason now I'm crying. How did that happen? Our hostess reaches out and rubs my shoulder.

Hey. I'm so sorry, she says.

And theatre woman leans across and also gives me a kindly look.

It's OK, she says, I do know how you feel, you know. My son's dyspraxic. What I mean is, I know what you're going through.

The boy's father says I behaved badly. In the taxi home, he's cool with me and, when I demand to know why he didn't stick up for me, he tells me that my reaction was completely over the top.

But she was attacking me, I say, feeling the frustration rise again. I didn't mean to be rude but I just couldn't take her fucking superior attitude.

She wasn't attacking you at all and you were rude. You brought the subject up –

Only when she asked me –!

Yes, but you didn't have to tell her anything at all and yet you chose to. You can't blame the poor woman for not knowing the whole story. She was just trying to engage with you, that's all.

Hmm. Well, maybe I don't want to be engaged with.

Silence as the red and blue lights of late-night London arc and bend across the cab.

I still think you could have stuck up for me, I tell him. Whether or not you thought I was right. Couldn't you see I was upset?

Yes, I could see that and I was trying to calm you down.

Oh great. Thanks very much.

Come on. He puts a hand on my knee. There's no need to be like that.

I pull my knee away and sigh.

I'm just so sick of trying to explain this thing to people. I don't want to know what they do or don't think. I just don't want this to be the story of our lives.

It's not the story of our lives. Don't be so dramatic.

OK, I don't want it to be how things turned out, that's all.

He looks at me for a moment in the half-light and I've no idea what he's thinking.

Back in Suffolk, I finally call Monica Churchill, the former church warden of All Saints, Woodton, whose number Steve and Elaine Hill gave me back in the spring. I ask her if she has any idea where the Yellolys were buried.

Well, let me see, she says, there were, if I remember rightly, two charts. One I think was made in the 1960s and another in the 1980s. We tried hard to do an updated version – some of the stones are really incredibly hard to decipher – but we tried. I'll look on the charts and see if I can see any Yellolys, and if I can, well, you're very welcome to borrow them – the charts, I mean. I expect you'd want to go up to the church and have a look, wouldn't you?

I thank her and arrange to phone on Thursday morning before I set off – just to check she's actually found the charts.

It's all very exciting, she tells me. I only hope I can be of help to you, that's all.

But Wednesday night she calls me to say she's already looked at the charts in detail and there's not a single Yelloly on them.

Really? I can't hide the disappointment in my voice. Not a single one?

I simply can't understand it. They have to be somewhere, don't they? Well, I'm stumped, I really am. It's a complete mystery. So frustrating. Oh dear, you've really got me guessing now.

Well, it's very kind of you to have gone to this much trouble, I tell her.

But it does seem strange, she goes on, because the oldest graves, you know, the ones in the long grass – someone's supposed to be cutting it but of course they haven't – well, all those ones right at the back of the church – it's a conservation area, that bit now – are from 17-something and therefore far pre-date your Yellolys.

So – what? You'd think the Yellolys would be round the front.

Exactly. You know, near the porch, near the entrance. Lots of the graves nearer the front of the church seem to date from around the early 1800s.

So that really is where Mary's should be.

Exactly, yes.

I ask her then if she thinks there might be some kind of family tomb or crypt in the church. Because the plaque for

279

Jane does say *near this place and in the same tomb*. The question is, how near? And Florence's book does also state that Nicholas was buried in All Saints, Woodton among the old Suckling tombs.

That's very interesting, Monica agrees.

But are there any tombs actually inside the church? When I was there looking around, I couldn't see where there would be the space for any.

Well, she agrees, I was warden there for all those years and certainly I never came across one. But then again – I know there are a lot of Suckling stones in the floor near the altar, for instance.

But would Sucklings actually have been buried under there, I mean actually under the floor of the church?

I've really no idea. I suppose I ought to know, but I don't. But even so, none of the stones say *Yelloly*.

That's true, I agree.

Monica sighs.

How very frustrating, she says again.

I thank her anyway and we agree we'll keep in touch and she'll certainly call me if she comes across any new information, but there's probably no point in my coming to see her tomorrow.

But next morning, at nine o'clock sharp, the phone rings.

Monica Churchill here. Well! I have to say, this is quite exciting. Because, you see, I'm a bell-ringer, and last night I was up at the church for practice as usual. And I was feeling so curious about everything we'd talked about and so, in our break – they don't give us long – I went in and had a good look around and just on impulse I pulled up a piece of carpet on the floor near the aisle and, would you believe it, there they were –!

There what were?

The two names!

Which names?

Dr John Yelloly and his wife!

Really? You mean – what? Right there under the carpet?

Yes, right there in the aisle. After all this time! You'd never have known it but there's definitely some kind of a large Yelloly gravestone under there – and I really think it may be more than just the two of them. And, well, you see I didn't have long to look as they don't give us much time off from the bell-ringing, but you might want to go and have a look yourself.

Is that OK?

Certainly it is. You're very welcome to roll back any carpets you like and if anyone queries it just say that Monica Churchill gave you permission.

I drive back to All Saints, Woodton that afternoon. Drive through the quiet, pale streets of Bungay, past the roundabout where there are always chickens pecking, and up along the Norwich road. The air is soft and bright and the late-June countryside is perfect – poppies and cow parsley in the hedgerows, specks of birds sailing high in the heat haze.

I park by the verge as usual. Deep tyre marks in the dried mud. Very different from when I came here with Julia in the winter. But just like on that day, there's no one around as I walk up the gravel path, past the graves from the early 1800s, no sound but the faraway putter of a tractor or combine.

I put my hand on the skinny metal latch. It lifts and falls with a satisfying clang. The porch gate with its wire mesh shudders behind me and I push open the familiar heavy door, catch the warm, waxy scent of flowers. The dim, muted silence of a church on a summer's afternoon. Lilies and dusty kneelers.

The first thing I notice is that there are actually several carpets. Leading from the door where I'm standing now and right up the aisles. Why have I never thought to look under them before? And how do I know which is the one that Monica pulled up?

I go right up the aisle towards the altar and start by pulling back the rubber edge of a smallish carpet to reveal – yes – a Suckling stone underneath. You can tell by its length that it's a grave. Another very long red carpet that goes all the way down the aisle, but looks as if it would be heavy to roll back.

So I decide to start again somewhere else. There's a much smaller blue carpet that leads horizontally from the door of the church as you go in. Might as well try that one. Not so heavy and easy to flip the edge of it back, so I walk over and do it.

And straight away there he is: *Nicholas Yelloly*.

I continue pulling the carpet back. *Jane Davison Yelloly*. And a couple of feet further along: *Mary Yelloly*.

You.

Just under the carpet, just behind the pew where Julia and I sat and talked on that winter's day. One long gravestone with three names clearly carved into it. *Nick, Jane, Mary*.

After all this time. Here you are. Here you always were. After all my wondering, all my searching, it really is this easy. I get down on my hands and knees and run my finger over those letters – the M, the A, the R, the Y.

But what are you? What exactly is under here? Teeth, hair, bones? Dense, hard, porous. Calcium. Phosphorus. Or dust?

It doesn't matter. Right now, crouching here on this floor on a hot, light summer's day, I'm the closest I'll ever be to what is left of you.

★   ★   ★

I'd always imagined your burial takes place outside – at night in that quiet churchyard, somewhere under those trees, Woodton Hall silhouetted against a dark navy sky. Dark-clad figures. A slice of moon illuminating the flat side of a shovel.

But I was wrong. That's not how it is at all.

Instead they must all come in here. Must all somehow file in and crowd round, standing right here in the cool heart of the church where I'm kneeling now.

But how? Are these pews here, or are they added later? And isn't it difficult to prise up Nick's heavy stone barely eighteen months after it's laid? How do they do it? Do they have to break the floor to lift it, to get it up?

And how does it feel to be your mother, your father, your brothers and sisters? To stand here and watch as the deep, dark space they haven't glimpsed in more than a year is smashed right open all over again and you and Jane are lowered in?

I'm thirteen, then fourteen. At night when we're staying there, Daddy comes to say goodnight and he asks me if I've started my periods yet.

I'm not quite sure about this question. Part of me understands perfectly that he might want to know – so many details of my life he never gets to hear about these days, so many things he's shut out of. But another part of me feels it's none of his business, it's my business. The secret velvety workings of the insides of my body are a mystery even to me and certainly not for anyone else to know.

I glance away and bite my finger. Not yet, I say.

Another thing he does that I don't like: when he kisses me goodnight – he's always kissed me goodnight and there's nothing wrong with that – he sort of half kisses and half breathes in my ear so it tickles. He always did this when I was little – it was one of our special jokes – but now I'm getting too old and I don't like it, but it's hard to know what to say. I don't want to hurt him. I'm so glad he's in a good mood. But I don't really like the smell of him any more and I don't like the wet feeling in my ear either.

After he's been to me, I hear him go and do the same to my sisters and I hear the shrieks of laughter. But it's easier for them, I think, because they're still young and they share a room.

I'm fifteen and I start my periods, but I don't tell him. At home, Mum's really good, just the kind of mum you need when your periods start. Coming to stay with him and managing all that stuff – sanitary towels and pains in your stomach and all that – is a bit hard, but I do it somehow. And I've started wearing make-up. A bit of kohl and mascara. He says nothing but I feel him looking at me and I know what he's thinking. He's thinking I look like my mother. He always said she wore too much make-up and somehow, in his head, I think he thinks that has something to do with why she left him.

I'm fifteen and at weekends there are quite often parties and, when I stay with him, I have to miss them. Part of me doesn't mind because I'm still quite shy about boys, but another part of me would really like to go.

Can't you ask your dad to pick you up? my friends say.

They ask it impatiently, innocently. It's the kind of thing their fathers would do, but their fathers are tall, smiley, stooping and kind. They don't realise what a big deal it would be for me, what a non-starter it is. Can I imagine my father doing that? Taking or fetching me from a party the way my mother and my stepfather do? Can I imagine even asking him? I tell my friends I don't mind missing the parties. It's quite nice actually to have a weekend off, relaxing and doing nothing much.

I take my O levels and I'm expected to do well. I work hard, I'm good at English, languages. I'm a linguist. You could do anything, says my mum. Be a bilingual secretary, work in Europe!

Sixth form will be great because I'm going to do just English, French and German and an extra O level in Spanish. No more sciences. And you get to wear your own clothes. We've already been allocated our tutor groups.

But at the end of the summer term, the headmistress – who I've never spoken to in my life except to shake her hand on speech day – asks to see me in her study. I go in, my face red and my limbs fizzy with nerves. I've almost never been in trouble in my life. The only school rule I've ever broken is the one about not eating your sandwiches on the tennis court. What can I have done?

She's standing there in the window, framed in sunshine. Her little dog at her feet. She looks just like the Queen and it's not just me, everyone thinks so. It's a school joke that she looks like the Queen. She waits a moment before speaking.

I'm so sorry, Julie, to hear that you will be leaving us, she says. We'd all rather hoped you'd stay on and go into the sixth form.

I stare at her. I don't know what to say. A whole new wave of blush rises from my chest and up my face.

But – I'm not leaving, I say, hearing how stupid the words sound as they come out.

She looks surprised and she goes to her desk and picks up a letter.

You don't know about this?

I shake my head.

Well, your father has written to say you're leaving at the end of term. I think you'd better speak to him. He's obviously in some financial difficulty. He says he can't afford to pay the school fees any longer.

Our boy is homeless again. He's moved out of his Brixton bedsit, leaving a guitar as hostage for the rent he owes his landlord. It's worth about £600, he assures me. No it isn't, his father says. I bought it for him. It's worth £200 new. The way he's treated it, probably a lot less.

The boy has become very hard to get hold of. Most of the time his phone is turned off. I try him all day and finally at 9 p.m. he answers.

Hey, Mum.

Are you OK? Why don't you ever answer your phone?

It's not fucking well charged. The charger's somewhere else. It only gives me about two minutes then it cuts out.

So – where are you?

Around.

What?

All I can hear are male voices in the background.

I said around.

Have you eaten today?

Not really.

Well, can I come and get you? Take you for supper?

Um. Not now.

Have you got somewhere to sleep tonight?

I dunno.

Well – come and sleep here.

It's not that simple, Mum.

I realise then what the jittery wobble in his voice is. His teeth are chattering.

Are you cold?

Nah. Just a bit wasted. Look, I gotta go, Mum.

But –

The phone goes dead.

I dial again. Voicemail. I sit for a few moments, take some breaths.

Things I think about when I think about my son. The shy, slightly half-hearted space he takes up when he stands in a doorway. The warmth and humour at the edges of his voice. The way when he was little he couldn't say the word *kangaroo* properly.

Kang-arrooo.

A thousand bath times when he was small. Hooking my hands under his arms, the swinging lightness of his small wet body, legs bent. The hooded towel with the yellow duck embroidered on it. The clean sweetness of his baby saliva, the warmth of his breath, the hard pink ridge of his gums.

The tickle of his hair on my face on a Sunday morning when he crawled into our bed and tried to kiss me awake. The sound of *Chuckle Brothers* on TV as his father and I struggled to go on sleeping. The flecks of hardened Weetabix that would never completely come off our bedroom carpet. The time we waited at the doctor's surgery while he was sick over and over again into a towel and was so brave and didn't complain once.

The way he walks down the street with his head slightly tilted to one side. His lopsided walk. His clever grey eyes. The unexpected depth of his voice. The fact that he has read Keats, Wilde, Joyce. And can write poetry that really moves me. The fact that he understands politics and history and philosophy. The fact that, having let go of his education, he may never have the thrill of learning any more about these subjects.

The way he dropped by one day recently and asked if he could play me a couple of songs he'd just written and I said yes, but let me just fetch Dad, because I so wanted to include him, and he said OK but you could tell he was shyer of playing in front of both of us. And how I wondered, then, whether I'd done the right thing, forcing these two together like this. And how I almost cried, watching him perched on the arm of the sofa just as if life was normal, looking at his fingers, then back into our eyes, singing and playing with such enjoyment and conviction.

The fact that I'll probably never live with him again. That I'll never again walk into a room and find him there, asleep, arms flung out, mouth open, cat curled against him, and be able to know that he's a hundred per cent safe. The fact that he asked me with real interest the other day what I was writing and I was so tempted to tell him. Tempted yet terrified.

The fact that it's getting cold outside again now and he hasn't got a winter coat. There are holes in his shoes. And the other day, when it was raining so hard, he told me he had plastic bags on his feet over his trainers and people in the café were laughing at him. The fact that he too was able to laugh when he told me this. His sense of humour. That and his warmth and his crazy, unnerving optimism.

The fact that I'm not allowed to buy him things because if I do I will be padding his corners, enabling and encouraging his dependency on drugs. The fact that he will only truly be able to hit rock bottom when he's cold and hungry and desperate and can go no lower. The fact that I find this fact very hard to think about. The fact that I ignored all of this the other day and topped up his phone and bought him a sandwich and didn't tell his father. The fact that I can't decide if I feel guilty about this or not.

Things I can't do any more: I can't go near the baby departments of any stores, not ever, not even to walk through them to get to another department. Just not worth the pain.

I can't open our photo albums. Not at the moment. I can't risk seeing that small boy smiling at me from between those pages, having fun in a time when the future was still a place alive with possibility. I can't risk seeing myself there either – a light-hearted, long-haired girl in a red Miss Selfridge coat, a girl who believed that, caring for her children as she did, only good things could possibly lie ahead.

I can't drive the car fast any more. I've accepted that. I haven't been able to drive on a motorway or even a fast A road in six months. I'm afraid of what will happen if my heart speeds up and I lose control. Obliterated by my own momentum. For the moment, I take the train. Better for the planet, I tell myself.

I don't want anyone to ask me how I am because I don't know how I am. OK, I do. I am raw. I am boring. I am flattened, deadened. I have nothing in my mind except the deep black hole that is the loss of my child. The feel of him spilling and spilling out of that hole. How do I feel? Please don't ask me. You don't want to know how that feels.

There is never a single moment when he's not in my head and heart, the backdrop to everything I think or feel or do. Whole days go by now when I don't really think of him at all. Both of these statements are true.

And then: I come into a room late at night, maybe our bedroom or maybe my study, or else I round the stairs on to the landing, and I catch sight of you for a moment. A quick, split-second blur of grey clothes. Grey or maybe blue. The soft, creased edge of your clothes. Hurrying away.

Mary?

Even though it's not possible, still there you are – a young, fair-haired woman, a curl bouncing on your neck, hand briefly on or near the door. Almost, but not quite, visible to me.

Mary? Is it you?

Silence. The cat yawns, gets up, stretches, lies back down again. Somebody laughs and I don't think it's me.

When my parents' divorce was originally settled in court, it was agreed our father would pay our school fees until we left school. Now he's saying I should leave school now. Because I'm sixteen, he's not paying. He says I can go and do a secretarial course. After all, he left school at fifteen, and hasn't he done perfectly well for himself?

My mother says I don't need to worry. She says that all she needs to do is go back to court and they will make him pay. She wants me to write a nice letter, addressed to him, telling him exactly why I want to stay on at school:

Dear Daddy,
I haven't got my O level results yet but I got very good results in my mocks, mostly As and Bs, and I want to stay on and do three A levels. After that I plan to go to university to study English or maybe languages. I may even sit Oxbridge . . .

I don't have to go to court with my mother, because I'm too young. But the letter is read out as proof of my serious academic intentions, and we win. He has to pay.

There was never any question really, my mother assures me. It was always agreed that he would pay for your education for as long as you wanted to study. Now at least there won't be any problem when your sisters' time comes.

I dread the next weekend I see him. I am terrified, tense with guilt and dread. What will he say, what will he do?

He says nothing at all. He is cool with me. He does not make eye contact, only speaks to me if he has to. He is normal with the girls, laughing, chatting about TV. Otherwise it's OK. Nothing terrible happens.

Now, every weekend I visit is the same – cool, tense, yet uneventful. Sometimes – in fact more and more – he cancels at the last minute and we stay at home and I am so relieved. And in my memory now, those cold, angry weekends are a blank. I've lost them, chosen to let them go. If anything else bad ever happened, it's slipped off the edge of my mind and is safely gone.

And then, finally, a letter comes – for me, from him. He says that, in the light of all that's happened, he thinks it would be better if he didn't see me again.

And I stand in the garage at the back of the house and I sob quite hard, but not for long. Tears cancelled out by the thought of all those free weekends.

I'm seventeen and my father doesn't want to see me any more. I don't tell many people. The only thing I know is that when I grow up I will be a better parent to my children than my father has been to me. No parent should ever reject a child. I will love my children. They will never be afraid of me. There will never be any terrible, stupid rules. I will love them. I will just love them.

Some days I feel I'm getting closer, getting so close. Other days I know what I think I've always known. That I'm never going to find you. That it's not even what I came here for. It never was. That everything I've done these last months, every place I've been, every step I've tried to take towards you has really just been one more step inside myself.

Following Jeremy Howard down the dark corridors at Carrow Abbey. Standing on the windy parapet at Narborough with Joanne and David – both the man and the boy, as the wind lifts his hair – the whole of Norfolk spread out before us. Watching the brown owl rise through the trees in the churchyard with Julia. Drinking tea in the converted stables with Steve and Elaine. Eating Bryony's stewed apple while Fred the greyhound and a whole undiscovered box of Yelloly treasures watch me do it. Your mother's little purse, found all over again and safe at my feet in the Town Hall where Regina Spektor sings. A family romance, a lifetime of faith and hope, drowning in volume, feeling the beat.

You go too fast and you can't slow down. So you panic. All those unanswered questions clenched like dust between your teeth.

But you discover little things about a person and you start to get a picture. You can't help it, you just do. And soon it's irresistible, you start to let yourself think this might not necessarily have to be all, might not have to be the end. Why should it all grind to a halt right here, right now, when there could just be a better resolution? A lovelier one. A more hopeful one. *Oh! Let it be Thy pleasure to turn these shadows to our eternal benefit.*

Turn these shadows.

Some days I even think I could have got to know you, been your friend. I could be your friend. And if that's true, then surely death could lose its grip? And it can't be long then before the inevitable happens.

★   ★   ★

I'll find myself one warm spring evening on some familiar rough track, maybe through farmland, maybe on the edge of a field. I don't know what month it is or even what year, but it feels warm, the air soft and light on my face. And I'll make my slow way along the track and, sure enough, there at the very end under the big old tree, the big old blazing tree, a slender, fair figure will be waiting for me.

You. Or, not you, but her. She.

She'll have her back to me − her slender, narrow-shouldered back. Pale-blue dress, white sleeves, tattered brown shawl, dirty blonde curls −

And after a moment, sensing me, she'll turn. And we'll both stand there looking at each other for a second or two. She'll regard me with calm curiosity, neither especially warm nor cold. She'll know who I am. I'll know who she is. It'll be just exactly as it's always been − as we always knew it would be. Except that now, for the first time, her face isn't blank.

Her face.

I stare, I do, I can't help it. I just can't take my eyes from that face, so very nearly familiar, but seen properly now for the very first time.

Greyest grey eyes, slim nose, pencil-dot freckles.

Hey. It's you.

Yes. It's me. Who are you?

I can explain. Can we talk?

Yes, but where?

The church. Can we go in the church?

She doesn't answer. You don't answer. I no longer even know who's asking the questions. Neither do you. But still, sensing an opportunity, we start to move towards the church. Because everything always leads back here − back to Woodton, back to the church.

Walking beside her, glancing downwards, I decide not to notice that her feet don't quite touch the ground.

Our son drifts from sofa to sofa. He busks. He takes a lot of drugs. When I see him – which I do, as much as I can – he treats me as if I am his friend. I'm grateful for this. I've reached a point where just being allowed some regular, relaxed interaction with him feels like – well, something. The opposite of loss.

The other day he rang and asked if he could borrow 3 quid.

I'm going busking and I'm meeting this girl and I need enough for a coffee and £1 to put in the hat. I don't want her to think I'm a complete scumbag.

But you are, aren't you? I said as softly as I could.

What?

A scumbag. What I mean is, you have no money. You have no home. You have nothing. You sleep all day and stay up all night. Don't you think it's time you kicked the drugs and tried to get a job?

I'm hardly doing any drugs and I don't need a job. I make as much as I need. The other day I made 40 quid in one hour's busking!

But – then where did that go?

I spent it.

Spent it on what?

On drink, I suppose. Maybe some coke.

The speed with which he said it made my heart tighten.

So you're admitting that?

Somewhere on the streets of London, I felt him shrug.

At least I'm being honest, he said. Surely that counts for something?

The speed with which he said it. The road slips under the car so fast, I can't keep my balance. What if I had to stop?

All you can do is keep on loving your children, keep on hoping. But what if loving and hoping aren't enough? What if you can't stop? What if you can't?

I see him one more time, my father. When our boy is born, his father asks me how I feel about the fact that he will never know his grandfather.

We should go and visit, he says. Take the boy, give him a chance to bury the hatchet. His first grandchild – how can he refuse?

I think my father could easily refuse, but I can also see that he is right. We should give him a chance. It's because he says things like this – and is prepared to act on them – that I love him. So I say OK, let's do it.

Well done, he says. He knows how terrified I am.

He lives in a different house now, in a small executive estate off a country lane. Clipped lawns, shiny cars, birds singing. We don't tell him we are coming because we don't want to give him a chance to tell us not to. We stand on the doorstep on a bright February day and press the bell. Our boy is a few weeks old, in my arms, a tight white bundle, fast asleep.

My heart bangs so hard it feels like my chest will explode. No one answers. Maybe he's out? I say hopefully. Then there's the slow sound of footsteps. A chain being taken off.

The man who opens the door is smaller, older, a mottled face. He looks puzzled, troubled, upset, wary.

Julie? he says – and I think it's funny that after all these years he knows exactly who I am, he knows it's me.

Hello, Daddy, I say. We've brought your grandson to see you.

★   ★   ★

The other day he came here for the first time in maybe six months. Into our house. He said he couldn't stay long. He always says that. I offered him a pizza anyway. OK, he said, but it will have to be quick.

And he washed his hands at the sink, drying them on the tea towel instead of the towel just like he always did. And then he sat there at the kitchen table and cut up some goat's cheese to put on it. Extra goat's cheese, just like in the old days. He sat at that same old circular pine kitchen table where he once knelt up on a chair to paint with finger paints. The table where he did homework. The same kitchen table where he must have blown out so many cakefuls of birthday candles over the years.

And I tried not to look too hard. I tried not to like it too much, having him here. His curly, unkempt head bent over the cheese. His dear head. The head that I wanted to go over and hold as close and hard as possible against me, bending to plant a kiss.

I tried so hard to be normal and light and to ignore him that I almost forgot what I was doing. I did. I almost forgot. I boiled the kettle and poured the boiling water down the sink. He didn't see. I refilled it and set it to boil again. Steam clouds in the sink.

And when the pizza was ready to put in, he went over to light the oven and, because he doesn't live here any more, he picked up the wrong lighter, the broken one that's just been sitting there but needs to be fixed. And then when that didn't work, he got down, frowning, on his knees to see if it was the oven itself that was broken.

I had to go over and show him that the oven was fine and which was the correct lighter to use and I don't know why but this fact really shook me up. Just the simple act of having to explain our own oven to our child who used to live here, who ought to live here, that was bad.

But, I pointed out to his father the other day, at least the boy is coming to us willingly, at least he's seeking us out. At least we still have some kind of a relationship with him. We should be grateful for that.

When the time comes, I said, when he realises he needs help, at least the channels will all be open. And, you know, I am sure he will come to us. I just know he will.

His father sighed.

What?

Well, he said, but when?

I think it could easily be as little as three or six months away.

He laughed. A sad little laugh.

Are you mad? No way. I'm thinking more like ten years. At the very earliest.

My stomach turned.

Seriously? That's what you really think? Ten years?

He hesitated and he sighed.

You know, on a bad day, I mean a really bad day, I don't think I will live to see it.

You won't live to see him come off cannabis?

That's right.

But how long are you intending to live? You're only forty-seven, for goodness' sake!

He looked away. He looked at nothing for a long time.

You know what I mean, he said.

We go into my father's house – he asks us in, even though his voice says he doesn't want to. I smell ash, soap, newish carpets. There's an electric organ, a very large TV.

And what happens next?

I think he makes us tea. He hardly looks at me, instead he addresses the boy's father, who says all the right things. He's not unfriendly and he's not that friendly either – he's civil, placid, patient, waiting for the moment when this will be over, when we'll go.

He shows us some of his gadgets. I demonstrate enthusiasm for the bits of grey plastic, the buttons and lights. I tell him how great they are and we all laugh – the old feeling of judging his moods, of wanting to please him. I am thirteen again and I am sixteen and I am twenty-eight, a mother now, a parent. I remind myself of this as I look at his old hands, distorted by a long-ago encounter with a flaming chip pan, hooking the tea bag out of the thick brown tea with a spoon. The grey counter in his kitchen. A tin of baked beans. A bottle of whisky.

We ask if he'd like to hold his grandson. He says no, he wouldn't.

I would if he was a girl, he adds. I like little girls.

Later the boy's father can't believe this. He repeats it again and again to me, to others, to anyone who will listen. His family doesn't contain anyone who behaves like this. He has never met a man who would not melt when confronted with the small, warm, alive package that was his grandson.

I don't know how long we stay there but it's all perfectly civil, so civil I can't quite believe we managed it, and then we go. We say a pleasant goodbye. We almost shake hands, but not quite.

As we drive away with our baby – slightly hungry now, almost ready for a feed, strapped in his little car seat – I feel emptied out, numb. The boy's father tells me he did a clever thing. He left one of the boy's muslin wipes there, a clean one. He left it deliberately, on the sofa.

So he has a solid reason to get back in touch, he explains, clearly pleased with himself. So he has something to return to us.

I try to imagine a world where this might happen. I tell him that was a good thing to do and, for a moment or two, I mean it.

But my father never gets in touch. He never returns the cloth. I send him a postcard and he never replies. That's the last time I ever see him.

The boy calls yet again to ask us to lend him money. He doesn't call his father, he calls me.

I'm waiting for this fucking loan to come through, you see. They're fucking me about as usual. All I need is the deposit for two weeks' rent on this room in Bethnal Green –

We want to help you, I tell him, but we're not lending you any more money. Not because we can't afford it and not because you won't pay it back – though you won't – but because we no longer think that's the right way to help you. I'm sorry, darling.

But what the fuck! Do you want me to be homeless for ever?

Of course not. I very much want you to have somewhere to live. But I think you should get a job. You're nineteen years old and you're free all day. And if you can't get a job, then you should admit it's because you've got a problem. And if you want help with that, we are always here and we know exactly how to help you.

He laughs.

You always have to say it, don't you, Mother dear? It really is quite funny, that way you always have to come back to this. The same old story: my son the drug addict.

Have you ever thought that perhaps the reason I come back to it, is because it's true? Because that is the story?

Well, I'm sick of this story of yours, this idea that it's about drugs. If you want that to be the story then go away and write one of your fucking novels about it, OK?

The thing about panic – the one really good and reliable thing about it – is that it has a peak.

Although the nature of panic is that it feels like an upwards arc, it feels like it can only go on and on, building and building, that's actually not true. It doesn't. It builds and then it peaks and then it subsides.

You think it will go on and on, crescendoing, till it kills you. But it won't. In fact, if you think about it sensibly, the very fact that you are at its peak, at the worst bit, means you are almost out of it. The worse you are feeling, the more likely it is to subside.

The dark hole opens up, and then it closes again.

If you can remember this supremely comforting thought, if you can believe it, then you can deal with panic. I think I really do believe this.

I've started doing breathing exercises. Every day. Making time for them. Mostly managing to remember. Feeling the slow beat of my own heart. Staying with it, trying to breathe. Remembering I'm here, I'm me.

Last week I almost drove to Suffolk. I felt I could have done it. I will do it. I almost did.

Mary Yelloly and I sit together in All Saints Church. She sits right here beside me, just to my left, in that dark-wood pew – exactly the same one that Julia and I sat in on that long-ago freezing March day.

She is close enough to me that I can see the softly curving detail of her. Close enough that the edges of our clothes can touch.

I'm trying not to let myself be too nervous, too daunted by her presence. I'm trying to remember that she's just a girl, a normal girl. Barely older than my daughter. A child, really. And anyway, I can't waste it. This is it. My only chance, a chance grabbed out of nowhere. After all this time, months and years, almost two hundred years, of waiting and searching, I really am finally this close to her.

I can see everything. The rough, dun-coloured wool of her shawl, a kind of fluted ribbon stitched around its edge, twisted where it's been pulled too tight. Her blue frock, dirt on its hem. The slightly frayed edge of her short cotton sleeve, threads unravelling, fabric so thin that the light bites into it.

I can see her bare girl's arms. Child's arms. Her skinny wrists. Thin and blue-veined. A long scratch on her hand, between thumb and forefinger, trying to heal but still pink and sore. On her left hand, a ring with an oval green stone. Shortish, oval nails, not that clean. The little finger on her left hand bitten right down.

If she looks at me, she can see my jeans – dark blue stretch jeans, five or six years old, tighter now, the knees worn pale. The edge of my mauve wool sweater. My tired, middle-aged hands, looking more unnervingly like my mother's hands every day. My wedding ring. The nails I used to bite but don't any more.

She can probably see the sharp little diamond that I wear in my ear lobe for weeks on end without taking it out. The small lines and creases that renew themselves more deeply every day on my face. The sweep of kohl and the skim of translucent powder, brushed under my eyes this morning, then forgotten about. The face I often forget to look at these days. The face I should take better care of. Right now emptied out with tiredness. Emptied out.

I can smell her. The warm skin and hair smell of young girl, of hormones. And a faint smell of sweat too – not exactly stale, but not too fresh either. On top of that, a scent I think I know, but can't place. Something old-fashioned. Violet? Hyacinth?

I don't know what I smell of. Prada perfume put on last night, probably. To me, I always really just smell of me.

I can see the curve of her pale lashes on her cheek. A small blue vein moving in her temple. A raggedy snag of skin where she has chewed her lip. A small pimple on her chin. Her pale, pale skin.

I'm trying not to stare too much, I really am. But after all this time, all this waiting, the close-up detail, the sheer, alive fact of her body right here next to mine – it's intoxicating.

She places her small slender hands on the hard shiny back of the pew in front.

I don't know who you are, she says stiffly, but I feel I know you. Please remind me how we met. Are you a London friend of my papa's?

I hesitate, unsure where to start.

We've never met before, I tell her, and she looks surprised, a little frown puckering her forehead. But we're not exactly strangers either. It's hard to explain exactly what we are.

She turns her gaze on me. Her grey gaze.

Well, I feel I know you, she says again. Please don't laugh.

Why would I laugh?

She bites her lip.

It's a bit of a puzzle, isn't it? Still, I feel quite comfortable with you –

Good. I'm glad.

But why are we here? Do you know why we're here?

The sound of her voice is strange. The faintest trace of an accent. Is it Norfolk?

I wanted to talk to you, I tell her as carefully as I can. I wanted to ask you some things.

She crinkles her nose.

You did?

Is that OK?

She thinks about this.

What's your name?

I tell her my name and she repeats it a couple of times. *Julie. Julie.* It is the strangest thing I've ever heard. Mary Yelloly speaking my name.

It's a French name, she says then, eyeing me carefully.

It might be.

You're French?

Not exactly, no.

Not exactly?

I'm not at all French.

She smiles then and is about to say something else but has to stop and draw breath for a moment in order to cough. A ragged, tearing sound, deep in her chest. She wipes her mouth with the back of her hand. I wonder whether to say something, ask if she's OK. But I don't want to interrupt her smooth line of thought.

She regards me with solemn eyes.

I don't know how I know this, Julie, but – you have a child?

I take a breath.

Three, I say, I have three.

Ah. Three?

Yes.

She shuts her eyes for a second. Her skin is so pale you could put your fingers through it.

Well, I feel – please don't mind me saying this – but I feel there's a child that you're feeling very upset about.

I wasn't expecting this. I shiver.

Yes, I tell her. Yes. You're right. There is.

Well, he's very lonely, she says. I don't know how I know that, but I do. I think he wants you to know that.

I touch my fingers to the corners of my eyes, holding back the tears.

I'm so sorry, she says, I'm so sorry to have to tell you that about your own child.

I twist on the hard, slippery pew, feeling around in my jeans pocket for a tissue.

Minutes go by. Her cool hand on my back. We are both so still. I don't know what we're waiting for. Neither does she. Early-evening sun slants into the church. It must be summer. A ribbon of light through the mauve stained glass.

I glance to my left at the Yelloly tablets on the wall. I can't believe she hasn't noticed them. Her name on the wall. If she sees them now, I think, if she glances that way, then she'll know. It'll all be over then. She'll go.

What is it? she asks me. What are you looking at?

Nothing, I say, and then quickly, distracting her: Can I ask you something?

What?

Do you love Charles Tyssen?

She doesn't look at me, but I notice that the edge of her pale nose quivers.

My cousin Charlie? Of course I love him!

304

I sneak a glance at her.

Not like that, I say, I don't mean like that.

What, then?

Come on. You know what I mean.

She turns her head ever so slightly. Holding her breath as she inspects my face.

Charles, she begins, you know him?

I shake my head.

Not at all, I say.

The thing about Charlie is – he's so serious. So very tight and closed up and serious. He makes me shy. I never know what to say. He makes me feel –

What?

I don't know. (A little laugh.) How do you know about Charles?

Most of what I know is from a book, I tell her truthfully. Someone wrote a book about your family –

What book? Who wrote a book? Oh, on account of my father, I suppose.

I say nothing. I let her think it. I mustn't tell her too much.

Well then, one thing your book probably won't tell you is that Charlie was a bit soft on me.

Was?

All his life. Since we were small. I think he's got over it now.

Ah.

Is that all you want to ask me?

I smile.

How many questions do I get?

She frowns and taps her fingers lightly on the back of the pew in front.

All right, I say, I have another.

About Charlie?

No, about Robert Suckling.

A long sigh.

Oh Julie, do I really have to talk about this now?

Sun slides around the church. The long beam pouring through the stained-glass window lengthens. Soft jewel colours lighting up the dust.

I'm sorry, I tell her, I know you must think it's none of my business. I must seem pushy. It's just – well, don't you see? This is my only chance.

What do you mean, your only chance? Only chance for what?

To talk to you. To know things.

But I'm always here.

Not always. Not for me, you're not.

She sniffs. Another little cough.

I'm sure I don't know why you're so interested in me.

I've been looking for you for so long.

And now you've found me?

In a way. I hope so. Yes.

She gives me a long look.

I do wish I knew who you were, she says again. I feel as if I know you. But why?

I smile.

I feel just the same. I feel like that too.

About me?

Yes. About you.

She coughs again. A slow racking cough. This time she pulls a small grey rag from her sleeve, wipes her mouth.

Are you OK?

Oh yes, thank you, I'm so much better than I was.

You've been very ill?

Not so ill. I'm definitely mending now. Papa says I am.

That's good. I'm glad you're better.

Silence for a moment or two. I'm not sure how hard I want to push her.

Do you mind telling me about the walk in the woods?

She turns to look at me with grey amused eyes. Eyes as grey as the eyes of my boy. Eyes that can go somewhere else in two seconds flat. Eyes that widen.

The walk in the woods? With Robert? You even know about that? That part is in your book, too?

And who's Mr Brown and why did Mrs Coulcher say you were piqued? Piqued at what?

Ah! Jane Coulcher! Now I understand. Is that where all this ridiculous information's coming from?

She's a source.

A source. Hmm. Not a reliable one, though.

No?

That woman. I don't want to say too much, but she has been no friend to Mama. You know her?

Not really. But one of her letters happened to survive – I think Florence Suckling knew her.

Florence Suckling? I don't know the name. Is she a relative of Robert's, then?

She's – it doesn't matter. Look, in the woods. What happened?

A sly little smile.

What do you think happened?

He kissed you?

She looks away quickly, bites her lip.

I'm sorry, I tell her. But it's so hard for me to know. I mean I really can't even begin to guess how things were in your time.

She frowns at me as if she doesn't understand.

Do you love him? I say then.

A long pause.

Love him? she says, and her voice is suddenly shy. I don't know. I don't exactly know what love is. Oh, I know what people say. Sophy and Groome, for instance, they love each other. You can see it in his eyes, and sometimes when he leaves, poor Soph weeps as if her heart is breaking. But I don't weep about Robert. He would never make me weep. Though I sometimes do wonder if I have a heart to break –

You have a heart, I tell her.

She smiles and hesitates again.

But Robert and I, we'll walk for hours and we'll talk and you've no idea the things he knows. Terrible things and wonderful things. Things you wouldn't believe. And we talk as if we just can't stop. And when he goes all I can think of is all the things I meant to ask him and didn't. So many things I just forgot to say!

I smile at her and she blushes slightly. Colour creeping over her face from her neck.

Not only that, but everything I tell him he understands. I never have to explain a thing. It's like there's this easy mood between us all the time. He makes me feel so – listened to. And I don't know what love is, Julie, but when he talks to me, when we've been walking and talking a while, then I'll look up and suddenly the whole world looks different.

In what way different?

It's like – everything's more beautiful, louder, more wide awake, all the colours undiluted!

I look at her face, lit up with her little speech.

That's the only way I can really describe it, she says, suddenly self-conscious, making a face.

I know what you're talking about, I tell her. And I think I would call that love.

She looks at me doubtfully and then she smiles.

You would?

I think so, yes.

I look at her now – the rush of her blood showing through the skin. The palest blonde hair looping over her ear. I can't take my eyes off her. I realise I don't want this to be over. I don't want her to go. I don't want to lose you, Mary. Please don't go.

I'm so sorry, I hear myself tell her, and she looks surprised.

Sorry for what?

Never mind. It doesn't matter.

She looks at the cool church floor. She sighs to herself but she looks happy. She's thinking about Robert. She does not look at me.

More minutes go by. After a while, she lifts her head.

I'm really sorry, by the way, she says. About your lad.

I look at her in surprise. *My lad.*

How did you know? I ask her, more out of curiosity than anything.

She brings her face closer to mine. I can smell the sticky heat of her skin, a faint hot smell of something a bit like fever.

I've been in your head so long, she says, I think I probably know everything.

OK, I say, unsure whether this makes any sense.

Do you think you'll get him back? she asks me then.

I think for a moment.

I don't know, I say truthfully. What do you think?

She shrugs.

I think there's still a lot of time.

You think so?

Oh yes. There's time. He's young. He has time. He has all the time in the world.

I shut my eyes.

Does he?

You don't believe that?

I don't know, I tell her, it's always hard, isn't it – to know about time.

What about it?

I twist the tissue in my fingers.

How much of it you've got. I mean, it's easy not to think about it when you have a lot of it. But once there's less –

She turns and fixes her grey eyes on me. Solemn grey eyes, full of questions, full of possibility. Eyes so like the eyes of my boy. She takes my other hand, the one without the tissue.

Your hands are so warm, she says. It feels like a miracle.

I smile. *A miracle.* A miracle of warmth, of life. She twists my wedding ring round the way my daughter would.

And yours are so cold, I tell her, but she doesn't seem to hear me.

She's thinking hard, listening for something. A voice in her head?

He'll come back, she says, I just know he will.

Oh Mary. No one knows anything, I tell her. I know you mean well and you're only saying that to be kind, but I'm afraid I've stopped listening when people say those things. You can't know. No one can.

She looks at me, suddenly fierce.

Ah, but it's not true – you forget. People do know things. The way you know about me.

I know about her.

It's true, I agree, I do. I know.

What do you know?

She looks right into my eyes and I look at her and then I have to look away.

Tell me what you know, she says.

And straight away I start to see what I didn't see before: how different the church looks. How the shadows have grown deeper and darker, how the floor is rougher, the pew we're sitting in much lighter and smaller, small leather prayer books on the shelf. Lilies haunting the air.

I glance at the Yelloly plaques. And of course, they're gone. No longer there. Not yet there.

She's still holding my hand and her own hand is warm now. I can feel the life beating through it, the hope.

Mary?

Yes?

What month is it?

She stares at me, puzzled.

You don't know what month it is?

Is it May?

She smiles.

Of course it's May.

May of what year?

She laughs as if I'm testing her.

1837!

You're twenty?

That's right. But in December I shall be twenty-one.

When I leave the church, the sun is low in the sky and an oldish man is mowing the grass between the graves on a sit-on mower. Leaving a wide wake of bright green behind him.

The air smells shrill and green too, of the beginning of life and the end of summer, the end of the day and the beginning of evening. The beginning, middle and end of this journey. The edge of the sky behind the church is bright orange. Shepherd's delight. A perfect evening. Tomorrow will be another lovely day.

As I walk back down the gravel, the man raises a hand and waves to me, and I lift my hand and wave back.

The years fold and pleat together. I don't know how they do that. Long stretches of time turn to nothing.

And even though you don't know it yet, one day you are buried in the dark, damp earth and another day I am born and then just three seconds after that I am eighteen, maybe nineteen, walking through the streets of an Italian town wearing a bright tomato-red sundress, the sun on my back. I remember the sundress. What happens to the sundress? And I am crying and then laughing and then I am twenty-one, the same age you were when you died, except that I'm alive, so intent on being alive – and this is the last time in my life that I will ever remember being alone.

Because not so many years after this – a quick pleat of years, a stretch of time so elastic you can barely feel it – I will meet someone and, not long after this, we'll have a child and we'll bring him home from the hospital and, just as I always knew would happen, his father will run me a bath and I will climb into it so very gratefully while he takes our son into the bedroom.

Our boy. That's what we call him. From that very first moment, even though he has a name, that's what he is.

Our boy.

Is he OK? I'll call from the bathroom, even though I know the answer. Is the boy OK?

He's fine. The boy's just fine. You relax, take your time. Stay in the bath as long as you like.

And I will. I will take my time. I will never know quite how to relax, but certainly I will take my time.

It's hard to know about time, but still I will lie in that bath, just as you lie in the dark earth, and it will seem like no time at all has elapsed between the Italian street and this deep warm bath. No time at all between one moment and the next. And if that is true, if time can stretch and stretch, or else snap back in an instant, then surely death can't be anything very important?

I'll lie there in that warm bath for a long time on that February afternoon – 1 February 1989 – feeling so happy and so complete.

And when I get out, carefully because I'm still stitched and sore, and the bath water drains out into the frosty air, I'll pad into the bedroom wrapped in my towel, the TV on, cartoon-hero music playing, and I'll see them both there, asleep in the armchair in front of *Mighty Mouse*.

A long-haired, soft-faced boy in a woollen jumper, mouth open, fast asleep. And a warm-haired, tiny-fisted one lodged in the crook of his arm.

I thought I'd never see my boy asleep again. But I was wrong. He's started sleeping here just occasionally, turning up now and then and asking if it's OK if he puts himself in his old bed, stays the night.

Well, sometimes it's night but usually it's more like day. But we always say yes. Just for the moment, anyway. We're not quite sure whether it's the right thing to do – some would say yes, some would say no – but, because there really are no concrete answers, for now we're doing it. We're doing it because right now we can't really manage to do anything else.

And he's here now as I write this, asleep upstairs, arms and legs thrown out of the duvet, mouth open, poor old Kitty curled against his leg, satisfaction spilling out of her face.

I thought I would never see him asleep again, but I was wrong. I was wrong about a lot of things. Maybe the best we can hope for in this unknowable, unguessable life is that we might turn out to be wrong. That the things we dreaded might not happen, or not as badly anyway. That those we thought we'd set our hearts on might turn out not to matter very much.

I used to think that love was the solution to everything, but I was wrong about that too. It's just the most irresistible part of the problem.

Mary is gone. She lies under the church floor at Woodton, her bones dissolved to nothing, her brief, unknown life turned to dust, and the fact that I know this — and have discovered that I do, after all, care very much about it — makes no difference to anything.

It makes no difference that I found her, that I know where she is. It makes no difference that I wrote this book, or that you chose to read it. I never met her, and neither will you, we never will.

The conversation in All Saints Church never happened, just like so many things that will never happen, however much you might want them to. And nothing I do or think or feel can bring that young girl back to life, and it took a while for me to be able to put up with that idea, but I know it now and I think I can live with it. I've learned to live with so many other difficult things.

I'll tell you one thing that did happen, though, that has happened, that will happen.

★   ★   ★

We will conceive our first child on a hot, light evening in May – an evening very similar to the one just a year later when his crying makes me cry, an evening almost identical to the one seventeen years after that when he knocks me to the ground. An evening probably not so very different to the one when Mary lost the rest of her life.

But we don't know any of this yet. All we know is that the birds are calling outside and particles of dust are drifting in these bright, warm shafts of evening light and we think we might love each other and our bodies are about to collide and in a few moments, in this bed, you will turn to me and then, in one of the long moments that follow, he will begin to exist. Our boy.

But that hasn't happened yet and right now this moment, so full of possibility, is all we have.

AFTERWORD

TWO MONTHS AFTER I finish writing this book, I pick my boy up in the pouring rain. I haven't seen him for weeks – he has no phone and he won't give me the address of his Peckham bedsit.

We go to a café, where he orders steak and fries and I order peppermint tea. I try not to snatch too many glances at his face. He looks OK, not as thin as last time and his hair has grown long and curly. He has his guitar wrapped in a bin bag to keep it dry.

I tell him how good it is to see him. He shrugs. I tell him I've got something to show him.

Remember that book – the one I started writing ages ago, about the girl who lived two hundred years ago?

Mary Yelloly?

I didn't think you'd remember the name. Well, I started finding out about her and it was just that her story was so unrelentingly sad. And all of this stuff with you – it was all happening at exactly the same time. And one day I suppose I just ground to a halt. I couldn't do it. And then I realised: I could only write truthfully about Mary if I wrote about what was going on with you as well.

He wipes a chip through ketchup and gives me a weary look.

So – what? My whole life story's in this fucking book?

It's not quite like that, I say, pulling out the manuscript. But please, I really do need you to read it, tell me what you feel about it. Don't worry, it's not so much about you – or at least it is – but it's more about me really. A mother's story. And I know you're not going to like everything in it. In fact there's quite a lot you might not like. But please, please try and remember that it's been written with nothing but love.

He sighs, eats another chip.

It's a book about how much I love you, I tell him again, though I realise you may not choose to see it quite like that.

He warns me that he won't be able to read it fast. (I'm pretty busy, you know, I've got a lot on.) But, just over twenty-four hours later, we're in another restaurant with the marked-up manuscript spread on the table between us.

It's so lovely to see you two days running, I tell him truthfully. I should write books about you more often.

He almost smiles.

Yeah, well, Mother dearest, you've been very clever with this so-called book.

But he goes on to tell me there are some things he objects to.

Really? Like what?

Well, for a start, this bit about selling my brother skunk. I never gave him skunk. Hash, yes. Big difference. And you say I encouraged him to get stoned on the way home from school, but that's not true. I was actually trying to stop him.

By giving him hash when he was only thirteen?

Yes! To prevent him having skunk!

Ah.

And another thing: when we're discussing the termination thing, you have me just sitting and fiddling with my Xbox as if I didn't give a fuck. And yet I remember sitting down in the sitting room with you and Dad and having a really serious conversation about it, both of you going on at me.

Really?

Definitely!

OK, I say. I'm sorry. I'll look at it. I can easily adjust it.

He turns the pages. He's marked up the bits he's unhappy with. So few bits. I'm amazed at how many pages have no marks on at all.

At one point, he shakes his head.

You and your short, snappy little sentences, he says. I know what you're doing, you know.

It's how I write.

Yeah, yeah. And then this bit, the bit where you and Dad throw me out for the last time and you have me saying *I'll take a knife and stab you through the heart*.

You don't remember saying that?

Fuck's sake! If I said it, I wouldn't have meant it!

I know that, I say slowly. It's not that I think you'd have done it. But you must admit it was a pretty aggressive thing to say.

He looks at me for a moment with his clear grey eyes, but he says nothing.

And then, when you say I finally dropped out of school, you very conveniently omit to mention that I'd already got myself on to the course at Goldsmith's.

I think about this.

That's true, I say, I'm sorry, I don't know why I didn't say that. And how is it, by the way? Are you still going?

He hesitates.

There've been some attendance issues, he says.

You haven't been going?

I'm going. But if I miss a single session now, they'll kick me out.

You'd be mad to give up on all that work, I tell him. Just stay and do the exam, for goodness' sake.

What d'you think I'm doing?!

He looks back down at the manuscript.

To be absolutely honest, he says carefully, I wasn't all that interested in the stuff about the Mary Yelloly person.

Well, that's understandable.

I'm not saying it's bad, necessarily. But maybe you have to be pushing fifty and female.

Thanks a lot!

But the bit in the church, at the end. I did think that was pretty good.

You did? I feel myself flush with pleasure. You really liked that bit?

He nods, takes a forkful of pasta. Moments pass. I realise I don't want this dinner to end.

But if you want to know, he says softly and he doesn't look at me now. You're right: it was then.

What was then?

When I started smoking.

You mean –

You and Dad. All those evenings. I'd be in bed holding Kitty and just watching this little dot on the wall while I listened to you two arguing.

My heart jumps.

Was it so many evenings? (In my head those bad months have shrivelled to something small and dark and tight.)

The first time I ever smoked a joint alone – I felt so guilty. Oh, darling.

He swallows and I think, He's still here, the exact same boy. The shape of his mouth when he was five years old. What did we do to him?

I'm so very sorry, I tell him slowly. We had no idea. We were so wrapped up in our own problems. We were idiots.

Yeah. You were.

I love you so much. We both love you so much.

Yeah, well.

We walk along Walworth Road in the cool dusky evening. Me in my old coat and trainers. His tall shape towering over me. I tell him how very much it means to me, that he's read the book like this. So quickly. So carefully and kindly.

I was dreading giving it to you, I tell him. But you see, I had to write it. It was just the only thing I could possibly write.

I know that, he says quietly. I understand about writing.

Well, you're good, I tell him, to understand that.

He says nothing, lightly strums his guitar.

But I've been very merciful, you know, he says as we walk past Co-op Funerals, Argos and Superdrug, litter blowing against our legs.

I know you have, I say, I know.

So don't you go thinking I approve of what you've done.

OK, I say, and I steal a glance at his face, which, despite his words, is warm, amused even. For a moment, I feel like the child.

When we turn into our road, he perches on a car bonnet and asks to play me a song he's written. It's rough, forlorn, full of passion. When he plays, his face changes and he turns into someone else, someone I don't really know.

I stand there listening to the song. People walk past. I don't know who they think we are or what they think we're doing. The sky has almost lost its light and I can smell cooking and exhaust. The boy who lives across the road – a boy who only a year or so ago was at school with him and is at university somewhere now – sticks his head out of the window, grinning.

Hey, man! I thought it was you! What you up to, then?

Just playin' a song to my mum.

Cool! You OK?

Yeah. You?

Yeah. Good to see you, man.

We walk on down the road towards our house. I ask if he'll come in for a bit. He says he won't.

But you could drive me to Brixton.

Where are you going?

The Academy. Gotta meet some people.

So I run into the house to grab my cardigan and car keys and, when his father hears that our boy is outside, he comes out to say hello.

The boy is sitting on the bonnet of our car, curly head bent, playing chords. He looks up slowly when his father approaches.

Hello, boy.

Huh.

How's things?

OK. (The smallest flicker of a smile.)

When we're almost at Brixton Academy, he tells me he's got another song he wants to play me.

One I wrote about you.

So I pull in on Brixton High Road and put on the flashers. Close my eyes as his music fills the car. I catch phrases: . . .

waiting for your hand . . . as daylight breaks over my shy bones . . .
I've made mistakes . . . lonely in the rain. Again, that unknown
young man's face.

And my tears start to fall, but it doesn't matter because he's
not looking at me, he's looking somewhere else – beyond,
apart. The car rocks every time a heavy lorry shudders past.
He's singing about me but he's gone somewhere else, somewhere I can't go.

When he's finished, he still doesn't look at me. I can't really
speak. My heart hurting. Salt in my mouth.

It's so beautiful, I croak. Thank you.

He smiles to himself, a wobbly little smile.

I knew you'd cry, he says. And he opens the car door and,
guitar under his arm, he's gone.

AN END

When you've finished painting me in red and black,
to suit your fiction, lies and facts,
and you've recognised the truth of me,
that over live or die I'll live in dreams.
My place of safety, liberty
is the only reason my heart still beats.
So when you're sick of war and you want me back,
overlooked aspirations of all I lack,
my ship will still be sailing on,
off the edge of ambition and into the sun,
where you can race to find the man,
who always was, and still is, your son.

ACKNOWLEDGEMENTS

This book owes a lot to so many people. Tony, Bryony and Julia Yelloly generously put their entire family archive quite literally in my hands. Every biographer dreams of stumbling upon a dusty old box that's lingered in an attic for a hundred years. That's what happened to me and I can't thank them enough.

Mary and Paul Sanders-Hewett also shared their precious and inspiring family treasures with me, as well as offering research back-up that was well beyond the call of duty. Patrick Baron lent me books, showed me his wonderful paintings and kindly allowed me to interrogate him at length. These three families – the Yellolys, the Sanders-Hewetts and the Barons – are Mary's direct descendants and their kind and imaginative support made the writing of this book a real pleasure.

Meanwhile, Steve and Elaine Hill of Woodton Hall generously let me interrupt their Sunday lunch and invade their home, as well as providing a great many interesting facts. The Reverend John Buchanan of Beccles proved a fascinating and informative email correspondent. David Turner of Narborough Local History Society and Joanne Nadelson of Narborough Hall kindly gave me a moving and memorable glimpse of Mary's childhood landscape. Jonathan Plunkett helped me track down the real Carrow Abbey with the help of his late father George Plunkett's meticulous and atmospheric photos, and Jeremy Howard of Robinson's (Britvic) spent several patient hours with me in the long, dark corridors at Carrow (not to mention giving me a lift to the station). Maggie Wood at the Warwick Doll Museum never managed to track down the Tyssen doll, but I very much appreciate all her efforts in trying. And the indefatigable Monica Churchill of All Saints, Woodton did finally find Mary for me when I had almost given up – what would I have done without her?

Though she's been dead almost a hundred years, thanks are also due to Florence Suckling. This book would have been so much harder to write without access to her excellent 1898 family history *A Forgotten Past* (now long out of print), which I've quoted at length. Thank you to Julia Yelloly for loaning me the published book, and to Mary Sanders-Hewett for giving me access to the wonderful original manuscript. I don't know what Florence would have made of my book – I suspect she thought she'd written the definitive Yelloly/Tyssen family history – but I came to rather love her bossy, judgemental, yet always vivacious, company.

However, if Simon Finch of Simon Finch Rare Books had not come across an album of paintings at a Suffolk auction and known it was special, and if Peter Straus of Rogers, Coleridge & White hadn't seen it and straight away thought of me, Mary and I would still be strangers to each other. A big thank you to both.

Finally, thank you is a very inadequate word to express what I feel about the countless people, teachers, doctors, counsellors, family and dear friends, who supported Jonathan and me as we struggled with a problem which some days – no, many days – threatened to overwhelm us.

You made us tea, you let us weep, you listened to us at length when we were boring even ourselves. You offered endless insight and wisdom and practical help, but you were also wise enough not to insist upon looking for answers. Best of all, you somehow continued to care for and believe in our boy and didn't recoil as we learned the terrible lesson that Mary Yelloly's parents must have also learned: that you can make your babies and you can love them with every single cell of your being, but you can't make them safe, you can't in the end choose how their lives turn out.

So many of you so often said: 'If only there was something we could do to help.' Well, there was, and you did it. You stayed with us through this big, sad, terrifying, momentous thing, and this book is also for you.

J.S.M., London, August 2008

A NOTE ON THE AUTHOR

Julie Myerson is the author of seven novels, including the bestselling *Something Might Happen*, and two works of non-fiction, including *Home: The Story of Everyone Who Ever Lived in Our House*, which was dramatised on BBC Radio Four. Her latest novel, *Out of Breath*, was published by Jonathan Cape in February 2008. She lives in London and Suffolk with her husband and teenage children.

A NOTE ON THE TYPE

The text of this book is set in Bembo. This type was first used in 1495 by the Venetian printer Aldus Manutius for Cardinal Bembo's *De Aetna*, and was cut for Manutius by Francesco Griffo. It was one of the types used by Claude Garamond (1480–1561) as a model for his Romain de L'Université, and so it was the forerunner of what became standard European type for the following two centuries. Its modern form follows the original types and was designed for Monotype in 1929.